BUILDING AI DRIVEN MARKETING CAPABILITIES

UNDERSTAND CUSTOMER NEEDS AND DELIVER VALUE THROUGH AI

Neha Zaidi
Mohit Maurya
Simon Grima
Pallavi Tyagi

Apress®

Building AI-Driven Marketing Capabilities: Understand Customer Needs and Deliver Value Through AI

Dr. Neha Zaidi
Symbiosis International Deemed University,
Symbiosis Institute of Business Management,
Noida, India

Simon Grima
Marsaxlokk, Malta

Mohit Maurya
Delhi, India

Pallavi Tyagi
Delhi, India

ISBN-13 (pbk): 978-1-4842-9809-1
https://doi.org/10.1007/978-1-4842-9810-7

ISBN-13 (electronic): 978-1-4842-9810-7

Managing Director, Apress Media LLC: Welmoed Spahr
Acquisitions Editor: Shivangi Ramachandran
Development Editor: James Markham
Project Manager: Jessica Vakili

Distributed to the book trade worldwide by Springer Science+Business Media New York, 1 NY PLaza, New York, NY 10004. Phone 1-800-SPRINGER, fax (201) 348-4505, e-mail orders-ny@springer-sbm.com, or visit www.springeronline.com. Apress Media, LLC is a California LLC and the sole member (owner) is Springer Science + Business Media Finance Inc (SSBM Finance Inc). SSBM Finance Inc is a **Delaware** corporation.

For information on translations, please e-mail booktranslations@springernature.com; for reprint, paperback, or audio rights, please e-mail bookpermissions@springernature.com.

Apress titles may be purchased in bulk for academic, corporate, or promotional use. eBook versions and licenses are also available for most titles. For more information, reference our Print and eBook Bulk Sales web page at http://www.apress.com/bulk-sales.

Any source code or other supplementary material referenced by the author in this book is available to readers on the Github repository: https://github.com/Apress/Building AI Driven Marketing Capabilities. For more detailed information, please visit https://www.apress.com/gp/services/source-code.

Paper in this product is recyclable

Contents

About the Editors

Dr. Neha Zaidi is an Assistant Professor of Marketing at the School of Business Studies, Sharda University. She has more than ten years of experience in academics and research and has worked with several reputed management institutions. She has received awards for her research at various international conferences and has published research papers and case studies in Scopus-indexed and ABDC journals in the areas of travel and tourism, sustainable marketing, social media marketing, and services marketing, which remain her prime domains of research.

Dr. Mohit Maurya has a PhD in Retail Management and has almost two decades of experience in academics, research, corporate training, and consulting. Some of his previous associations were with the NIILM Centre for Management Studies, Siddaganga Institute of Technology, Kirloskar Institute of Advanced Management Studies, and ICFAI University. He has published several research papers in national and international journals of repute. He has trained over 1200 executives at various companies like JSW Steel Ltd., Wadhawan Food Retail, Aditya Birla Retail Ltd., Trident Powercraft Private Ltd., GMR Infra., Adecco India, Seminis, Monsanto Agro, Kirloskar Brothers Ltd., Kirloskar Oil Engines Limited, Kirloskar Pneumatic Co. Ltd., and Kirloskar Ebara Pumps Ltd.

Prof. Simon Grima is the Deputy Dean of the Faculty of Economics, Management and Accountancy, Associate Professor, and the Head of the Department of Insurance and Risk Management at the University of Malta. There, he coordinates the MA and MSc Insurance and Risk Management degrees together with the undergrad degree programs in insurance. Simon is also a Professor at the Faculty of Business, Management and Economics, University of Latvia, and a visiting Professor at UNICATT, Milan. He served as the President of the Malta Association of Risk Management (MARM) and President of the Malta Association of Compliance Officers (MACO) between 2013 and 2015 and 2016 and 2018, respectively. He is also the Chairman of

---

The original version of the book has been revised. A correction to this book can be found at https://doi.org/10.1007/978-1-4842-9810-7_17

the Scientific Education Committee of the Public Risk Management Organization (PRIMO). His research focus is on governance, regulations, and internal controls, and he has over 30 years of experience in financial services, academia, and public entities. He has acted as co-chair and is a member of the scientific program committee on some international conferences and is a chief editor, editor, and review editor of several journals and book series. He was named outstanding reviewer for *The Journal of Financial Regulation and Compliance* in the 2017 and 2022 Emerald Literati Awards. Additionally, Simon acts as an independent director for financial services firms; sits on risk, compliance, procurement, investment, and audit committees; and carries out duties as a compliance officer, internal auditor, and risk manager.

Dr. Pallavi Tyagi is an Associate Professor at the Amity College of Commerce and Finance, Amity University Uttar Pradesh, Noida, India. She has earned her MBA from Banasthali University, Rajasthan, India. She earned a Doctor of Philosophy in Human Resource Management with a concentration on employee empowerment and organization performance in 2018. Pallavi has 12 years of professional experience. She has published various case studies and research papers in reputed journals and presented papers at various national and international conferences. She serves as an editor of *The Global Journal of Management and Sustainability* (ISSN 2583-4460). Her areas of interest include diversity, equity, and inclusion (DEI), employee empowerment, and social entrepreneurship. She has edited various books with international publishers, such as Emerald and Rivers Publishers. She also has several patents and copyrights to her credit.

Using Social Media for Improving Customer Engagement

Dr. Harish Kumar*, Professor and Head, Department of Mass Communication, St. Xavier's University, Action Area III, B, Newtown, Kolkata, West Bengal 700160, Email: harish.kumar@sxuk.edu.in

Customer engagement is an essential aspect of corporate success, as engaged customers are more likely to purchase products and services, refer friends and family, and provide valuable feedback. Social media has not only become a powerful platform for corporate houses and marketers, but at the same time, it's helping them to connect with customers on a personal level, which was difficult through traditional marketing channels. Recent technological developments have also made it possible to personalize the information. Another important development is the use of artificial intelligence for the purpose of understanding customers' issues and engaging them for better

N. Zaidi et al. (eds.), *Building AI Driven Marketing Capabilities*,
https://doi.org/10.1007/978-1-4842-9810-7_1

relationships. The integration of AI with different social media platforms is helping the marketers to be more connected with their customer base. Therefore, this chapter is going to give us an insight about social media and its use for better customer engagement.

Introduction

Social media has changed the way we used to communicate. It has also paved the way for better engagement with customers. Boyd and Ellison (2008) defined social media in this way: "a networked communication platform in which participants create, share, and/or exchange information and content (including user-generated content) and engage in social networking." Social media has transformed the way business communication used to take place with their customers. Social media platforms, such as Facebook, Twitter, Instagram, and LinkedIn, offer businesses the ability to engage with customers in real time. Social media is becoming very important because according to the latest statistics, as of January 2022, there were approximately 4.87 billion social media users worldwide, representing around 62.4% of the total global population. In India, as per the data of January 2022, the number of social media users reached 517 million, making India the second-largest social media market in the world after China. This represents around 37.5% of the country's total population.

In this way, its global presence is encouraging different multinational companies to also use social media platforms for better communication and engagement with customers. Let us understand the concept of customer based on the following definitions given by renowned scholars:

According to Marketing Guru Philip Kotler, "a customer is a person who buys goods or services for personal use or consumption and not for resale or manufacturing" (Kotler, 2003, p. 6).

In the field of customer relationship management, Peppers and Rogers define a customer as "someone who has interacted with your company in any way" (Peppers & Rogers, 2016, p. 21). This includes not only purchasers but also prospects, influencers, and even dissatisfied customers who have made complaints.

In relation to social media, a customer may be defined as "an individual or group who engages with a company or brand on social media platforms, by interacting with their content, posting comments, asking questions, or providing feedback" (Kietzmann et al., 2011, p. 243).

Therefore, we can say that customers are very precious for us, and in recent marketing communications, they are being treated as king. As we discussed earlier about social media, let us learn about the different types of social media platforms which are frequently being used by different companies and corporate houses.

Important Social Media Platforms

Social media is becoming an integral part of marketing communication which is being used for the purpose of better customer engagement. Some of the important social media platforms that are widely used for customer engagement and marketing are as follows:

- **Instagram**: Instagram provides a platform where users can share photos and videos. We can witness its popularity with the fact that it has more than one billion monthly active users. It helps marketers in sending appropriate audio and visual content reels for creating better engagement which helps in a strong visual identity. As we know, Instagram stories also do the job of creating better engagements with their customers and showcasing their products or services.

- **YouTube**: YouTube is an important platform for sharing audio and video content. It's also very important because it has over two billion monthly active users. It is an ideal platform for corporate houses that want to showcase their products or services through interactive video content. With different advanced tools like creating channels, playlists, and other tools, marketing activities can become more engaging and could result in motivating and convincing customers to drive traffic to their website.

- **Facebook**: Actually, Facebook is also a very popular social media platform for customer engagement. It's very important because it has a monthly active user base of more than 2.7 billion. It offers a range of features such as pages, groups, messenger, and formulation of social groups based on their liking, interest area, and profession.

- **Twitter**: Twitter is one of the microblogging platforms that is being used frequently by corporate houses and marketers. It also comes with different features like the blue tick facility and sharing information through text and audio/visual elements. Twitter has more than 330 million monthly active users. Twitter is also being used for the purpose of updating new information and announcement.

- **LinkedIn**: LinkedIn is also a social networking platform which is being used by professionals. It also offers a range of services, such as company pages and showcase pages, and at the same time is used for the purpose of workshops, sessions, and seminars which might be related with customer engagement.

- **TikTok**: TikTok was once one of the most popular social media platform in India. Still, it has a monthly user base of more than one billion. TikTok has different tools like duets and challenges that are also being used by marketers for the purpose of customer engagement and awareness.

- **WhatsApp**: WhatsApp is a messaging app that is widely used for personal communication. However, businesses can also use WhatsApp to engage with their customers through features such as WhatsApp Business and WhatsApp API. These features allow businesses to provide customer support, send transactional messages, and engage in conversations with their customers.

- **Pinterest**: Pinterest is used for visual discovery and for the purpose of bookmarking. It has more than 400 million monthly users. It is an ideal platform for businesses that have a strong visual identity and want to showcase their products or services through images. Different tools such as boards and pins are encouraging customers and being used to increase the traffic of different websites.

- **Snapchat**: Snapchat is a multimedia messaging app that is widely used by younger audiences. With the help of tools like filters and lenses, different marketers used to engage with their customers and build brand awareness.

- **Reddit**: It is used for news aggregation and discussion. More than 52 million active users are using it daily. It is being used to engage with niche communities and drive traffic to their website.

Important Studies on Social Media and Customer Engagement

Chen and Chen (2017) conducted a study to investigate the impact of social media engagement on customer loyalty. Their findings showed that social media engagement had a positive effect on customer loyalty and that social media was an effective tool for building customer relationships.

Sharma and Joshi (2018) conducted an empirical study on Indian brands and their use of social media for customer engagement. The study revealed that Indian brands are increasingly using social media to engage with their customers by building brand awareness, creating user-generated content, and providing customer support.

Singh and Srivastava (2018) conducted a study on the Indian FMCG sector and analyzed the impact of social media marketing on customer engagement. The study found that social media marketing has a significant positive impact on customer engagement, and companies should focus on creating relevant and engaging content.

Chauhan et al. (2019) conducted an exploratory study on Indian consumers and their engagement with social media platforms. The study identified that Indian consumers are highly engaged with social media platforms, with a focus on entertainment, socialization, and information seeking. The study also revealed key factors that influence customer engagement, such as trust, social influence, and interactivity.

Singh and Saini (2017) conducted a study on the Indian fashion industry and examined the impact of social media on customer engagement. The study found that social media has a significant positive impact on customer engagement, and companies in the fashion industry should focus on creating visually appealing and informative content.

Singh and Saini (2018) conducted a study on the Indian hospitality industry and examined the impact of social media on customer engagement. The study found that social media has a significant positive impact on customer engagement, and companies in the hospitality industry should focus on creating personalized and engaging content.

Leung et al. (2013) explored the effects of different types of social media engagement on customer loyalty. Their findings suggested that proactive engagement, such as responding to customer queries and complaints, was more effective in building customer loyalty than reactive engagement, such as promotional posts.

Hajli (2014) investigated the impact of social media on customer engagement and found that social media was a useful tool for businesses to engage with their customers, improve customer satisfaction, and enhance brand image.

Verhoef et al. (2010) studied the relationship between customer engagement and loyalty. They found that customer engagement had a significant positive effect on loyalty and that social media was an effective platform for engaging with customers.

Finally, Kaplan and Haenlein (2010) proposed a framework for businesses to engage with their customers through social media. The 4Cs framework emphasizes the importance of providing relevant and engaging content, creating a community of engaged customers, and customizing content to meet customer needs and preferences.

Conclusion: The literature highlights that social media engagement is an effective tool for businesses to build customer loyalty, enhance customer experience, and improve brand image. By engaging with customers through social media, businesses can build strong relationships and create a loyal customer base.

Impact of Social Media on Customer Engagement

Different social media platforms are being used for the purpose of marketing communication and for better engagement of customers. Therefore, we can have a lot of examples through which we can say that it's having a great impact on customer engagement:

- **Provide customer support**: Social media provides businesses with a platform to provide customer support in real time. Customers can reach out to businesses through social media, and businesses can respond promptly, providing solutions to their queries or complaints, leading to improved customer satisfaction and loyalty.

- **Strengthening relationship with customers**: Social media is helpful for corporate houses to build and strengthen relationships with their customers. Through social media, better engagement is possible; it can create a sense of belongingness and leads to the formulation of better relationship with customers. Generally, satisfied customers are more loyal, and sometimes they are also doing the job of advocacy.

- **Create brand awareness**: Social media provides businesses with a platform to create brand awareness. The way people used to share the content on different social media platforms is helpful in reaching toward a wider audience, increasing brand visibility and awareness which is helpful in increasing profit.

Advantage of Social Media Strategies for Customer Engagement

The following are strategies for leveraging social media to improve customer engagement:

- **Engage with customers**: Engage with customers on social media by responding to their comments, queries, and complaints promptly. This can help build relationships and create a sense of community.

- **Share valuable content**: Share valuable content that is relevant and engaging to customers, such as blog posts, infographics, and videos. Valuable content is very helpful in building trust with customers, and on the basis of it, credibility can be ensured.

- **Provide exclusive offers**: Provide exclusive offers to customers on social media. This can incentivize customers to engage with your brand on social media, leading to increased engagement and loyalty.

- **Personalize communications**: Personalize communications with customers by addressing them by their first name. This can help create a more personal connection and foster a deeper relationship with customers.

Disadvantages of Social Media Strategies for Customer Engagement

Despite the benefits, social media and customer engagement present several challenges; these are as follows:

- **Negative feedback**: Social media allows customers to provide negative feedback publicly, which can damage a brand's reputation and lead to decreased customer engagement and loyalty.

- **Privacy concerns**: Privacy concerns are a significant challenge associated with social media and customer engagement. Customers may be hesitant to engage with businesses on social media if they feel their personal information is not secure.

- **Competition**: Competition is another challenge associated with social media and customer engagement. With so many businesses competing for customer attention on social media, it can be challenging to stand out and engage customers effectively.

Hence, social media platforms helps in different aspects of marketing communication, for instance: to build relationships, provide customer support, and create brand awareness. To improve customer engagement, businesses should engage with customers, share valuable content, personalize communications, and provide exclusive offers. While there are challenges associated with social media and customer engagement, corporate houses can overcome these challenges with the right strategies and approaches.

Social Media Engagement vs. Mainstream Media Engagement

As we discussed about social media use for better engagement with customers, we must be familiar with why it's different from mainstream media in relation with customer engagement. The following are the elements which make it different:

- **Interaction**: Social media engagement is interactive, and it's very helpful in ensuring a two-way communication. Customers can ask questions, provide feedback, and engage with companies in real time, while mainstream media is typically a one-way communication.

- **Cost**: Social media engagement is generally more cost-effective than mainstream media engagement. Creating and posting content on social media platforms are typically free, while advertising in mainstream media can be expensive.

- **Speed**: Social media engagement is faster than mainstream media. Customers can contact companies through social media platforms and receive an immediate response, while mainstream media engagement may take longer due to the need for approval.

- **Reach**: Social media engagement can reach a larger audience compared to mainstream media, as it allows companies to engage with customers from all around the world.

Based on the preceding elements, we can say that customer engagement through social media offers a faster, more interactive, wider-reaching, and cost-effective option for companies to engage with their customers compared to mainstream media.

Innovative Technologies and AI in Social Media

Artificial intelligence is becoming an integral part of marketing communication. The following are the important AI-based tools and cases which are related with the application of artificial intelligence:

- **Chatbots**: One of the most common uses of AI for customer engagement is through chatbots. Chatbots can be used to provide 24/7 customer support, answer frequently asked questions, and help customers with their purchasing decisions. Chatbots use natural language processing (NLP) to understand customer queries and respond in a conversational manner, making it a seamless experience for customers. Chatbots have become a popular tool for customer engagement on social media platforms. Many Indian companies are leveraging chatbots to provide 24/7 customer support, answer frequently asked questions, and provide personalized recommendations. Some examples of Indian companies using chatbots for customer engagement include

  - **HDFC Bank**: HDFC Bank uses Eva, a chatbot that provides instant responses to customer queries related to banking products and services.

  - **ICICI Lombard**: ICICI Lombard, a leading insurance provider, has developed a chatbot that helps customers buy insurance policies, renew policies, and get claims settled.

  - **OYO Rooms**: OYO Rooms, a hotel booking platform, uses a chatbot to assist customers with booking inquiries, room availability, and other questions.

- **Kotak Mahindra Bank**: Kotak Mahindra Bank uses Keya, an AI-powered chatbot that provides customer support, helps customers find the nearest bank branch, and offers personalized product recommendations.

- **Flipkart**: Flipkart is one of India's ecommerce platforms that uses a chatbot to help customers track their orders, get information on products, and resolve complaints.

Personalization

Artificial intelligence is also used to personalize customer experiences. In this regard, customer data such as browsing behavior, purchase history, and preferences are recorded. AI algorithms can use this data to provide personalized product recommendations, targeted marketing messages, and customized offers, leading to increased customer engagement and loyalty.

Personalization has become an essential aspect for Indian companies in meeting the individual needs and preferences of their customers. Here are some examples of personalization approaches that Indian companies use:

Customized products and services: Companies in India offer customized products and services that cater to their customers' unique needs and preferences. For example, Lenskart, an Indian eyewear company, provides its customers with a virtual try-on feature to choose frames that fit their face size and shape.

Targeted advertising: Indian companies use targeted advertising to personalize their marketing messages and promotions based on the customers' interests. Myntra, an online retailer, uses machine learning algorithms to suggest personalized recommendations to customers based on their purchase and browsing history.

Personalized customer service: Indian companies provide personalized customer service to enhance customer satisfaction. For instance, ICICI Bank uses AI-powered chatbots to deliver personalized support to its customers and respond to their queries instantly.

Personalized loyalty programs: Indian companies offer personalized loyalty programs that provide customers with personalized offers and discounts based on their purchase history. Tata CLiQ, a loyalty program by the Tata Group, is an example of such a program. Swiggy, a food delivery platform, sends personalized messages to customers with recommendations based on their order history.

Another type of content is the video content which exhibits product demos and showcases a product's features and benefits in action. Testimonial videos can also be used to feature satisfied customers sharing their positive experiences with a product or service. In addition, brand story videos can be created to highlight a brand's history, values, and mission. Finally, live videos can be streamed in real time, allowing viewers to engage with the content in real time. By creating engaging and informative video content, businesses can enhance their brand awareness and connect with their audience on a deeper level.

BYJU'S, an edtech company, uses video content as the centerpiece of their learning platform. BYJU'S offers a vast library of video lessons and lectures, covering a wide range of subjects and topics, presented by India's best educators. These videos are not only informative but also engaging, with animation, graphics, and interactive elements, making learning a fun experience for students.

Myntra, an online fashion retailer, has also been leveraging video content to showcase their products and engage with their customers. They created a series of short, fashion-focused videos, featuring their models in different outfits, styled for different occasions. These videos not only showcase the latest fashion trends but also demonstrate how their products can be styled to create different looks.

Finally, Tata Sky, a direct-to-home television provider, uses video content to promote their services and entertain their customers. They created a series of short, humorous videos, featuring popular Bollywood actors, showcasing the different features and benefits of their service. These videos are widely shared on social media, generating buzz and engagement among their customers.

Frequently Used Online Tools for Customer Engagement

- **Predictive analytics**: Artificial intelligence helps strategists to anticipate customer needs and provide proactive support. Predictive analytics can be used to identify potential issues before they occur and take proactive steps to prevent them. This can help businesses improve customer satisfaction and loyalty.

- **Sentiment analysis**: AI can be used for sentiment analysis, which can help businesses understand customer feedback and sentiments. Sentiment analysis helps in understanding and identifying customer sentiments and related issues, allowing businesses to take immediate action to resolve them. Sentiment analysis can also be used to identify customer trends and priorities, allowing corporate houses to provide more personalized experiences. Sentiment analysis is a versatile tool that can be applied in different ways to analyze customer feedback and gauge the overall sentiment toward a particular product, service, or brand. The following are some examples of how sentiment analysis can be utilized:

  - **Product reviews**: Companies can utilize sentiment analysis to assess customer reviews of their products and services to determine customer sentiment. This can aid in identifying areas for improvement and enhancing customer satisfaction.

  - **Social media monitoring**: Sentiment analysis is used by various social media platforms for identifying brand, product, or service mentions. This can help companies track customer feedback and sentiment in real time and respond to customer inquiries or complaints proactively.

  - **Brand reputation management**: Sentiment analysis can be used to monitor and manage a company's brand reputation. Companies can track mentions of their brand on various social media platforms, news websites, and blogs and use sentiment analysis to determine the overall sentiment toward their brand.

- **Customer surveys**: Sentiment analysis can be utilized to analyze customer survey responses and determine customer sentiment toward a particular product or service. This can aid companies in making data-driven decisions to enhance customer satisfaction.

- **Customer feedback tools**: Customer feedback tools such as surveys and feedback forms are used in India to collect feedback from customers. For instance, hospitality brand OYO uses customer feedback tools to collect feedback and improve customer experiences in its hotels.

- **Live chat**: Live chat is another tool used in India for customer engagement. For example, online education platform BYJU'S uses live chat to provide instant support to students and resolve their queries.

- **Mobile apps**: Mobile apps are increasingly being used in India for customer engagement. For example, food delivery app Swiggy uses its mobile app to offer personalized recommendations to customers and provide 24/7 customer support.

Overall, these effectively provide better customer support and ultimately drive business growth.

Indian Companies Using Social Media Platforms for Better Customer Engagement

Social media has become a vital tool for customer engagement in India, and several Indian companies have successfully leveraged it to engage with their customers. Here are some examples of Indian companies that have used social media for customer engagement:

- **Zomato**: Zomato, a food delivery and restaurant discovery platform, has built a strong reputation for customer service by the support of different social media platforms. In this regard, Zomato is using Twitter and Facebook to engage with its customers. The company has a dedicated Twitter handle called @ZomatoCare that addresses customer complaints and issues in real time, demonstrating its proactive approach to customer service.

- **Ola**: Ola, a popular ride-hailing platform in India, has used social media to provide real-time customer support and address customer issues. The company has a dedicated Twitter handle called @OlacabsSupport that addresses customer complaints and issues. Ola has also used social media to run promotional campaigns and offer discounts to its customers, further increasing customer engagement.

- **Flipkart**: Flipkart, one of the leading ecommerce platforms in India, has used social media to build a loyal customer base and drive sales growth. The company engages with its customers on platforms like Twitter and Facebook, providing updates about its products and services and running promotional campaigns. Flipkart's social media strategy has helped it build strong customer relationships and increase customer engagement.

- **HDFC Bank**: HDFC Bank, one of the leading banks in India, has leveraged social media to provide 24/7 customer support and offer exclusive discounts and promotions to its customers. The bank engages with its customers on platforms like Twitter and Facebook, resolving customer issues and building strong customer relationships.

- **Lenskart**: Lenskart, a popular eyewear brand in India, has successfully used social media to build brand awareness and drive sales growth. The company engages with its customers on platforms like Facebook and Instagram, providing updates about its products and services and running promotional campaigns.

- **Amul**: Amul is an Indian dairy brand that has successfully used social media to engage with its current and prosperous customers. The brand has a strong social media presence and is known for its witty and humorous posts that connect with its customers. Amul has launched various campaigns, like the "Amul Topical" campaign through social media.

- **BigBasket**: BigBasket is an Indian online grocery delivery platform that is also using various social media platforms for connecting with customers. The brand has a dedicated customer service team that addresses customer queries and grievances on social media. BigBasket also uses social media to promote its offerings, launch campaigns, and engage with its audience through interactive posts and contests.

- **Swiggy**: Swiggy, a popular food delivery platform in India, has a strong social media presence and engages with its customers through various social media channels. The brand uses social media to address customer queries, complaints, and feedback, as well as to promote its offerings and launch campaigns.

- **MakeMyTrip**: MakeMyTrip is an Indian online travel company. This company is having a presence on various social media platforms in order to engage with the customers. The brand has a dedicated customer service team that addresses customer queries and solves the problem on social media. MakeMyTrip also uses social media to promote its offerings, launch campaigns, and engage with its audience through interactive posts and contests.

- **Mahindra Group**: This multinational conglomerate uses tools like Brand watch to monitor its brand reputation and gain insights into customer sentiments and preferences by tracking mentions of its brand on social media platforms.

These examples demonstrate how Indian companies are leveraging social media to engage and strengthen relationship with customers, address their concerns and feedback, and to promote their offerings and campaigns. By using social media effectively, companies can build a strong relationship with their customers and drive customer loyalty.

Conclusion

Engaging with customers through social media has become an essential strategy for businesses to stay relevant and competitive in today's digital age. Companies are using various tools and techniques to enhance customer engagement through social media, such as personalized messaging, social listening, sentiment analysis, chatbots, and more.

For example, Indian companies like Tata Sky, Vodafone, and HDFC Bank are using chatbots to engage with their customers and provide them with personalized recommendations based on their preferences. The chatbots are available 24/7, and they can handle many queries simultaneously, reducing the response time and improving the overall customer experience.

Similarly, many Indian companies are using social listening tools to monitor online conversations and gather customer feedback, which helps them to understand their customers' needs and preferences better. For instance, Amul, a leading dairy brand in India, uses social listening to track online conversations related to its brand and products. This information is used to develop new products and marketing campaigns that are tailored to meet out the needs and expectations of its customers.

Apart from the preceding things, social media has transformed the way marketing companies used to engage with their customers, and it has become an essential tool for customer engagement and marketing. Indian companies are leveraging various social media tools and techniques to enhance customer engagement and improve their overall business performance. As social media continues to evolve and become more sophisticated, it is expected that more innovative and effective strategies will emerge, leading to better customer engagement and increased business growth.

In summary, we can say that social media has provided us with different features and tools, and especially in India, it is being used by various companies for better and continuous customer engagement. Companies are also using it to provide 24/7 customer support and to resolve issues in real time.

Applying AI for Product Life Cycle Management

Ambika Khurana*, Assistant Professor, School of Business Studies, Sharda University, Greater Noida, Uttar Pradesh, India, Email: ambika.khurana@sharda.ac.in

Shelly, MBAI (Pursuing), School of Business Studies, Sharda University, Greater Noida, Uttar Pradesh, India, Email: 2020518243.shelly@ug.sharda.ac.in

Tirthankar Dey, Integrated MBA (Pursuing), School of Business Studies, Sharda University, Greater Noida, Uttar Pradesh, India, Email: 2020435851.tirthankar@ug.sharda.ac.in

AI has been getting a lot of attention lately in the manufacturing industry. Considering it is the foundation of Industry 4.0, so smart manufacturing strategies are really interested in it. PLM (Product Life Cycle Management) covers all the engineering, enterprise, and administrative tasks related to a product throughout its life cycle, from the creation of an idea to the recycling of finished goods. In this chapter, we look at a few AI theories, methods, and technologies related to the key PLM stages of intelligent manufacturing (e.g., product design, manufacturing, and service). We also provide a road map to help guide future research and use cases for AI in PLM. We also look at the potential and challenges of AI for PLM.

Introduction

Product life cycle management encompasses engineering, commercial, and managerial tasks related to a product throughout its entire life cycle: from the ideation of an abstract concept to the disposal of a final product.

Modern production is changing rapidly due to the rapid development of information-related technologies such as the IoT, cloud computing, AI, and big data which impact every aspect of product life cycle management.

International production strategies and innovations, such as the Industrial Internet strategy in the United States, Industry 04 strategy in Germany, Manufacturing Innovation 03 strategy in South Korea, Industry 2050 strategy in the UK, and Made in China 2025 strategy in China.

Artificial intelligence (AI) refers to a variety of theories, approaches, technologies, and tools that are designed to mimic and augment human intellect. Artificial intelligence (AI) applications have recently become widely used in a wide range of industries, contemporaneous with the fast growth of big data, machine learning (ML), and computer chips. In order to do complex jobs demanding noticeably improved dependability, precision, and efficiency, human operators must be supported, helped, and sometimes even replaced by AI. A few examples of well-known AI applications are Google's DeepMind AlphaGo in board games, security systems for all transportations, facial recognition systems for payments, speech recognition systems for smart devices, and carriage security systems.

In the context of advanced manufacturing, there aren't as many AI applications for product life cycle management as there are in other disciplines. On the one hand, manufacturers are naturally apprehensive to embrace AI in product life cycle management owing to the extremely high requirement for quality, dependability, precision, and cost-effectiveness in manufacturing. This particularly stands for small- to mid-sized organizations (SMM). The benefits of AI to product life cycle management, however, are too many to mention. The first benefit is that a complicated production process may be optimized for a less labor-intensive phase since AI can easily replace people in repetitive and risky activities. Second, a costly manufacturing process may be made more affordable given that verified AI solutions can last a very extended period. Third, because countless AI algorithms are becoming more compatible with industrial-scale big data, production decision-making is moving more in the direction of data-driven approaches. Manufacturers are better prepared to respond to a changing industrial environment because of their improved capacity for handling massive volumes of data. Finally, many advanced AI programs may be easily modified for use in industrial settings. Computer vision has been used, for instance, to automate quality control, visual localization, dimension measuring, object sorting, bar code identification, and other processes.

Recent Trends in Product Life Cycle Management

Product life cycle management (PLCM) was originally designed to capture the three phases of a product's life cycle in the open market: promotion, maturation, and depreciation. With the advent of concurrent engineering in the 1980s, PLCM gradually gained traction in manufacturing engineering. This led to a new division of product life cycle management operations: market research, product development, process design, production, distribution, utilization, after-sales service, and recycling. Different academics understood product life cycle management differently in view of the constant changes in the production pattern. The product design phase, the product production phase, and the product service phase are the three distinct phases that AI technology is categorized into to classify their techniques and goals in various stages. Substages are further separated into each stage: the planning phase, manifestation layout, design specification, and trial manufacturing are all parts of the product design stage. Substages of the product manufacturing stage include material procurement, production scheduling, manufacturing, and warehousing/logistics. The service stage encompasses a variety of value-added services, including recycling, sales, use, and after-sales support.

A comprehensive information structure that integrates diverse data, information, and technologies is crucial for product life cycle management deployment in practice. Information integration for product life cycle management calls for general theories and methodologies, as well as specialized technologies for data analysis, information and semantic integration, information interaction, and web service connectivity, among other things. The requirements and components of the product life cycle management extension are continually improved by the new manufacturing processes. However, given the wide range of product life cycle management, the majority of the current frameworks are particularly designed for a single application situation, which hinders their general applicability.

Various optimizing and assessment strategies have been introduced inside the product life cycle management framework. Common evaluation criteria for the design phase include aesthetics, functionality, development time, and environmental friendliness. Typical evaluation techniques include the Analytic Hierarchy Method, the Method for Orders of Preferences based on Resemblance to the Perfect Solution, the Impact Matrix, the Kano Model, etc. Prevalent assessment pointers for the production cycle include production span, cost, resource usage, and energy consumption; common optimization techniques are embodied by theme and subtheme algorithms. For the registration phase, the service quality is a crucial metrical system for assessing service performance since it shows how much personalization is provided to clients.

The data of product life cycle management has experienced marvelous growth as a consequence of the extensive usage of implanted technology such as RFID tags and of course cutting-edge sensors in the manufacturing and service stages. Newly formed approaches to product life cycle management data modeling, synchronization, connection, transformation, and removal are being actively developed as of now. The measure and diversity of product life cycle management data will keep on increasing as new age technologies such as the Industrial-grade Internet and the digital counterpart expansion traction. When it comes to analyzing great quantities of data with several dimensions, numerous AI algorithms are bigger than orthodox practices. One of product life cycle management's most striking potentials across their design, production, and service stages is the interface among product life cycle management and data science.

AI: What Is It?

Depending on their research specialities, disciplinary backgrounds, and domains, researchers describe and interpret artificial intelligence (AI) differently. Personification and intelligence are two terms that appear in several definitions of artificial intelligence.

Symbolisms, which proposed that cognition, knowledge representation, application, and reasoning were at the core of AI, are credited with first introducing the concept of AI. The creation of several expert systems was one of symbolism's greatest contributions. According to connectionism, AI is developed from bionics (or engineering that is inspired by biology), particularly concerning our knowledge of animal and human brains. The development of artificial neural networks, which were motivated by the biological neural networks that make up the core of animal brains, was a significant contribution to connectionism.

Actionism, a relatively recent school, specializes in the study of cybernetic model of systems about auto-organization, auto-learning, auto-adaptation, auto-stabilization, and auto-optimization. Based on the pre-existing characterizations, the authors define artificial intelligence (AI) as the applications, theories, tools, and methodologies designed for simulating intelligent behavior, create artificial intelligence in computer systems, empower artifacts to perform intellectual tasks, and understand human intelligence.

"Artificial narrow intelligence" (ANI), "artificial general intelligence" (AGI), and "artificial superintelligence" (ASI) are the three subcategories of AI. A single domain-specific job may be carried out by artificial systems thanks to ANI. Three other subcategories of ANI include perception, cognition, and learning, in addition to behavior. A further developed stage of AI is represented by AGI, where AI is viewed as being roughly similar to human intelligence when compared to their capacity to carry out general intellectual-based activities. The present state of our knowledge of AI, however, is further away from sufficient to create a fully operational ASI system. It is a potential AI state in which AI has higher intelligence levels than human intellect. As a result, it can do jobs that are too difficult for the human intellect to handle. Authors of this chapter primarily discuss the use of ANI in product life cycle management.

AI systems must possess the cognitive and learning intelligence to learn, analyze, evaluate, and make decisions based on observed information. Logic, planning, knowledge representation, reasoning, machine learning, and other important technologies are included. Before the development of AI, logic was a well-developed academic field. Logic refers to the general principles of the reasoning used in various problem-solving scenarios. It facilitates analysis, characterization, and programming while describing and simulating intelligence and resolving challenges with intelligent thinking. Propositional logic and first-order logic are both parts of the common logic branch.

In order to control the behaviors of artificial systems, behavior scientists integrate computer-based systems, sensory systems, feedback-generating systems, and communication tracker systems (such as automation software, robot process, and intelligent robots). Complex tasks can be accomplished by intelligent robots through manual instruction or auto-learning. It can communicate with human handlers using everyday language, and they can even work along with human handlers using more sophisticated sensory abilities. Human operators can be replaced by intelligent robots that are more productive, less expensive, and more reliable. Prescription dispensing, medical material handling, direct material handling, patient care, inventory replenishment, product packaging and picking, order fulfillment, help with shopping, package delivery, security, customer service, etc., are a few examples of potential applications. Interface recognition and workflow execution technologies are combined by robot process automation software. Screens and keyboards are used to control programs and carry out system activities automatically, simulating human actions. Software for robot app automation is a "bridge" technology which combines several systems to carry out more sophisticated tasks than automation.

Product Life Cycle Management

Product life cycle management had their beginning in the automobile and aviation business and then spread to other related and unrelated sectors including electronics, packaged products, fashion, and healthcare. Product life cycle management was industrialized as a result of technology development in product data and their management, computer-aided design (CAD), and computer-aided engineering (CAE) (PDM). These expansions made it possible for manufacturers to integrate design and production, reducing the lead times and production cycles. Because of the complexities and the sheer number of processes involved within the production, it was likely possible to boost the competition by restructuring the methods and centralizing all information involved. Product life cycle management is more than concerned with integrating these available technologies with the procedures, humans, and theories as a product moves through their life cycle, though.

Product life cycle management is the process of not only managing a product when it passes through their several lifetime phases but also including the introduction of the product and implementation of the production, further development, managed timescale, and ultimately the collapse.

The production of goods and then their marketing are both an integral part of their management. While making business-related decisions, from factors like pricing and advertising to their growth or necessary cost-cutting, the idea behind the PLC can be helpful.

The definitive goal of effective PLM is to generate an item that outclasses their rivals, is incredibly lucrative, and lasts for as much as the consumer prefers and future technologies allow. This is accomplished by getting together the multiple corporations, departments, and relevant personnel in the product's production to modernize their operations. The process involves more than just generating Bills of Material (BOM).

Product life cycle management solutions help businesses in overpowering the engineering problems and growing complexities of the product development process. They can be assumed as one of the four standards of a production company's information-based systems structure, among which are the management of infrastructures with clients ("customer relationship management," CRM), relations with suppliers, resources held by the company, and supply chain management such as ERP.

The marketing strategies for a product are decided by the stage of their life cycle. For example, a newly made model (that is still in the beginning phase) is in need of explanation, but in the case of a matured product, it requires differentiation methods. Product life cycle management has a huge influence on a product's most basic elements as well. A product can still continue to be developing even after it reaches the maturity phase, principally if it is being upgraded or improved in some other way.

Effective product life cycle management offers various advantages, including accelerating product launch, releasing a product of higher quality, enhancing product safety, boosting revenue prospects, and minimizing mistakes and waste. Product life cycle management can be supported by specialized computer-based software programs that perform activities like documentation, design integration methods, and procedure administration. Product life cycle management lowers the total cost involved and reduce lead time for "new product development" (NPD). In case the newly made products consist of increasing or imitative changes to the already made old products, ground-breaking new items, and the next-gen of the platform, there needs to be a method for each department to manage them. This new "product development process" (PDP) uses the product life cycle to determine what the basic shape and arrangement of the method will look like. A good product life cycle management is all-inclusive, secures and manages the product info, and ensures that business procedures use and are built upon the information generated.

The three key essentials of product life cycle management are as follows:

- Information and Communication Technology (ICT): The essential integrated platform and processes, including the architecture, resources, and standards, are at the center of this.

- The Processes: These cover all the parties, faculties, and organizations concerned.

- The Methods: These are the protocols, laws, and customs.

Product life cycle management is increasing in scale as a result of the globalization of the world economy. Giving rise to shorter production run window, new supply chain processes, and outsourcing all necessitate the need for businesses to have accurate and current manufacturing information. Moreover, the Internet allows us to communicate swiftly with partners who happen to be located far away. The modification of production requirements may now be done during the production period because of the product life cycle management. With segregated engineering and production divisions, this procedure would commonly take days and even weeks, particularly if the production plant was located abroad. Product life cycle management upsurges the speed to market in numerous different ways:

1) Keeping track of your changes throughout time

2) Keeping your company knowledgeable about the products

3) Adding the company's systems together

4) Recording the components and raw materials

5) Monitoring the manufacturing processes

6) Handling consumer expectations and product action

7) Citation of the physical and chemical features

8) Upholding version control management

9) Preserving records of opinions and goods from history, today, and beyond

10) Documenting adjustments to prices, rules, improvements, and consumer expectations

The Product Life Cycle Management Stages

With the prospect of reducing any wastage, the procedures must be integrated since countless businesses must harmonize the resources available and personnel stationed at more than a few locations. On top of that, unity keeps the procedures focused on the product itself and increases the possibility of their commercial achievement. Product life cycle management business models come in a diversity of forms these days, which can be one of the following:

- Beginning of Life (BOL): The design and production processes, which include the original idea and then development as well as any samples created, are all included in the onset of life stage. There are several sub-actions involved in the early development stage that lists all the concepts, criteria, and testing that are obligatory. The business is required to withstand the BOL phase irrespective of the production structure. The product, complete with its production procedure, supply requirements, and specifications, happens in the BOL.

- Middle of Life (MOL): Post-manufacturing, during which your product is sold, utilized, and maintained, is the intermediate period of a product's life. The client now has the product in their ownership. To generate information for both instant solutions and imminent developments, one may have to generate data on any faults, service rates, and customer experience.

- End of Life (EOL): The phase known as "end of life" involves recycling, retiring, or dumping the product. Business now does the process of reverse logistics. EOL commences when the customers no longer require the given product. Companies then start generating data on which materials and components involved are still somewhat useful.

AI in PLCM

AI (artificial intelligence) has made a significant impact on various industries, including product life cycle management (PLM). PLM refers to the process of managing a product from its initial concept and design through its manufacturing, distribution, use, and disposal. AI technologies can enhance various stages of the product life cycle in the following ways:

- Design and Development – Generative Design: AI algorithms can generate multiple design options based on specified constraints and objectives. This helps designers explore innovative solutions.

- Predictive Modeling: AI can analyze historical data to predict potential design flaws or performance issues, allowing designers to make informed decisions early in the process.

- Simulation and Testing: AI-powered simulations can accurately predict how a product will behave under various conditions, reducing the need for physical prototypes.

- Manufacturing and Production – Process Optimization: AI can optimize manufacturing processes by analyzing data from sensors and production lines, identifying bottlenecks, and suggesting improvements.

- Quality Control: AI-based computer vision can inspect products for defects during manufacturing, ensuring high-quality output.

- Predictive Maintenance: AI can predict when manufacturing equipment needs maintenance, reducing downtime and improving overall efficiency.

- Supply Chain Management – Demand Forecasting: AI algorithms can analyze historical data, market trends, and external factors to provide accurate demand forecasts, aiding in inventory management.

- Supplier Selection: AI can analyze supplier data and performance metrics to help in selecting reliable and cost-effective suppliers.

- Risk Management: AI can identify potential risks in the supply chain, such as disruptions due to weather or geopolitical events, and propose mitigation strategies.

Enhancement in marketing and sales includes

- Personalization: AI can analyze customer data to personalize marketing messages and product recommendations, improving customer engagement.

- Market Insights: AI can analyze social media and online trends to provide insights into customer preferences and sentiment.

- Price Optimization: AI algorithms can adjust pricing based on real-time market data and customer behavior, optimizing revenue and profitability.

Enhancement in service and maintenance includes

- Remote Monitoring: IoT devices and AI can be used to monitor products remotely, identifying potential issues and enabling proactive maintenance.

- Troubleshooting: AI-powered catboats can assist customers with troubleshooting and provide real-time solutions to common problems.

- Spare Parts Management: AI can predict when spare parts are likely to be needed, optimizing inventory levels and reducing downtime.

Enhancement in end-of-life management includes

- Recycling and Disposal: AI can assist in identifying components suitable for recycling and proper disposal methods, minimizing environmental impact.

- Data Analytics: AI can analyze usage and performance data to gather insights for future product iterations.

Overall, AI in PLM streamlines processes, enhances decision-making, improves product quality, and accelerates innovation by leveraging data-driven insights throughout the product life cycle. However, it's important to note that implementing AI in PLM requires careful consideration of data privacy, security, and ethical implications.

AI in Product Design

AI makes product design easier by looking at what's going on in the market and using AI algorithms to figure out the best way to mine PLM data. It also helps designers make smarter decisions, so they can create products faster and independently. AI's product design framework has a database with case studies, plus libraries like knowledge, algorithm, and application libraries. The design database takes PLM data from all over the place (the Internet, sensors, robots, and more) and provides data support. The case library has successful design cases that can be studied and referenced. Knowledge libraries store reusable design guidelines and know-how used in the design process. And the algorithm library has AI algorithms designed and stored, and they're triggered automatically based on applications.

The AI chip is responsible for improving parallel speed for AI algorithms and optimizing data reading/storage. The preceding elements work interactively and support various product design processes as the AI chip calculation speed increases.

AI in the Production of Goods

The artificial intelligence–enhanced framework for the production of goods covers resource allocation, planning for production, machining, assembly, quality control, logistics, and more. Artificial intelligence (AI) improves the product manufacturing stage primarily through two methods: (1) refining the manufacturing execution and management process of AI algorithms and (2) substituting AI devices for human labor. Additionally, major advancements in machine-human interaction, defect forecasting, wise decision-making, and more areas result from AI and manufacturing system integration.

AI in Goods and Service Sales

Standard service sales rule, based on highlighted scenario adaptation for evaluation and advice for products is challenging. A major difficulty for the current sales service is how to make knowledgeable product suggestions while taking into account both unique product attributes and changing customer wants. By analyzing the demand-related data of the user set and product set, using deep learning and recommendation algorithms together (e.g., DNN + collaborative filtering) can improve the personalized decision-making authority of advice based on the sales big data. Additionally, the time-series network can extract preference characteristics based on the user's preferences from the content of the product sales network and user group, past purchasing behaviors and generate suggestions.

Future Prospects of PLM with AI: Promoting the shift of the business model of the manufacturer, the resources, skills, and the importance of the manufacturer all play a role in the flexibility and responsiveness of the conventional manufacturing model. This type of model is sensitive to market changes. With the help of AI, the manufacturer may make the transition to mass customization and personalization. Customers can make direct personalized order requests on the basis of intelligent recommendations. Manufacturers can fulfill the requests using extremely flexible manufacturing lines within smart factories. Smart customization is most helpful in the design and manufacturing of consumer goods. Consumers demand distinctive, customized, and individualized goods and services. Successful uses of smart customization include cars, computers, clothing, furniture, and home appliances. Red Collar Group has been running intelligent shop floors and industrial Internet platform in China for ten years. Customers can customize suit designs through the Internet and mobile device apps. Thereby changing perspectives from "Business to Customer" to "Customer to Business"

Enhance Product Design Effectiveness and Quality: When combined with existing techniques and tools, artificial intelligence (AI) can significantly improve product design quality. For example, Autodesk's Fusion 360 product design platform and Netfabb's 3D product design platform both incorporate AI and machine learning (ML) modules. Depending on their perception of the requirements and constraints, intelligent design modules provide design solutions. Furthermore, the "Internet of Things" provides producers with access to extensive production data, increasing the simulation capacity of digital design solutions. Digital twin systems enable the monitoring, management, and optimization of physical product activities through their digital counterparts.

In order to enhance product manufacturing reliability, artificial intelligence (AI) can be employed in a variety of ways. These include detecting unexpected occurrences during the production process, simulating job completion procedures to anticipate future issues, and enabling proactive equipment maintenance. Additionally, AI systems can be used to identify discrepancies in equipment performance and to request suppliers to limit fraying components, as well as to anticipate and prepare for unexpected breakdowns. Finally, AI can take the place of humans in tasks such as ML-based product quality assessments and computer-based workpiece location.

Guaranteeing individual safety on the shop floor: An increase in shop floor safety can be attributed to the use of intelligent robots in place of human workers. The behavior of people, equipment, and vehicles is also gleaned from the surveillance footage in workplaces utilizing picture segmentation, feature extraction, and target recognition. These behavioral data serve as the data foundation for the creation of intelligent security systems, which hold great promise for guaranteeing human safety because they can recognize operator behaviors.

Building Smart Supply Chains

The traditional linear supply chain model is undergoing a profound transformation through the integration of artificial intelligence (AI) and big data. This technological fusion equips manufacturers with the ability to not only optimize supply chain processes but also proactively detect and address network disruptions. It extends its impact to areas such as risk management in inventory, supplier performance enhancement, data-driven decision-making for product sales and market demands, efficient manufacturing scheduling, and improved transportation linkages. AI and big data, thus, empower businesses to navigate the complexities of today's supply chain landscape with agility and strategic foresight.

In this exploration, we delve into the pivotal role of AI and big data in reshaping the traditional supply chain model. We will examine how these technologies enable manufacturers to identify risks, enhance performance, and thrive in the competitive arena of modern commerce:

- Risk factors for inventory
- Supplier performance
- Product sales
- Market demands
- Manufacturing scheduling
- Inadequate transportation linkages

A common use for big data analytics is to predict risk factors for inventory. With ML capabilities, manufacturers can adjust inventory levels, reduce time to market, and cut costs by predicting atypical shifts in market demand.

Challenges: There are numerous theoretical, methodological, technological, and operational obstacles to the comprehensive integration of advanced manufacturing and artificial intelligence in PLM.

- Data Collection, Transfer, and Integration: Large training data are crucial to the effectiveness of AI applications, particularly in the areas of perception, cognition, and learning. The complexity of AI algorithms rises correspondingly to the extent of unstructured data in PLM, which makes it harder to check data consistency. The efficient gathering, transport, and integration of high-quality data are thus a major challenge.

- The AI Algorithm's Dependability, Interpretability, and Adaptability: The core of artificial intelligence in perception, cognition, learning, and decision-making is an intelligent algorithm. In order to increase the dependability, precision, and timeliness in industrial settings, complex PLM needs increasingly sophisticated AI algorithms. The 90% accuracy rate of object recognition, however widely accepted in many contexts, is insufficient for the majority of industrial applications. For instance, when accuracy falls below 99% in a facility that produces millions of products every day, product trustworthiness may be in doubt.

- Influence of External Factors: Unlike a lab setting where there are few uncertainties, the actual PLM environment is full with unknowns that have an impact on the data quality and algorithm reliability. The majority of AI programs are built and evaluated. The accuracy of visual identification algorithms can be impacted during the production stage by fluctuations in light and shop floor dust. Speech recognition algorithms are less accurate when there are mechanical noises. To ensure reliability, the device must undergo thorough testing and validation while being used in challenging outdoor conditions in the service stage. Many AI systems are built to discover new rules using huge data, but they are unable to handle unplanned, low likelihood emergencies. Solving these low-probability emergencies via human intervention is more advantageous. Determining how to set up a system that combines AI and human input is thus a significant task.

- Security of Information, Equipment, and Trust: The foundational requirement for intelligent design, production, and services is security. Information security, equipment security, trust authentication, and other issues are all part of PLM security. Enable seemless data flow across the product life cycle, ensuring easy access for customers, suppliers and manufacturers. Therefore, it necessitates secure, dependable, user-friendly, and adaptable information security measures for businesses outfitted with cutting-edge technology for firewall, intrusion detection, and authentication.

Conclusion

Artificial intelligence (AI) research and applications have grown exponentially in contemporary industries due to the increasing discoveries of platforms, algorithms, and interface techniques. Complex and exciting applications of AI in PLM were discussed in this chapter. By mapping customers' wants and preferences to a product's characteristics, capabilities, and performance in a highly customized manner, artificial intelligence (AI) can improve design judgment during product conception, actualization, and finely tuned design phases of product development. Artificial intelligence (AI) helps with perception, analysis, and decision-making throughout product manufacturing, including sourcing decisions, product schedules, shop floor organization, and storage logistics. The primary purpose of AI during the product service phase is to enhance computer-human interaction, behavioral aspects of customer service, product maintenance, disassembly and recycling, exercising control, and making smart decisions. This will improve intelligence, informationization, and the long-term growth in product-service ecosystems.

Empowering Customer Experience with AI Tools and Technologies

Reena Malik*, Chitkara Business School, Chitkara University, Punjab, India, Email: reenamalik2008@gmail.com

Ambuj Sharma, Ballabh Pant Social Science Institute, Jhusi, Allahabad, India

The knowledge potential of the business can be improved with technology, and such technological advancements can also help in improving customer interactions. Intelligent technologies, such as artificial intelligence, are

© Neha Zaidi, Mohit Maurya, Simon Grima, Pallavi Tyagi 2024, corrected publication 2024
N. Zaidi et al. (eds.), *Building AI Driven Marketing Capabilities*,
https://doi.org/10.1007/978-1-4842-9810-7_3

transforming businesses by gathering and analyzing huge amount of data which further improves customer interaction and experience. The objective of this chapter is to analyze the role of artificial intelligence in improving customer experience and to examine tools and techniques of artificial intelligence which are being used by businesses to reach out to customers and engage with them. We'll review secondary data for showing how companies are utilizing the power of artificial intelligence and reaping the benefits of advanced technologies by providing seamless experience to the customers. This chapter explores various tools and techniques used for customer engagement with real-life examples of the companies' providing implications for academicians and marketers.

Introduction

The biggest growth opportunity for companies nowadays is the customers' transition from offline to online; being tech-savvy consumers, they spend most of their time online, and this also calls for a great online experience which today's customers want. Companies are creating influential customer experiences, as with the advancements in technology, the complex things have become much easier with a single click. In order to provide enhanced customer experience, companies are utilizing artificial intelligence. Artificial intelligence (AI) is a disruptive technology enabling machines to mimic human and cognitive functions. The term is also used to represent the various capabilities of a learning system which are representative of the intelligence level perceived by humans. The different capabilities can be of different types like processing of natural language, automating, predicting, decision making, etc. Applications of artificial intelligence also include image and video recognition, understanding natural language, generating natural language, smart automation, interactive agents, analytics, and predicting.

Artificial intelligence (AI) can perform various tasks like solving various problems and reasoning as using this technology machines can mimic human effective and cognitive which is required for performing such tasks [1]. In order to take real-time decisions like predicting and other marketing-related actions, machines present, learn, and store the information on the basis of past and present knowledge as well as experience [2]. Machines learn while assessing the decisions, and this enables machines to respond and adapt as per the dynamic business environment which was not possible earlier with traditional approaches. AI is being widely used in different fields, and certainly it has changed the entire landscapes, especially in marketing where a transition has happened from traditional approaches to digital approaches like usage of chatbots, etc. Artificial intelligence has multiple things to offer like personalization, automation, prediction, and recommendation which has brought a revolution AI has unfolded various avenues of competitive advantage, but AI has its limitations and challenges too. The challenges include complex designing, privacy compromise, etc. The chapter will discuss various tools of artificial intelligence for customer engagement, AI-driven customer journey, and enhancing customer experience. It will also discuss the challenges posed by it.

In order to draw a conclusion, data can be processed from various platforms with the help of AI technology. With the emergence of modern marketing, the power has shifted from industry to consumer. Companies are increasingly focusing on their customers' interests and spending heavily on marketing designing appropriate marketing strategies to reach out to their customers [22–25]. With extensive data available on social media platforms, companies are taking more interest in what their customers are feeling, liking, and buying. This data can quickly be converted in real time which can be easily modified for maximum effectiveness. Further, deeper insights can easily be availed for optimizing digital advertising and account-based marketing [11].

Customer Interaction and AI

The use of artificial intelligence in one or the other form is widespread. Car voice interfaces are being widely used in automotive. Companies like BMW are even working on providing premium and more natural experience by introducing gesture and gaze recognition capabilities in their 2021 series. People are using AI to interact with the government as well; students are benefiting from the introduction of artificial intelligence in the education sector. Chat interfaces are being used for resolution of government (policies) related queries. Especially during the COVID-19 pandemic, chat interfaces were widely used in French cities to assess health symptoms. In countries where native languages are being spoken more than English, daily interactions have grown.

Technologies Empowering Customer Experience

Big Data Analytics

The power of data is significant today and has the ability to transform different sectors on the basis of compiled data. The data gathered provides crucial information which helps managers to make good decisions. With the unprecedented increase in online shopping, a huge amount of data is available online which can be utilized by AI tools to understand choices and preferences, track location, identify dislikes and feedback, etc. Such information can also be utilized for the purpose of forecasting demand, estimating the next purchase pattern, modifying products, track online orders, etc. [16]. Most of the companies are nowadays using big data for making such big decisions and providing their customers a seamless experience. With utilizing such advanced technologies, Amazon's giant retailer in order to surprise their customers they implemented anticipatory shipping which deals with delivering those products which they could think of buying in the near future. Big data analytics also enables companies to develop a competitive advantage by utilizing such new technologies [29].

Recommendation Systems (RS)

Due to online platforms, there is so much information in the form of data that is available on ecommerce platforms. However, the availability of data in large amount may create dissatisfaction in decision making [14]. AI tools provide solutions to such dissatisfaction to the customers by recommending them what they should buy as per their taste and choice. With such recommendations, customers end up buying the right products.

Conversational Agents (CA)

Another tool of artificial intelligence is the conversational agent that is transforming businesses. It is a form of communication that the customers can easily make with brands through digital assistants. Consumers are buying through conversational agents nowadays and are very satisfied. This is also called a conversational commerce. Digital assistants or personal assistants like Alexa, Siri, and Google Assistant are widely used by customers for listening music, ordering food, etc. People consider these assistants as their companions at home and at the office [13–16].

Service Robots

Robots equipped with AI features are used for various services to enhance the customer experience. Such robots are built with features like image processing and biometrics. They may be physically present or in virtual forms in the future. Common questions of customers can be dealt with by such robots in shopping malls, hospitals, hotels, airports, etc. Service robots can be physically embodied robots and can be in virtual formats in the future. These robots can also be used for the purpose of dropping parcels to customers which will also be very cost effective and environment friendly.

Internet of Things (IoT)

The connected things or their network which is capable of connecting with humans with the help of the Internet is IoT. Various electronic devices use sensors for operating automatically like air conditioners, washing machines, microwaves, etc. Such technologically intelligent devices are capable of ordering on their own if something falls short, for example, refrigerators can order food, fruits, vegetables, etc., according to the stock left. Devices are becoming more smarter and advanced with the use of the Internet, and one can operate them by sitting far away from home. Imagine your refrigerators showing information related to price, important dates, specifications, etc.

Technological advancements like the Internet of Things are transforming the shopping experience immensely. IoT has immense potential to transform the shopping experience. With the help of IoT, information like price, usage, manufacturing date, specifications, expiry date, etc., through smartphones with the help of the Internet.

Extended reality (XR), augmented reality (AR), virtual reality (VR), and mixed reality (MR) technologies give customers a unique experience by enhancing their view of the real world. Computer-generated information provides an entirely different view utilizing AR, for example, Lenscart uses a 3D mirror where users can try different glasses as per their face and can actually see how it looks on them. Another virtual reality technology provides an entirely virtual environment using 3D wearables [9]. VR technology is widely used in the gaming industry, but now it is widely used in healthcare, education, and retailing for giving seamless experience to the customers. Businesses are developing AI-driven customer journey in order to provide a magical experience to their customers [10].

Significant Applications of Artificial Intelligence (AI) for Marketing

Artificial intelligence is delivering relevant information to clients on the basis of their preferences. The information delivered is being examined by AI technologies, which has made things easier and more accessible. It may be considered as a tool to guide marketing programs to achieve high-end objectives [33]. Undoubtedly, artificial intelligence is assisting marketing managers to reach out to modern customers at individual levels by using hyper-personalization including timely and relevant messages.

Tracking and Assessing

Technology has the ability to track and assess a visitor's activity on-site and quickly show the material which is highly individualized. The data being collected is utilized for future content updates and modifications as per the visitor preference. Sellers are being leveraged with this personal data which empowers them to focus on outcomes. The purchasing patterns, desires, and goals are being utilized to understand the purchase influence or decision making while purchasing using artificial intelligence [23].

AI-Enabled Customer Support

Artificial intelligence provides customers with support throughout the journey, which is intelligent yet convenient to customers. For a seamless customer experience, it is critical as well. Marketing automation is transforming the way marketing programs are handled with the help of AI operations. The technology is capable of interpreting data in real time. It makes complex data easier by separating sorting and prioritizing the data. Platforms like AI are addressing the needs of the next generation by providing hyper-personalized offerings to clients.

Customer-Centric Choices

AI utilizing the advanced technology gathers valuable insights in order to understand their customers and make choices which are customer-centric. AI systems provide market information to the marketers by evaluating and analyzing different platforms on the Internet, which enables marketers to develop personas of consumers. Developing personas needs information like purchasing patterns and habits, interests, referrals, previous interactions and communications, etc.

Customize Shopping Processes

By making simulation models and interacting with virtual assistants, artificial intelligence can customize the shopping process as per customer convenience. Various companies are using AI technology to interact with their customers. These technologies are intelligent as they can propose the inventory by utilizing the data on previous purchases and searches made by the customers. AI is outperforming humans in varied areas and growing rapidly. They can predict the market trend more precisely and provides valuable inputs for decision making. The user experience can be enhanced immensely utilizing the information provided by AI.

High Conversion

Companies are able to improve their operational efficiency with the help of these intelligent technologies, making the customer experience better. The target customers can easily be identified utilizing the data made available by AI, and the conversion rate can also be improved with minimum effort [34].

Customer Preferences

Demographic data of the customers and data on their preferences can be availed by using AI tools, and marketers can target the customers with personalization and customization. Future marketing strategies can easily be built on the information availed through AI tools to make the customer experience better and more seamless.

Timely Delivery of Message

A better understanding of the customers through AI enables marketers to give away the right message to the actual and potential customers. A comprehensive profile of each consumer can be prepared with the help of AI while having an interaction with the customer. Utilizing this profile, personalized content can be created and forwarded to the customers [17]. With the advancement of technology and tools like AI, data can be collected from various sources easily, as on the Internet, it is present everywhere like profiles of consumers, browsing history, keyword searches, etc.

Artificial intelligence can be used for identifying and forecasting trends for the future by the marketers, as on the basis of this forecasting, they can take significant decisions like allocating budgets and target audience. Spending on advertising can be done cautiously, especially digital marketing, and more focus can be done on other important works [3, 5]. AI plays a crucial role in all the phases from planning to the conversion and finally to the loyalty phase. Marketing strategies or campaigns designed utilizing AI having more chances of success. Thus, companies can also develop a competitive advantage using AI to those in the industry not utilizing it [6, 19]. With the help of AI, marketers can generate engaging content like short stories and videos targeting their audience.

Artificial Intelligence Tools Used for Engaging Customers

A variety of AI tools can be used at different touchpoints to interact with customers. A few among them are as follows.

Voice Assistant

Voice assistant is one of the technologies that engages customers as it provides hands-free operations of the devices. The technology can interact with humans by responding to the spoken commands. Voice assistants are capable of recognizing the voice and providing expected response to the one who is interacting through the system of IVR, that is, interactive voice response which functions as a virtual digital assistant. With the emergence of such platforms, customers are expecting and looking forward for more such options and opportunities where they can interact solely [28].

Chatbots

Another AI technology, chatbots are conversational software which have the ability to replicate human behavior. Chatbots being conversational are widely used in different fields like healthcare, education, etc. Chatbots are also being used in businesses on a large scale in order to interact with the customers. These are activated on the basis of text and queries rather than speech. Every type of request requiring information is being fulfilled by chatbots as they have the ability to use the stored information while replying to the query. Chatbots have the ability to learn continuously and use the already stored information to give the appropriate answers to the queries asked. Effective use of chatbots in business is capable of providing positive impact and high engagement with the customers [30, 32].

Sentiment Analysis

Online conversations using digital devices are very significant as they provide valuable insights on customers' choices, interests, and preferences. In fact, while having online conversations, sentiments of the consumers can also be known and can be utilized for framing marketing strategies. AI tools for sentiment analysis have the ability to capture sentiments from sources like posts on social media, reviews, survey, blogs, etc.

Attitude toward brands can easily be identified as this will help marketers to frame their messages in such way which is more appealing to customers. The text-mining tool can assess emotions and assist in optimizing customer service to engage loyal customers [22].

Facial Recognition

AI tools like facial recognition is a smart technology and capable of matching faces accurately from the digital database. Facial recognition can easily detect the face of a person from an image as well. This technology extends a variety of information about a person after recognizing the face like gender, age, visit frequency, etc. Such information about an individual is very crucial for marketers as it provides the opportunity for designing personalized messages and marketing programs [29]. Personalized messages can be sent to the customers suggesting options for eyewear or cosmetics as per their facial features.

NLP

It is the process of converting human language in such computer structured programs that it can be understood by computers. The computers understand the human language and provide output accordingly which helps in understanding customer requirement that too with no challenges of syntax error. Furthermore, businesses can derive meaningful insights from what customers say in their own words and make more relevant strategies based upon these insights [18].

Visual Search

In this search, people can search with the help of images and not text. Customers can simply search with the image of what they have captured or found online. AI tools respond to the picture by identifying the picture in the image and suggest results on the basis of the image put to search. Visual search offers convenience to customers and curated results as per customer requirement. Thus, this tool enhances overall customer experience [8].

Kiosks

Kiosks are touchless devices integrating voice and gesture control features. Kiosks are able to understand different requirements of a customer. They can perform their tasks with greater efficiency and more accuracy while interacting with the customers. Kiosks are capable of providing engaging customer experience.

Real-World Examples

Many companies are using AI tools to engage and interact with their customers and provide them smooth and seamless experience throughout their purchase journey.

Starbucks, a well-renowned name in beverages, uses predictive analytics in order to gather and analyze the data of consumers by offering loyalty cards and other mobile applications. Such prediction helps in sending personalized data to the consumers. Users by using mobile applications can easily place their orders with speech commands on mobile. Utilizing such tools also helps companies to increase their profits year on year.

- Wowcher, by using AI-powered copywriting, ramped up social media and brought a revolution as the AI tool was able to study the emotions as part of writing patterns. After utilizing this technology, the leading ecommerce company was able to cut cost drastically [24].

- Nestle or Unilever used artificial intelligence in order to identify insights on food trends from the information floating on social media or in public domain. They analyzed that people are inclined toward having ice creams in their breakfast, and companies modified their marketing mix accordingly to become pioneers in the field just by utilizing AI tools and providing a better experience to the customer by launching the products which well suited the customer needs [27].

- Utilizing AI, Alibaba, a giant retailer, launched the "FashionAI" outfitter which was able to provide a unique experience to the customers. As, by using smart labels on garments and smart mirrors, the system was able to recommend customers matching outfit that they can take in pairing with the tried or purchased item. They also worked on virtual wardrobe where customers can easily try clothes virtually without actually trying them [31].

- Another big giant in footwear, Nike, utilized AI tools and provided customers the pleasure of designing their own shoes. The customers can choose the soul, type, color, design, fabric, pattern, print, etc., and can get customized shoes as per their chosen designs. This provides customers another level of customized experience. Nike would also be able to predict the sales and trend as per the information received by the customers. It was also able to recommend products as per their choice in present and in future as well.

- Amazon launched a new checkout system in their selected stores which were touch free, and customers can easily walk out of the store without wasting their times at checkout. Amazon with the help of AI was able to provide these checkout-free physical stores as the sensors on the products and carts automatically picked and charged customers of the Amazon Go application [35].

- Netflix, an online streaming giant, uses AI and able to provide personalized recommendations on the basis of information gathered and customers like the suggestions or recommendations provided as per the taste and preferences of the customer regarding various shows, movies, new releases, etc. [37].

AI and Personalization

Companies are using automation and data points to target customers and provide them with a personalized message so that customers can have better experience and get engaged; this form of target marketing is also known as personalized marketing. Previous researches have proved that developments in artificial intelligence helped companies to better target their customers by providing them with individualized and personalized content [12]. Micro marketing through artificial intelligence enables companies to meet individual needs of the customers. Companies can adjust and modify their marketing strategies as per customer views without getting into their privacy zone [36, 39]. Customers are increasingly making interactions through chatbots as they can ask any information and query anytime, anywhere. This interaction with chatbots collects data about the nature of queries, products and services preferred, content usage and preference, etc. [20].

AI and Hassle-Free Service

Every customer wants a hassle-free experience while purchasing; it should be systematic and trouble-free so that the customers get their needs fulfilled without any problem or barrier [21]. Previous researchers have proved that AI can be used to improve digital marketing and serve customers better without any confusion throughout the process. Customers found their experience with chatbots more flexible as the interaction is more accessible. Customers need not wait for a long period of time for long durations for any response, which makes this interaction hassle-free. The paper by [25] discussed the role of chatbots in the front end as chatbots are widely used for the purpose of billing and searching out desired products; chatbots are even used as a shopping companion, which reduces the extra effort by the customers. This also helps chatbots gather more relevant data about purchase patterns and preferences.

AI and Service Quality

Artificial intelligence is also improving the quality of service (QoS) which is the overall experience a customer experience during the journey of purchase. The paper by [20] has discussed and proved that AI improves efficiency and provides quality of service to customers. Previous research has also discussed the ability of artificial intelligence to make accurate predictions, which ultimately helps in increasing profits by reducing expenditure on inventory. The paper by [26, 38] states about the rapid adoption of bots and artificial intelligence to improve the QoS especially in the domains of tourism and hospitality. Better interactive methods, communication, and customer engagement provide better service delivery.

Challenges

The following are the challenges in applications of AI:

- AI systems have high-speed ability to compute and require organizations to have good infrastructure and fast processors. Such systems are not easy to set up and maintain as artificial intelligence systems need a stable and adaptable environment for applications to function [14, 37].

- Another challenge is the budget requirement which organizations fail to deploy for AI applications. The installation and maintenance of advanced software and huge hardware are a big challenge for organizations that are not fund sufficient. Requires Huge Budget Another challenge is that businesses do not have funds for deploying AI technology. Funds required for AI are a big hindrance for companies to reap the benefits of AI tools and applications.

- In order to analyze the data and provide information for decision making, AI needs unified data. To arrange and unify the dispersed data from across all the different platforms is a huge challenge. This is required for taking crucial decisions on segmentation, targeting, pricing, and framing effective marketing strategies.

- Skill human resource is another issue in order to utilize the data of AI. An existing talent pool is insufficient in properly installing and interpreting the results generated by AI. Companies need to provide proper training to the employees to make them skilled so they can interpret the data and provide better results to the organization.

- Human interaction will always be preferred, and AI can never replace that human touch in the interactions. Also, customer service agents are required to handle human queries and requests that AI cannot handle. Customers especially in high-involvement products prefer to have an interaction with humans and not with AI chatbots as it provides a feeling of human touch as compared to a machine voice.

- The privacy of the customers is at stake as the data of each and every move is collected from online platforms. The ethical concerns and privacy concerns are somewhere at stake. The data is the backbone of the system, and collecting it from various platforms may hurt the sentiments of the customers [16].

Managerial Implications

In this era of advanced technology, companies are working on providing better customer experience. Customer experience is something which cannot be quantified; it can only be felt. Earlier researches have proved that AI contributes positively toward enhancing customer experience. In this highly competitive market, AI tools are helpful in understanding and retaining customers. The information gathered and analyzed by AI tools help marketers in framing and modifying marketing strategies. Technologies like virtual reality and augmented reality are capable of providing virtual cum real environment for enhancing customer experience. AI tools help marketers to understand their customers better, and with the power of data availability, hyper-personalization can be done by marketers, which will provide the wow factor to the customers as the only desired products and services will be available to them. The study provides implications for marketers and practitioners in designing effective marketing mix strategies in order to enhance customer experience. It also has implications for researchers and academicians in terms of understanding and designing new technologies in the marketing domain where customer satisfaction is of paramount importance.

Conclusion

Customer satisfaction is the main parameter for companies to consider in this customer-centric era, but the cut-throat competition has made it even more significant for companies. Intelligent and advanced technologies are widely used by companies to better understand their customers by collecting data on purchase patterns, searches, keywords, preferences, etc., from various online sources. Companies are providing more personalized experience to customers in a hassle-free way by utilizing various tools and techniques of artificial intelligence. This chapter has highlighted various tools which are used by companies to engage, entertain, and provide information to customers. AI is capable of providing accurate predictions on the basis of data collected which can be further utilized by companies to target customers in a better way, leading to build loyalty as well.

Interactive Fashion Textiles: Marketing New Technologies to Target Tech-Savvy Millennials

Dr. Rishab Manocha*, Associate Professor, School of Fashion, Pearl Academy, Jaipur, Rajasthan, India, Email: rishab.manocha@pearlacademy.com www.linkedin.com/in/rishab-manocha-5935bbb8/ https://orcid.org/0000-00026754-4040 www.researchgate.net/profile/Rishab-Manocha

There has never been a higher demand for intelligent materials like textiles that can be combined with technology in a seamless manner because of the integral role they play in our daily lives. A new interdisciplinary field, interactive fashion textiles (IFTs), calls for innovative methods of design. Experts in electronics, IT, microsystems, and textiles work together in this complex interdisciplinary sector to find new ways to improve the design of wearable

© Neha Zaidi, Mohit Maurya, Simon Grima, Pallavi Tyagi 2024, corrected publication 2024
N. Zaidi et al. (eds.), *Building AI Driven Marketing Capabilities*,
https://doi.org/10.1007/978-1-4842-9810-7_4

electronics. Fiber assemblies that can generate, transmit, modulate, and detect electrons are a pressing requirement, and designers and brands all over the world are responding to this demand by developing novel materials and methods. Due to their superior performance and unique immersive features—including portability, pliability, comfort, and minimal strain even under significant deformations—IFTs may offer viable platforms for virtual/augmented reality and artificial intelligence (AI) applications. Apparel producers and manufacturers perceive a need to adapt cutting-edge tech trends and start a broad extension of IFT applications into the clothing business in order to suit the expectations of millennial consumers as the Internet of Things, Big Data Analytics, and the Metaverse continue their meteoric rise. Some of the numerous recent shifts in the global textile industry include mass customization and personalization. AI and 3D textile rendering software are making this possible by assisting manufacturers by allowing them to construct bespoke clothing to meet the growing demands of Millennials. In an effort to provide a more in-depth examination of the IFTs' smart applications to the textile and garment sectors via a case study analysis, this chapter provides a basic introduction to the concept and classifications of the IFTs. It provides evidence of a contribution to scientific endeavors to understand the perspective of textile stakeholders and to question and evaluate their views on IFTs. The chapter further examines how customers, experts in the field, and firm shareholders feel about AI's part in the pursuit of IFTs. Indicative of the chapter's most important findings, corporations will be forced to rethink their whole business strategies, plans, marketing strategies, and production designs as a result of Millennials' newfound preference for tech-driven products. As a further scope, this chapter lays out some of the foundational elements for future studies of the interplay between artificial intelligence, the textile industry, and consumer preferences.

Introduction

Technology is utilized by businesses in the fashion industry of all different types and sorts in order to recognize and predict market demand and to immediately respond with fashionable designs and individualized trends. As a direct consequence of the development of artificial intelligence, the method by which businesses conceive of new products and put them into production is on the verge of undergoing a profound transformation. This shift will center on an organization's ability to foresee what consumers will wish to buy in the future. On the other hand, it is not likely that computer programs will ever be able to take the place of human designers in the design process. The network was trained to interpret colors, textures, and other "aesthetic aspects." Following that, the group that was working on Project Muze[1] developed an

---

[1] The innovative application of machine learning in the fashion industry is explored in

algorithm in order to generate designs based on the network's analysis of user interests and preferences in terms of aesthetics. In the course of the last few years, the textile sector has been making rapid strides toward the implementation of AI automation in order to meet the ever-increasing demands that customers have about the product quality. The practice of automating textile production through the implementation of applications that make use of artificial intelligence is swiftly becoming more widespread as a direct result of developments in related areas of technology as well as an increased emphasis on modeling and simulation. This is occurring as a direct result of developments in related areas of technology. The textile business is being increasingly mechanized as a means of meeting the ever-increasing demands of its consumer base. It is conceivable for manufacturing facilities to install AI systems in order to reduce the amount of waste they produce and save money. It is utilized all the way through the process of making textiles, beginning with the planning stages and continuing all the way through the process until the finishing touches are applied.

The term "artificial intelligence" (AI) is increasingly being used in a broad variety of contexts, some of which include the following but are not limited to these:

- The development of a design
- Production planning and control
- The laying out, cutting, and bundling of fabric
- A variety of sewing processes
- Pressing, ironing, and packaging
- Quality control
- Supply chain management, etc.

In the textile industry, one of the most widespread applications of artificial intelligence is the use of artificial neural networks, often known as ANNs,[2] which are also utilized in a variety of other fields discussed herewith.

Project Muze, a collaboration between Google and online fashion retailer Zalando. It's like being your own muse for fashion; your interests and personality serve as the source of inspiration for distinctive styles.

[2] ANNs are a subset of machine learning models that are constructed utilizing connectionism's concepts of neuronal architecture in the organic neural networks that make up animal brains.

Detection of Defects

The value of the thing will suffer as a direct result of the existence of flaws in the item's creation, if there are any. If there are defects in the fabric, then there is a greater chance that the end product will also have the same kinds of defects. This is due to the fact that the fabric comes before the finished product in the production process. As a result of this, it is an absolutely necessary step to carry out quality control checks on the fabric before it is woven into a garment. Trained members of the staff visually evaluate the fabric on the tables by hand, utilizing the tables. The tables are equipped with the appropriate lighting and testing technology. This tactic requires a large amount of time investment, and as a result, it almost always ends up producing work that is of lower quality than desired. When applied in this context, the use of AI makes it possible to do the operation more quickly, with a higher level of precision and without putting an excessive amount of pressure on the system in the process. It is possible to utilize artificial intelligence in the form of neuro-fuzzy or another system to create predictions about the properties of the fabric before the fabric has ever been produced. This is something that could be done even before the design of the fabric has been created. Utilizing the yarn in conjunction with the other components of the fabric's composition that are in play is one way that this objective can be achieved.

Pattern Inspection

Weaving, knitting, braiding, finishing, printing, and a variety of other processes, as well as any combination of these and other methods, can be used to create a pattern on a fabric. This pattern can then be printed on. It is possible for manufacturers to lessen the likelihood of human error and tiredness when it comes to the detection of flaws and innovations by switching from a visual examination system to a vision-based inspection system. This would allow the manufacturers to detect flaws and innovations more quickly and accurately. Because of this, the producers would be able to lessen the possibility of errors caused by human fatigue and carelessness. The textile industry makes use of methods that are related to artificial intelligence, such as ANN, in order to locate flaws in the materials that are being inspected during the process of quality control inspection. The primary objective of this endeavor is to ensure product quality. In order to carry out a fabric analysis, the very first thing that has to be done is to get an image of the material from the device that was used to take the photograph and then save it, utilizing the standard image format that is relevant. This is the first step that needs to be taken (JPEG, JPG, PNG, etc.). After this step, a variety of multilayer backpropagation strategies are employed in order to incorporate these photographs into an ANN system. In the following steps, the system will learn the proper weaving pattern as well as the quality of the yarn, the color, and any imperfections in the fabric.

Color-Related Issues

In the textile industry, the use of color is given a great deal of importance. It is common practice to judge the quality of a textile product based on how it appears to have been manufactured. The color of a product may be deemed acceptable or unacceptable, or it may be subdivided into more precise categories such as "too light" or "too dark," "too red," or "too green." The development of AI equipped with a "pass/fail" feature presents an opportunity to realize improvements in both the accuracy and efficiency of the process.

Garment Construction Defects

Stitching refers to the process of joining together two or more separate pieces of fabric by using seams and stitches. Sewability is a measurement of how well a seam can be formed and how well it performs. The ability of the fabric to be sewn may be affected by the low-stress mechanical qualities of the fabric, such as its tensile, shear, and bending strengths, among others. In the production process, an AI system might be utilized to determine which kinds of materials are most suitable for sewing.

Computer-Aided Design (CAD) Systems

The generation of patterns is an essential part of the process of producing textiles, which is why this stage has been ranked as the fifth most important one. The designers begin by hand sketching the fundamental patterns, which are later scanned and entered into the computer system. Pattern making, digitizing, grading, and marker planning are just some of the many jobs that are completed with the use of CAD software in the textile business. The use of CAD software contributes to increases in both productivity and the quality of production as a whole.

Production Scheduling and Flow Management

The goal of production planning and control, sometimes known as PPC, is to ensure that delivery deadlines are followed and that customer orders are completed as quickly as possible. This is accomplished by coordinating the activities of everyone involved throughout the various stages of production. The balancing of sewing lines, the assignment of operations, and the positioning of machines are all examples of tasks that can benefit from the application of artificial intelligence. PPC's ultimate goal can be accomplished with the help of AI.

Final Inspection

Final inspections of textile goods are absolutely necessary in order to reduce the number of rejects produced at each stage of the manufacturing process. In most cases, the final quality check of manufactured apparel is performed by specialists. It's possible that the length of time it takes to finish this process could be affected by both a person's physical and mental state. Because of this, utilizing automated inspection that is powered by AI is vital if one wishes to achieve the sought-after levels of accuracy and efficiency. Using artificial intelligence (AI) and image processing, it is possible to carry out automated inspections of the product's overall quality. The distribution of raw materials, components, completed items, and retail outlets is referred to as "supply chain management" (SCM) in the apparel industry. The generation of value for the client is the objective of supply chain management (SCM), which is performed through the coordination of a diverse range of operations, data sources, and assets located both internally and externally. The management of expenses and the promotion of the company's competitiveness are both made possible by the use of standard supply chain management.

Interactive Fashion Textiles

The term "interactive fashion textiles" (IFTs) refers to a broad field of research as well as a variety of products that enhance the functionality and value of fashion textiles. IFTs are defined as textile products such as woven, knitted, or nonwoven fibers, filaments, and yarn that have the potential to interact with either the wearer or the environment. E-textiles, which are a hybrid of textiles and electrical components, can be utilized in the production of intelligent materials. IFTs, or interactive fashion textiles, are fabrics that have been designed with the use of innovative technology in order to give the wearer additional benefits. Within works of literature, there are many different kinds of IFTs. On the other hand, the categorization of clothing according to grounds of both aesthetic and functional value is generally recognized. The functionality of the physical interface is increased because of IFTs. A design for a successful textile interface would take into account applications that are typically used. IFTs have the potential to become the next model for the development of creative methods for incorporating electronics into textiles and garments. They are able to learn to observe ambient circumstances or stimuli, react and modify their behavior intelligently, and give prospective solutions for problems in a range of industries, including the health industry, the sports industry, the automobile industry, and the aerospace industry. IFTs have the potential to become an integral part of our lives, much like the way we use mobile devices; they could even integrate the functionality of smartphones into our clothing, making them one with our bodies. The capabilities of IoT devices are gradually transitioning to become more analogous to those of mobile devices. The use of portable electronics has become so normal that we frequently do not give them the consideration they need. What do you think the next step is going to be for mobile devices? Which technological innovation would be daring enough to take the place of the existing smartphone and carry us into the next era of technological and cultural development? The incorporation of electronics into textiles will, in the not-too-distant future, make it possible for new communication opportunities to arise in a world in which pervasive and ambient computing will be the norm and in which we will be surrounded by textile interfaces that make our digital lives easier.

New Earth-Friendly Textiles

Alternate materials, such as leather that is created in a lab and is based on plants, could make a substantial contribution to the sustainability of the fashion industry. Numerous technological endeavors can be found within the scope of this topic. After fermenting certain strains of yeast to produce collagen, which is one of the primary components of traditional leather, and then processing this protein to create an animal-free leather material, the biotech company Modern Meadow,[3] which is based in the United States and has raised more than $180 million, creates a material that mimics leather without the use of animals. Another firm that creates a material called "Mylo"[4] that is analogous to leather is called Bolt Threads.[5] This company employs proteins that are obtained from mushrooms. "When you touch our material, it feels close to genuine leather," adds Jamie Bainbridge, who is the vice president of product development for the company. If no one told you otherwise, you would remain there and speculate as to whether or not the substance was leather. Bolt has produced collections in conjunction with a number of well-known fashion and retail brands, including Stella McCartney, Adidas, and Lululemon, among others.

---

[3] An American biotechnology business called Modern Meadow employs biofabrication to produce sustainable materials. In 2011, Andras Forgacs, Gabor Forgacs, Karoly Jakab, and Francoise Marga cofounded the business, which has its headquarters in Nutley, New Jersey.
[4] Mylo is a substance that resembles leather and is produced from the subterranean root system of mushrooms known as mycelium. As a more environmentally friendly substitute for Styrofoam packaging, the company that specializes in textile fibers called Bolt Threads collaborated with Ecovative, a leader in the field of mycelium fabrication technology, to produce MyloTM. Mylo was designed to be soft and flexible.
[5] Bolt Threads is a material solutions company. With nature as their inspiration, the company invents cutting-edge materials for the fashion and beauty industries to put themselves on a path toward a more sustainable future.

Rethinking "End-to-End" Design to Achieve Circularity

These attempts at sustainability in the fashion and technology industries by companies to be more environmentally conscious highlight how difficult it is to achieve sustainability. It is challenging to create circularity since it requires altering operations all along the supply chain. However, long-term sustainability cannot be achieved without it. Circularity is essential for this. Circularity is something that an increasing number of fashion firms, such as Lululemon, Patagonia, and Nike, are working to achieve. This is often done by taking trade-ins of used clothing and either reselling the items or reusing the fabric to produce "new" garments. The goal is to reduce the need for the production of new fabrics as much as possible by recycling the old ones and maximizing the amount of time that clothing may be worn before it needs to be replaced.

"A circular fashion industry is a regenerative system in which clothing is circulated for as long as its maximum value is preserved and then returned to the biosphere in a safe manner when it is no longer useful," according to one definition of the term "*circular fashion industry.*"

Yuima Nakazato,[6] a designer specializing in haute couture, reimagines the manufacturing process in order to create "garments for life" with the goal of achieving circularity. He employed 3D printing to limit the amount of waste produced during the manufacturing process by making only the elements that were required. He did this by using the precise proportions of the wearer's body. Without the use of needles and thread, Nakazato manufactures "modular" clothing with a computational knitting machine that operates in three dimensions. It is possible to disassemble and reassemble various parts of a garment, which makes it possible to make repairs and change the look of an item without having to replace it. The goal of the designer is to create clothing that is "permanent," which would eliminate the requirement and desire to throw it away. In addition to the prototype, Nakazato has released a variety of shirts that are already ready to be worn and make use of this technology.

It is possible that in the future, novel fabrics that have been made from materials of the next generation will find commercial application in the fashion industry. It has been reported that Tom Brady wears pyjamas with a "bioceramic print" that, when combined with body heat, produces far infrared

---

[6] Nakazato, who was born in 1985, grew up in an atmosphere that encouraged him to explore his creativity through a wide range of mediums. Before enrolling in the Fashion Department at the Royal Academy of Fine Arts in Antwerp, he taught himself how to sew.

radiation (FIR).[7] FIR is said to alleviate inflammation, improve circulation, and speed up the recovery process. Alternating hues are conceivably on the horizon for the world of fashion. The decade of the 1990s saw a rise in popularity for hypercolor T-shirts and mood rings, but the most recent renditions are significantly more sophisticated.

Researchers at MIT created a technology called ColorFab 3D, which allows users to print three-dimensional objects with "photochromic inks." These inks alter their color when exposed to certain wavelengths of ultraviolet light. The first item that ColorFab has manufactured with the help of this technology is a ring that can be pre-set to change into a number of different colors according to the user's preferences. Ebb is a color-changing fabric technology that is being developed by the same team that is responsible for Google's Jacquard Threads. This technology was created in collaboration with researchers from UC Berkeley, and it may one day be able to be programmed to respond to your mood or the environment. "If you can weave the sensor into the textile, you're moving away from electronics as a material," Ivan Poupyrev of Google explains. For example, "By making the components of our world and the surrounding world interactive, you, and with the same app connectivity as the Levi's Jacquard jacket." Even more incredible, researchers from Harvard University announced in January 2022[8] that they had developed temperature sensors that are stretchable and flexible, making them suitable for use in intelligent clothing and soft robotics. This is a significant step forward in terms of the development of wearable electronics because sensors are typically rigid.

Case Study Background

The textile industry is responsible for a significant portion of the environmental damage that is occurring today because of its inability to recycle its raw materials and its heavy reliance on chemicals that are widely acknowledged to be harmful to human health. At the current moment in time, the total yearly greenhouse gas emissions from the manufacture of textiles amount to 1.2 billion tons of CO_2 equivalent, which is a greater figure than the sum of all of

---

[7] The electromagnetic radiation spectrum includes a region known as far infrared (FIR), which is located at the end of the infrared spectrum. Many sources agree that the CIE IR-B and IR-C bands encompass the far infrared spectrum, which spans from 15 micrometers (m) to 1 mm (or around 20 THz to 300 GHz).

[8] The research was coauthored by Kun Jia, Shuwen Zhang, Hyeong Jun Kim, Yang Bai, and Ryan C. Hayward. The research was supported in part by the National Science Foundation through the Harvard University Materials Research Science and Engineering Center under grant DMR2011754.

the emissions that come from international flights and shipping combined. The intrinsic linearity of the manufacturing pattern in the textile sector is the most significant barrier that must be overcome in order for that industry to advance. At the moment, more than 100 billion articles of clothing are produced each year on a global basis, with the vast majority of these items (more than 97%) being made from unprocessed virgin raw materials. When it gets close to the end of these products' usable lives, they are typically thrown away in landfills or incinerators (which account for 87% of the total), or they are mechanically recycled to a lesser value (sometimes referred to as downcycling), which accounts for 12% of the total. Less than 1% of waste textiles are currently being recycled through the use of cutting-edge recycling processes in order to get them ready for use as a raw material in the production of new clothing. This represents a significant increase from just 1% of waste textiles being recycled in the past. It is anticipated that this percentage will increase in the not-too-distant future. In this scenario, recycling one type of fiber into another would eliminate the extraction and manufacturing of virgin fibers, in addition to the waste of resources that is caused by landfilling and incinerating garbage. This would be possible because recycling would convert one type of fiber into another type of fiber. For a good number of years, it would have been possible, from a practical standpoint, to regenerate fibers through the use of chemical recycling processes. This would have been the situation for quite a few years at this point. Extremely exact information is required in order to determine the actual content of the articles of clothing that are going to be recycled. Because the present techniques for sorting do not permit the completion of this activity, it is impossible to carry it out in its current form. The feedstock that is fed into fiber-to-fiber recyclers must not contain any of the chemicals, fibers, or material combinations that are indicated on the prohibited lists that accompany the recyclers. These lists are included with the fiber-to-fiber recyclers. These lists are typically included in the user manuals that are distributed alongside the recyclers. Because the technology that is now available for recycling fiber into fiber produces pollutants and toxins, there are significant challenges that occur as a result of these pollutants and toxins. Even in extremely low concentrations, coatings based on fluorocarbons, such as those found on impregnated outdoor materials, present a significant barrier for the processes of chemical recycling. Materials that have been impregnated can have coatings like this applied to them. There is a possibility that these coatings will be applied to the materials. This is still the case even if the overall fluorocarbon content of the material is on the lower end of the spectrum. In addition, the vast majority of recyclers demand that particular colors be eliminated entirely from the processing step or removed entirely from the equation. Because of this, the variety of suitable feedstocks is limited to either clearly defined production waste (pre-consumer) or easily identifiable clothing with recognizable characteristics (such as blue jeans stained with indigo). These two groups are included in the pre-consumer category (e.g., indigo-dyed blue jeans). The German Federal

Environment Agency[9] came to the conclusion that one kilogram of potentially hazardous chemicals is used in the process of textile finishing for every kilogram of material that is treated. This was stated in their report. The German Federal Environment Agency is the source of the estimate that led to the creation of this value. The fact that a large amount of the auxiliary materials that are utilized in the textile industry are ultimately discarded as waste has a negative impact on the natural environment. According to the findings of research that was conducted by Greenpeace, the textile sector is accountable for more than 20% of the discharge of organic pollutants into bodies of water. There is general awareness that some of these compounds are notoriously difficult to break down, and it is also common information that biological wastewater treatment plants can only decrease them to a certain degree. The amount of reduction that can take place is subject to this restriction in any case. The removal of pieces of clothing that can be reused and resold with the intention of selling them on the secondary market is the principal preoccupation of conventional sorting factories. This is done with the purpose of selling the eliminated products on the secondary market. The material-specific sorting for textile recycling, which is performed on a relatively insignificant portion of the remaining textiles, makes extensive use of haptic identification throughout the course of the process. This sorting is done in order to recycle the textiles in a more efficient manner. The purpose of this sorting is to prepare the textiles for recycling. In pilot sorting facilities, the use of optical detection in conjunction with near-infrared (NIR) spectroscopy has the potential to produce discoveries of higher quality. This is because NIR spectroscopy is able to better distinguish between different types of materials. These sorting plants devote the vast bulk of their efforts to recognizing cotton, polyester, and wool, but they make little effort to look for any other potentially dangerous pollutants. This section provides a high-level explanation of the approach that will be utilized for an upcoming project, which will be discussed further in subsequent sections. By determining the precise material composition of contaminated textiles as well as the quantity of contamination that is contained within those textiles, the purpose of this research is to make it possible to recycle used textiles back into their original state of fiber. This will be accomplished by identifying the precise material composition of contaminated textiles. In order to properly categorize the information, this method will make use of a combination of multispectral analysis, artificial intelligence (AI), and convolutional neural networks (CNNs). It is possible that used clothing that has been contaminated with hazardous substances

---

[9] In the Federal Republic of Germany, the German Federal Environment Agency (UBA) serves as the primary environmental regulatory body. It is included in the portfolio of the Federal Ministry for the Environment, Nature Conservation, Nuclear Safety, and Consumer Protection, along with the Federal Office for the Conservation of Nature, the Federal Office for the Safety of Nuclear Waste Management, and the Federal Office for Radiation Protection.

could be isolated from other hazardous waste and sent for recycling, thereby reducing the risk of further contamination of future garments. This would be accomplished by isolating the clothing from other hazardous waste. To accomplish this, the garments would first be separated from any other hazardous trash that was present. A contamination study that is conducted during the entire recycling process provides a reliable and tangible source of data regarding the level of exposure to harmful compounds that consumers have. The findings have the potential to be utilized in the formation of guidelines and principles that can be used during the decision-making process for the purpose of environmental protection.

Aim of the Case Study

The fundamental objective of this case study ought to be to close the current gap in textile recycling, which will ultimately result in the textile sector becoming less harmful to the environment. The case study concentrates its attention on three separate aspects in order to demonstrate all of the different aspects of this difficult challenge:

   (i)   Increasing the likelihood that clothing will be worn again (small cycle) by utilizing computer vision to categorize the many different types of previously worn garments into their respective categories

   (ii) Enabling the recycling of textile fibers (big cycle)

   (iii) Assessing whether or not textiles contain potentially harmful substances

The accomplishment of these three facets would correlate to a number of different elements of sustainability and would have a substantial impact on both social and economic levels. Because an in-depth description and discussion of part (i) would go beyond the parameters of this case study, the focus of the remaining content of this chapter is on parts (ii) and (iii).

The subsequent sections of this chapter will concentrate on parts (ii) and (iii) because it would be outside the purview of this case study to provide a thorough explanation and discussion of component I.

The purpose of the project case study's section (ii) is to demonstrate how spectroscopy[10]-based automated detection that is assisted by an AI classifier may identify raw materials and contaminants in order to enable a sustainable circular economy for textiles. This will be accomplished by presenting a demonstration of the many methods of detection that are available. A technology that combines spectroscopic analysis with an appropriate categorization based on artificial intelligence will be used to collect important information from the articles of clothing in order to make the sorting process as effective as it can possibly be. This will be done in order to maximize efficiency. Because of this, the sorting process will be able to function more efficiently.

This case study (subproject (iii)) is still investigating the problem of pollutants found in textiles from both an environmental and recycling perspective. This subproject will, on the one hand, produce a mapping and market overview of regularly used chemicals and the impact that these compounds have on the recyclability of materials. Additionally, this project will establish an inventory of materials that can be recycled. On the other hand, a process will be constructed that will involve the construction of an algorithm that compares the chemical list of textiles to recycling requirements and environmental regulations. This comparison will take place during the development of the procedure. Following the completion of this functional component, the results will be made available to the spectroscopic AI in the form of newly developed capabilities. As a consequence of the findings of this inquiry, it is anticipated that manufacturers will alter the designs of the products they produce. These modifications will take into account the existing environmental goals that are already being pursued and will include any suitable substitutes for hazardous compounds. This technique ought to, over the course of time, be able to identify and cut back on the utilization of pollutants that are obtained from the material flows of the textile sector.

A Spectroscopy- and AI-Based Sorting Method for Fiber-to-Fiber Recycling

It is planned to develop a dependable optical detection system in order to determine the material composition of worn textiles as well as the level of contamination present in them. The integration of sensors capable of multispectral analysis will allow for the accomplishment of this goal. When many spectral ranges are used in conjunction with one another, it will be feasible to sort materials in line with the criteria for fiber-to-fiber recycling.

---

[10] Quantitative assessment of the reflection or transmission qualities of a material as a function of wavelength is the focus of spectrophotometry, a subfield of electromagnetic spectroscopy. In order to quantify the intensity of a light beam at various wavelengths, spectrophotometers are used in spectrophotometry. Modern spectrophotometers may investigate large swaths of the electromagnetic spectrum, including x-ray, ultraviolet, visible, infrared, and/or microwave wavelengths, despite the fact that spectrophotometry is often applied to ultraviolet, visible, and infrared light.

Because NIR spectroscopy produces continuous and broad spectra, it is possible to execute coarse presorting depending on the fiber material. On the other hand, Raman spectroscopy (RS)[11] in the visible and ultraviolet ranges consists of clear and defined lines, which are more difficult to understand but enable a great deal more material-specific classifications. These spectra are typically found between 300 and 400 nanometers in wavelength. Therefore, RS is able to establish a molecular fingerprint of the textile and has the capacity to provide information regarding the existence of chemicals that have been expressly banned from the list of substances that are permitted for the recycling process. A neural network–based classifier will be constructed as part of the scope of this project in order to classify a vast number of different kinds of materials. This method has been deemed preferable to the conventional approaches to chemometric analysis, such as principal component analysis (PCA), because the conventional approaches are regarded as inferior to this method. For example, the presence of a very large number of different compounds may cause an increase in the dimensionality of principal component analysis (PCA). There is a good chance that a good number of these configurations will have low eigenvalues. They are not present, despite the fact that their presence is necessary for providing a correct illustration of the source data. Neural networks, on the other hand, have been utilized outside of the textile sector for the interpretation of RS with great success and have proven their worth as an instrument of analysis for chemical fingerprinting. This illustrates that neural networks have the ability to completely change the way chemical fingerprinting is done. It is essential to make use of a variety of data sources if one wants to achieve the maximum achievable level of dependability. The clothing type information that was generated by machine vision from the first subproject will be added to the data set when it is next updated. This information will be added to the multispectral data that has already been collected. On the basis of this vast and varied data set, artificial intelligence will categorize the material composition and estimate the pollution load in order to identify which recycling channel is the most appropriate. In contrast to the standard procedures for spectroscopic analysis, the most important consideration in this particular instance is not the precision of the match but rather the certainty that distinct classified features are present. This is because the accuracy of the match is not as important as the certainty that distinct classified features are present. For instance, recyclers have varying criteria when it comes to the precision of component determination. Some recyclers will accept bulk fractions of elastane in their processes that fall within the range of a single-digit percentage, but they must be able to remove other pollutants that fall within the range of a few parts per million (ppm).

---

[11] Raman spectroscopy is a method of nondestructive chemical examination that can reveal specific information regarding the chemical structure, phase and polymorphy, crystallinity, and molecular interactions of a substance. It is predicated on the interaction of light with the chemical bonds that are contained within a substance.

It is essential to have exceptionally high precision over the entire spectrum in order to solve the problem and acquire enough convergence of the fit when using a conventional method in order to arrive at a sound conclusion. When taking into consideration the needs that are in place at the moment, one approach is to use a deep neural network. As a direct result of this, the methodology takes into consideration the anticipated results before actually performing the analysis. In order to provide complete spectroscopy, this integration brings together two procedures that are typically handled independently: data analysis and result interpretation. In addition, incompatible components can be taught, such as staining that is material specific. It is important to take into account not only substantial correlations but also anticorrelations between characteristics. In addition, fiber-specific dyes and finishings, which are examples of exclusionary chemicals, serve the purpose of resolving degeneracies of the spectrum components, which in turn contributes to the robustness of the technique. When trying to determine whether or not a textile has been classified with an adequate level of precision, the degree of confidence that is connected with an estimate is of utmost importance. In this particular scenario, the limitations imposed by recycling operations do not have to be satisfied for every single article of clothing; rather, they have to be satisfied for every sorting unit (such as a container or a bale). One has the ability to maximize the rate of recycling while simultaneously optimizing their utilization of the limit values by making use of a stochastic strategy in this manner. In the event that the estimation is questionable, the system has the capability of remeasuring or altering the integration time of the measurement on its own in order to achieve a higher signal-to-noise ratio. The required integration time can be used as feedback to estimate the appropriate integration time based on prior knowledge (such as absorption coefficients from UV-VIS-NIR[12] pre-characterization), and this can be done in a variety of ways. Because of this, an evaluation that is time efficient is produced. If the signal-to-noise ratio has been optimized in the past without sufficient classification, this may be an indication that an unidentified drug exists. In order to arrive at a conclusion regarding the composition of fabric, additional laboratory analysis, such as chromatography or nuclear magnetic resonance (NMR),[13] could be performed. The findings of the most recent analysis that was carried out serve as the basis for the comment made in this review. Because of this, the system is able to continuously learn RS that had not been identified before, which improves its recognition capacity in comparison to

---

[12] An effective analytical method for identifying the optical characteristics (transmittance, reflectance, and absorbance) of liquids and solids is UV/VIS/NIR spectroscopy. It can be used to describe glass, coatings, semiconductor materials, and many other research and production materials. Optically, UV, VIS, and NIR function between 175 and 3300 nm.

[13] An electromagnetic signal with a frequency characteristic of the magnetic field at the nucleus is produced when nuclei in a strong constant magnetic field are disrupted by a weak oscillating magnetic field (in the near field).

the spectra that it learned for the first time during the development phase. The information gathered on contaminants through sorting will also be used to evaluate whether or not the textile industry is in conformity with the Registration, Evaluation, Authorization and Restriction of Chemicals (REACH)[14] regulation or with more stringent criteria such as Zero Discharge of Hazardous Chemicals (ZDHC).[15] Regardless of the numbers provided by the manufacturer, this technology makes it possible to determine and reduce the actual amounts of pollution produced by the textile production cycle. As a consequence, over the course of time, the general level of safety that textiles offer will gradually improve. There is a method for separating textiles that do not comply with REACH, and the textiles that are separated include those that were manufactured prior to the adoption of REACH or originated from markets that are located outside of the EU. In a similar vein, filthy work clothing and other types of soiled textiles that have gotten polluted through use are eligible for recycling under the hazardous waste category. The gradual removal of potentially harmful substances from the cycle of producing textiles is made possible as a result of this.

Conclusion

There is a possibility that artificial intelligence might dramatically cut down on the expenditures that are connected with the creation of items, which would ultimately lead to significant cost savings. This would be beneficial since it would allow for more efficient production. As a direct result of this, it presents a vast array of potential applications for usage in the manufacturing of a variety of garments and other types of accessories. It is a fantastic instrument that decision-makers can use in order to successfully organize and carry out complex production processes, discover and deal with major quality difficulties in a timely manner, and produce things that match the special requirements. The garment business is comprised of a number of subfields, the most prominent of which are the following: retailing of garments, manufacturing of apparel, designing of apparel, and management of the supply chain. According to the findings, the types of artificial intelligence methods that are utilized

---

[14] The European Union established REACH as a legislation to strengthen the protection of human health and the environment from the risks that chemicals might cause while also boosting the competitiveness of the EU chemical sector. Additionally, it encourages the use of alternate approaches to lessen the need for animal testing when determining a substance's hazards.

[15] Over 320 signatories from throughout the sector, including brands, suppliers, solution providers, and chemical suppliers, are part of the multi-stakeholder ZDHC organization. The ZDHC Roadmap to Zero Programme guides the fashion industry in removing dangerous chemicals from its worldwide supply chain while laying the groundwork for more environmentally friendly manufacturing to safeguard employees, customers, and the ecosystems of our planet.

most frequently in applications related to garment manufacturing are neural networks, hybrid intelligent systems, simulated annealing, multi-agent systems, genetic programming, artificial immune systems, fuzzy logic, and genetic algorithms. Other sorts of artificial intelligence methodologies, such as fuzzy logic and genetic algorithms, are utilized in the implementation of these technologies. These applications also make use of other kinds of artificial intelligence, such as fuzzy logic and evolutionary algorithms. When the researchers came to the realization that the research challenges studied in prior studies were limited, they gained another exciting finding. The finding was that the research difficulties were limited in scope. They came to the conclusion that the research did not adequately address or investigate a variety of concerns, which led them to make that judgment. This fresh piece of knowledge is stunning and really interesting. The commercial deployment of technologies that make use of artificial intelligence is still in its infancy in the garment industry. Because of this, the garment industry is considered to be a sector that is still in its infant phases. This is only one of the many reasons why the clothing business is still considered to be in its formative years. This is due to the fact that significant obstacles need to be conquered at a variety of different stages during the process. This is the rationale behind why things are the way they are. Because of this, incorporating AI techniques into the garment business requires careful analysis of the many different functional aspects that already exist within the apparel sector in order to guarantee the most effective solutions. This is necessary in order to make sure that the most effective solutions are implemented. This is essential in order to guarantee that the most efficient solutions are put into action. Additionally, there is a need for research to be conducted in order to evaluate the impact that various AI model parameters have on the output of solutions. This will make it possible to design approaches that may be used to modify parameters to meet the requirements of individual problems as they are encountered. Consider, for instance, the settings for the structures that are implemented in artificial neural networks. In spite of everything that is happening, it is unavoidable that artificial intelligence will play a part in the world that we live in. This presence will most certainly bring with it a number of opportunities and problems of varying degrees. As a consequence of this, researchers working on artificial intelligence and specialists working in the garment industry need to work closely together in order to overcome non-examined functional decision-making challenges in the apparel sector and to increase the efficiency of AI approaches that are already in use. This is important in order to improve the effectiveness of AI approaches that are currently being utilized in practice.

AI-Based Decisive Model for Customer Segmentation in the Fashion Industry

Pooja Chopra*, Assistant Professor, School of Computer Applications, Lovely Professional University, Phagwara, Punjab, India, pooja.27304@lpu.co.in, ORCID: 00000002-7624-9000

Munish Gupta, Associate Professor, Chandigarh University, Mohali, Punjab, India, gupta.munish2005@gmail.com, ORCID: 0000-0002-1982-4136

The use of AI in the fashion business has altered traditional practices. In numerous ways, AI has benefited the fashion industry. Tools like predictive analytics and comparative vision are used to identify product characteristics. Artificial intelligence has become increasingly prevalent in the fashion industry, particularly in analyzing search behaviors and providing similar product recommendations based on consumer preference. Artificial intelligence is used to analyze user search history and return more relevant results in the future based on criteria such as brand, color, size, current fashion trends, and price. This research endeavors to create an AI-powered recommender system for a website, focusing on women's clothing, accessories, and footwear. The AI model will consider customer attributes to prioritize their preferences, leading to personalized advertisements. The primary objective is to enhance sales through this approach. Inputs such as gender, income, marital status, salary, profession, and location will be collected to form datasets from the target audience. Training will employ 80% of the data, while 20% will be reserved for testing. Data cleaning precedes integration into the system. Users will be grouped based on input attributes, facilitating targeted ad delivery to each group. This study seeks to harness AI to optimize sales by tailoring recommendations and ads to individual customer profiles. The model built will be Fuzzy Logic based. Customers' tastes are uncertain. So, to handle uncertainties, this model will work well. Also, this model will go well in case of accuracy as this is Fuzzy Logic based. Also, we plan to keep the data of premium customers in the private cloud and regular customers' data in the public cloud. So, this model will promote security as well because the private cloud provides security features. To balance the cost, we prefer here a hybrid cloud-based model.

Introduction

Over the past few years, we've seen a sharp rise in the use of artificial intelligence in the fashion industry, particularly in monitoring customer preferences through their online search habits and making suggestions for related products [1]. Traditional methods in the fashion industry have changed due to the introduction of artificial intelligence. Through the use of AI, user search histories are analyzed to provide users with more relevant results in the future. These factors may include brand, color, size, current fashion trends, and price [2], [3]. Artificial intelligence has contributed to the fashion industry in many ways. The artificial intelligence–based model using problem-solving techniques can help the fashion industry identify and prioritize customer preferences based on inputs derived from customer demographic information [4].

Problem-solving techniques can be hard computing, like symbolic logic reasoning, and soft Computing, such as approximate reasoning, probabilistic models, fuzzy logic, randomized search, neural networks, evolutionary computing, etc. In complex Computing, a system has a finite set of instructions to solve a particular problem written in sequence, like the approach followed in C, C++, and other computer languages. A system cannot do anything without specific instructions [5]. In soft Computing, a system doesn't have any instructions; rather, a system learns by examples to solve a particular problem. Soft Computing is applied in real-life applications that work more efficiently and effectively. Artificial intelligence techniques are soft computing techniques that contain Fuzzy Logic, artificial neural networks, genetic algorithms, etc. Soft Computing consists of various techniques to exploit the indulgence for vagueness and imprecision to achieve low-cost way out, robustness, and traceability. Soft Computing is obtainable with a vast diversity of real-life applications to industrial systems and software products and hypothetical developments. Exploiting this has allowed sorting out human-like perplexity and authentic flaws into a generally hard PC program. Soft Computing helps in likely believe a real part in building programming models by lessening time, cost, and support. Several computational methodologies come within the range of Soft Computing. Some of them are machine learning [6], Fuzzy Logic [7], probabilistic reasoning [8], and evolutionary computation [9]. There are various benefits of Soft Computing. To illustrate, consider that a computer with hard Computing has no idea what we mean when we say that the water is hot, lukewarm, or cold. Computational models like Fuzzy Logic allow the computer to determine the temperature of the water and draw conclusions about whether it is hot, cold, or in room temperature [10]. Hard Computing cannot perform these kinds of calculations. Soft Computing is a capable tool that can offer problem resolution, optimization estimation, and search methods [11]. Soft computing techniques are used in diverse areas such as wireless communication, data mining, communication systems, transportation, healthcare, robotics, consumer appliances, etc. [12].

Fuzzy Logic

In mathematics, we all have studied a branch of algebra named Boolean algebra [13], [14], which means that there are two possible values of a variable, that is, true or false or simply 0 or 1, which we also call truth values. Computers rely on these truth values. But our human mind is not limited to simple true (1) or false (0) as the degree of truthfulness varies between these two values: true (yes in the case of the human mind) and false (no in the case of the human mind) [15]. The human mind considers many possibilities between "yes" and "no." Many options are there between this "yes" and "no," like somewhat, little, may, may not, cannot say, etc. For example, if someone asks whether x is a member of set A, as per Boolean Logic, the answer may be "yes" or "no" [16]. So, Boolean Logic entirely incorporates or prohibits a specified element in a set. But if someone says that x has a partial membership in set A, this can only be supported by Fuzzy Logic, as Fuzzy Logic wholly and partially includes something. Classical systems fail to capture the inherent ambiguity present in natural language [17]. On the other hand, Fuzzy Logic emerges as a solution for navigating decision-making in situations characterized by vagueness and imprecision. By embracing Fuzzy Logic, we gain a framework for making decisions even when the input information is characterized by vagueness, ambiguity, inaccuracy, or absence [18]. Fuzzy Logic is an imprecise, unclear, and unreliable framework for drawing inferences from the knowledge base [19]. Fuzzy Logic deals with uncertainty. It differs from bi-valued and multivalued logic in the following sense:

- In two-valued logic, truth values are limited to either true or false. However, in multivalued logic, the truth value of a proposition extends beyond just true or false, encompassing various intermediate values between these two extremes [20]. Fuzzy Logic introduces yet another dimension, where the truth value of a proposition can belong to a fuzzy subset, as exemplified by terms like "Very Bad" [21]. Let's take an example of weekend days in the case of Fuzzy Logic. The answer to the query "Is Saturday a weekend day?" will be 1 (yes). The answer to the query "Is Wednesday a weekend day?" will be 0 (no), and the answer to the query "Friday, a weekend day" will be 0.8 (for the most part, yes, but not completely). So Fuzzy Logic supports the concept of partial truthfulness.

- In two-valued logic, predicates are always crisp, but in Fuzzy Logic, predicates may be crisp or fuzzy, like few, much heavier, etc. [22], [23]. Fuzzy Logic supports different shades of truthfulness like "*Is this tea hot?*"

- The crisp output will be yes or no, but the fuzzy output can be cold, hot, etc.

- In two-valued logic, only two quantifiers are used, all or some, but in Fuzzy Logic, various quantifiers are used, that is, few, very, many, much, etc. [24].

- Fuzzy Logic uses linguistic variables to signify nonnumeric values of fuzzy variables, for example, execution time has linguistic terms: very low, low, medium, high, and very high [25]. In another example, let's take the age parameter. It has three linguistic terms: young, middle-aged, and old. While defining the crisp value, we will take a value of *30*, which is only one value among so many values, but the *young* linguistic term can contain so many values out of the preceding three linguistic terms. So, it is a form of data compression [26].

- Fuzzy Logic can make precise decisions with imprecise, insufficient, and conflicting information. Fuzzy Logic is an accurate logic of vagueness and inexact logic [27].

Let's take an example of a statement about the weather status in the city. According to classical logic, *"Today is sunny"* can be 0 or 1, where 0 means cloudy, and 1 means sunny. But this does not apply practically. In Fuzzy Logic, there is partial membership of an element to a particular set. Like in the preceding case, 1 means sunny, 0.8 means there are few clouds, 0.5 means it's hazy, and 0 if it rains all day.

So, we rely on Fuzzy Logic for dealing with imprecision and vagueness. Fuzzy Logic finds extensive application in expert systems and diverse other contexts.

History of Fuzzy Logic

Aristotle and his forerunners planned their hypothesis of common sense and arithmetic; they stated the law, which states that each plan should be true or false [28]. An apple is either red or not red; it cannot be both red and not red. Plato specified a third side, apart from true and false [29]. In the Aristotelian theory, logic is treated with two values. During the 19th century, George Boole formulated an algebraic system and set theory to address two-valued logic, representing true and false states [30]. In the early 20th century, Jan Łukasiewicz introduced a three-valued logic (true, possible, false), which unfortunately didn't gain significant recognition [31].

In 1965, Lotfi A. Zadeh, a researcher at the University of California, Berkeley, published *Fuzzy Sets*, a seminal work that established the mathematical foundation for fuzzy set theory and, consequently, Fuzzy Logic's development [32]. Zadeh observed that traditional binary logic was insufficient for handling data imbued with subjective or fuzzy concepts. To bridge this gap, he formulated a theory of Fuzzy Logic, enabling computers to navigate distinctions within data that possess various degrees of uncertainty, akin to human reasoning processes.

This technology was introduced within the United States, but at that time, scientists and researchers mostly didn't accept it for years. Some mathematicians argued that Fuzzy Logic was just a chance in disguise [33]. However, countries like Japan, China, and other Asian countries accepted Fuzzy Logic. There are over 10,000 scientists in China, the best range of researchers. Although Japan is considered at the vital edge of fuzzy studies, fewer individuals are engaged in fuzzy analysis [34].

Fuzzy Set Theory

The real complication between Fuzzy Logic and Boolean Logic of reasoning is that possible regards reach out from 0.0 to 1.0 (comprehensive, not just 0 and 1). For example, you could state that the fuzzy truth value (FTV) of the statement "Ram is tall" is 0.75 if Ram is 2 meters tall. To create this more formally:

m is an enrollment work and the capacity that draws meters to an FTV of 0.75. For example, a moderately straightforward participation capacity could be as shown in Equation 1.

$$m\big(TALL(x)\big) = \begin{cases} 0; x < 5 \\ \dfrac{x-5}{2}; 5 \le x \le 7 \\ 1; x > 7 \end{cases} \qquad \text{(Equation 1)}$$

A prescribed sense of an enrollment capacity can be expressed as an ability that maps each point of fuzzy set A to the real interim [0.0, 1.0] with the end objective that m(A(x)) approaches the evaluation of contribution for x in increments.

The Essential Particulars of Fuzzy Logic

The most important particulars about Fuzzy Logic are as follows:

- **Fuzzy Logic is not unreliable**: Fuzzy Logic cannot be measured as unreliable as it does not ignore its decision-making aptitude to output clear-cut outcomes.

- **Fuzzy Logic is different from probability**: The effort to decide something about the probable significance of obviously represented events that may happen purposelessly. With fuzzy reasoning, we are trying to decide something about the chance of the event itself. Fuzziness is progressively conveyed as unimportance, not inaccuracy or weakness; it is usual for observation and consideration.

- **Scheming fuzzy sets is easy**: Demanding out a fuzzy set's inaccurate state is often fast and easy. Later on, after some testing or knowledge, we can alter its right behavior.

- **Fuzzy systems are even and easily tuned and can be validated**: It's faster and tension-free to make fuzzy sets and engineer a fuzzy framework than to generate imitative knowledge-based systems since the fuzzy rule handles all the interlocking degrees of suppleness. These frameworks are accepted much like usual, yet altering them is usually significantly less difficult.

- **Fuzzy systems are not neural networks**: Fuzzy framework activities resolve the crossing point, extra or union of the fuzzy control causes. Whereas this is, to some extent, parallel to both straight programming and neural systems, fuzzy frameworks move toward these issues in an unanticipated method.

- **Fuzzy Logic is more than process control**: It is considered mainly as a tool chiefly as a tool, for the most part as an instrument for process control and flag study; its clarification is extremely restricting. Fuzzy Logic is a method for speaking to and breaching down data, independent of exacting applications.

- **Fuzzy Logic is a way of thinking and figurative procedure**: Fuzzy Logic is an influential and elastic equipment for discussing doubtful, vague, and indistinct data. It can't handle all issues but encourages us to demonstrate difficult, even fixed, issues.

Applications of Fuzzy Logic

Fuzzy Logic applies in various real-life applications. Some of the research of experts regarding Fuzzy Logic have been captured in various areas, which are as follows:

- **Anti-lock braking system**: Fuzzy Logic is employed in an anti-lock braking system successfully. The classical braking system, when used, can make the vehicle skid on the road, resulting in nonlinear movements. In contrast, the Fuzzy Logic used in this system helps to overcome this problem, resulting in stable behavior of the vehicle. The proposed system is tested and simulated on the experimental car to show the results [35].

- **Aircraft engine**: A controller based on Fuzzy Logic is proposed to control Piper Seneca V aircraft engines. Here, fuzzy input parameters are Cylinder Head Temperature (CHT), Vertical Speed Indicator (VSI), and Manifold Pressure. The output is the Cowl Flap Control Signal that will be opened or closed. The proposed system also helps in reducing pilots' workload [36].

- **Clinical decision support system**: Fuzzy Logic is also employed in the clinical decision support system that helps dentists make decisions in case of vague patient information. Fuzzy input variables like the extent of tooth loss, pain, tooth mobility, etc., are input to the system, and the output will be the possible treatments concerning the symptoms. The output is checked against dentists' predictions, and the results show that both are consistent. The system can increase doctors' confidence levels in treating patients according to their symptoms.

- **Energy systems**: Various artificial intelligence tools like Fuzzy Logic, neural network, and genetic algorithms are used in various energy systems like solar, wind, bioenergy, etc. Various applications exist, like in energy management and building using photovoltaic, voltage control, and power control stabilizers. Fuzzy DSS (decision support system) can be used as a decision model. The neuro-fuzzy system can be used as an expert system for maximizing available resources. Fuzzy Logic is used for estimation and optimization purposes for developing DSS in wind energy. Various techniques like Fuzzy PSO, QPSO, fuzzy honey bee optimization, fuzzy expert, etc., are used in various energy models. Fuzzy Logic and artificial neural networks have been used for estimating wind speed. All these applications are reviewed by the researchers [37].

- **Forecasting electricity load**: Fuzzy Logic can also be applied for forecasting electricity load. The researcher takes two fuzzy input variables: humidity and temperature. The result gave output in the form of projected load with a mean absolute percentage error of 0.71% as compared to the mean absolute percentage error of 3.18% with the conventional technique, which shows the reliability of the Fuzzy Logic tool in getting results [38].

- **Forecasting automobile fuel consumption**: A model named ANFIS (Adaptive Neuro-Fuzzy Inference System) is implemented to forecast automobiles' fuel consumption. For this, the model utilizes diverse automobile data, including attributes such as acceleration, cylinder count, displacement, horsepower, weight, and model year, encompassing vehicles like Ford Ranger, Toyota, and others. The model's outcome is the use of fuel in miles per gallon. The model's root mean square error (RMSE) is compared with the root mean square by using linear regression, and the result shows that the RMSE of the model is quite less than RMSE by using other techniques [39].

- **Software cost estimation**: Fuzzy Logic–based model is implemented to estimate software cost in terms of efforts spent. The model takes five inputs – complexity, data, tool, line of code, and skills – and gives one output in software cost estimation. The result of this model is compared with Constructive Cost Model (COCOMO) I and COCOMO II, and the results show an improvement in accuracy in predicting software cost estimation [39].

Design of the Model with Fuzzy Logic

As in the earlier section, we have explained the Fuzzy Logic applications in various areas. This section aims to provide an elucidation of the procedural intricacies inherent to the Fuzzy Logic process, along with its bespoke application within the scope of our undertaking. The graphical representation of the Fuzzy Logic control system, as depicted in Figure 5-1, serves to visually augment this exposition.

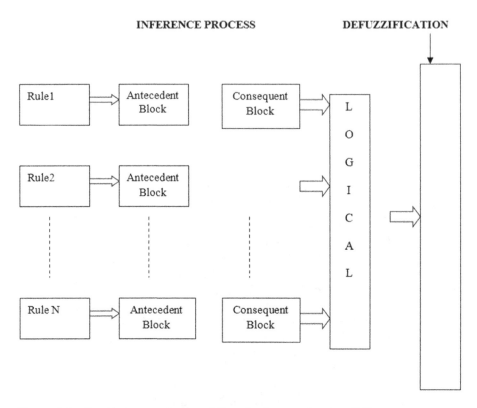

Figure 5-1. Graphical representation of Fuzzy Logic control system [41]

Fuzzy Logic Inference Mechanism

The Fuzzy Inference System: Essential Decision-Making Component in Fuzzy Logic

Within this system, the primary function revolves around decision-making. It leverages "IF…THEN" statements combined with fuzzy operators like "OR" or "AND" to formulate crucial decision rules. The resultant output from the Fuzzy Inference System (FIS) is consistently a fuzzy set. Notably, while the input to the system can be either imprecise or crisp, the resulting output maintains its fuzziness. A defuzzification unit is essential, which converts the fuzzy output into crisp output. When FIS is used as a controller, it is essential to have a fuzzy output.

The fuzzy inference process (as shown in Figure 5-2) consists of five steps, each of which is explained in the following sections.

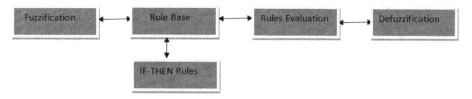

Figure 5-2. Fuzzy Logic process [41]

Step 1: Fuzzification

Fuzzification defines membership functions and linguistic variables for fuzzy variables [42]. In mathematics, variables take numeric values, but in Fuzzy Logic, fuzzy variables take nonnumeric values or linguistic variables [43]. Now the question arises what the use of linguistic variables is. Consider an example of a fuzzy variable: let us say the age of a process we have taken in our work. Its linguistic values are very low (VL), low (L), medium (M), high (H), and very high (VH). However, if we take here a numerical value, the case will be simple, but it represents only one value, say 22, but low represents a range, say 15–35 (more than one value).

The following are the characteristics of linguistic variables:

- The variable name

- Term set of the variable

- Rules governing the generation of variable x values at the syntactic level

- Rules of semantics that connect each x value with its corresponding implication

Fuzzification involves the establishment of membership functions, which are curves representing the degree of belongingness of an element to a universal set. Higher values on the curve indicate a stronger membership. Represented by the symbol "μ," its value ranges from 0 to 1. The membership function serves as a visual portrayal of a fuzzy set. In its graphical representation, the x axis represents the universe of discourse, and the y axis denotes the degree of membership within the range of [0, 1]. A variety of membership functions are available. But the choice of a membership function depends upon the application as it varies from application to application. There has been no research, till now, on where to apply a particular membership function. Applying a membership function in a particular application depends on common sense.

The following are various features of membership functions:

- **Core**: The core of the membership function for a fuzzy set A is defined as that area whose membership value is equal to 1, that is, $\mu_A(x) = 1$.

- **Support**: Support of the membership function for a fuzzy set A is defined as that area whose membership value is greater than 1, that is, $\mu A(x) > 1$.

- **Boundary**: The boundary is the difference between support and core.

In general, [32] categorized membership functions into three main categories, as shown in Figure 5-3 and discussed in the sections that follow.

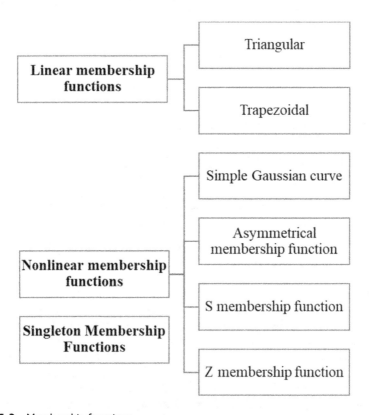

Figure 5-3. Membership functions

The utilization of nonlinear functions extends computation time. Hence, the majority of applications opt for linear functions.

Linear Membership Functions

Linear membership functions are made of straight lines. The various linear membership functions are as follows:

- **Triangular membership function**: A triangular membership function is a linear function made up of straight lines, as shown in Figure 5-4. It has a function name trimf. Triangular membership functions are used in cases having sharp boundaries.

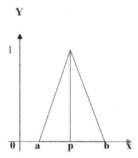

Figure 5-4. Triangular membership function [44]

Here, a is the lower limit, b is the upper limit, and p is the center point.

- **Trapezoidal membership function**: A trapezoidal membership function is easy to design and implement [45]. Here, the slope goes up, then consistent for some time, and then moves down (Figure 5-5).

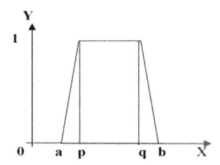

Figure 5-5. Trapezoidal membership function [46]

In Figure 5-5, *a* is the lower limit, and *b* is the upper limit.

Nonlinear membership functions

Nonlinear membership functions are not made of straight lines [47]. They are curves in shape. The various nonlinear membership functions are as follows:

- **Simple Gaussian curve**: The Gaussian membership function is selected where an element needs a smooth transition from one set to another. It is bell shaped, follows a normal distribution, and has more center density than corners, as shown in Figure 5-6.

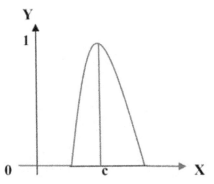

Figure 5-6. Gaussian membership function [48]

- **Asymmetrical membership function**: The asymmetrical membership function is opposite to the symmetrical one, which means half has the same mirror image, as shown in Figure 5-7. It can also be used using two sigmoidal functions. It is also known as a closed membership function.

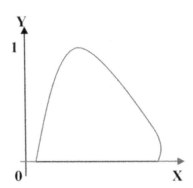

Figure 5-7. Asymmetrical membership function [49]

- **S membership function**: The S membership function is opposite to the Z membership function that opens to the right, as shown in Figure 5-8. Like in the case of "Permanent Teeth," we can apply this type of membership function.

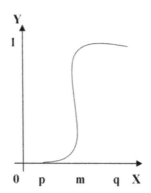

Figure 5-8. S membership function [50]

- **Z membership function**: The Z membership function is a membership function that opens to the left, as shown in Figure 5-9. Like in the case of "Temporary Teeth," we apply this type of membership function.

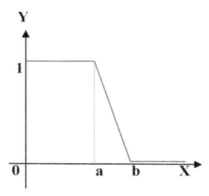

Figure 5-9. Z membership function [51]

Singleton Membership Functions

This membership function takes only two values, "0" or "1," as shown in Figure 5-10.

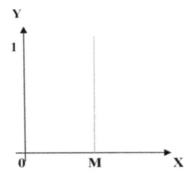

Figure 5-10. Singleton membership function [52]

The interpretation of fuzzy IF-THEN rules can be made in the following three ways (assignment statement, conditional statement, and unconditional statement):

- **Assignment statements**

  These types of statements use the operator "=" to assign value to variables. They take the following form:

  $$a = hi$$

  $$Weather = sunny$$

- **Conditional statements**

  These statements employ the form of "IF-THEN" rule base to assess conditions. They adhere to the subsequent structure:

  $$IF\ security\ is\ high,\ THEN\ priority\ is\ hot.$$

  $$IF\ ice\ cream\ is\ yummy,\ THEN\ eat.$$

- **Unconditional statements**

  They adhere to the subsequent structure:

  $$GOTO\ 20$$

  $$Switch\ the\ light\ off$$

Step 2: Designing Rule Base

In general, there are three approaches to designing a fuzzy rule base (Mamdani systems, Sugeno systems, and Tsukamoto models).

Mamdani Systems

This is the most commonly used approach to design a fuzzy rule base that uses antecedent and consequent approaches in the If-Then rule format [53].

The general format is shown in Equation 2.

$$\text{If a is } A_1^{\,k} \text{ and b is } A_2^{\,k} \text{ then c is } B_2^{\,k} \qquad \text{(Equation 2)}$$

A_1 and A_2 are antecedents, a and b are fuzzy inputs, and c is the fuzzy output variable.

And $K = 1, 2\ldots\ldots n$

In the preceding format, we have two antecedents and one consequent.

The Mamdani system is widely used to capture experts' knowledge embedded in the system. Finally, it decides in a human-like manner, so it is widely used in decision support applications. It differs from other systems in how the output is computed, as we use the defuzzification technique to compute the crisp output [54]. It also has an output membership function. If there are multiple antecedents and multiple consequents, they can be joined by using fuzzy operators like Fuzzy And, Fuzzy Or, and Fuzzy Not.

Sugeno Systems

The Sugeno system is used where we have a function like inputs. Here, the antecedent is fuzzy, but the consequent is a function of inputs [55].

The general format is shown in Equation 3.

$$\text{If a is } A_1^{\,k} \text{ and b is } A_2^{\,k} \text{ then c is } f^k\left(a,\, b\right) \qquad \text{(Equation 3)}$$

Here, the weighted average method is calculated to obtain the crisp value, as no defuzzification technique is needed. This system works well with optimization and adaptive techniques [56].

Tsukamoto Models

In this technique, antecedents are fuzzy, consequents are fuzzy, but membership functions should be monotonic [57]. Here, no defuzzification technique is needed as the weighted average method is used to compute the crisp value.

Step 3: Rule Evaluation

Utilization of Fuzzy Operators in the Antecedent

After the fuzzification process, if the antecedent part of a rule has many parts, they can be connected through fuzzy operators to get one number that will answer [58]. The resultant number is subsequently assigned to the output function. While the input for the fuzzy operator consists of two or more truth values, the output comprises a singular true value.

Deriving Consequences from Antecedent

Rule weighting is another crucial consideration. Prior to employing the implication method, it is necessary to determine the weight assigned to each rule. Each rule carries a *weight*, represented as a number within the range of 0 to 1. Typically, this weight is set at 1; nevertheless, the impact of a rule can be modified by adjusting its weight value to deviate from 1. Following the assignment of weights to individual rules, the implication method is executed.

Aggregation of the Consequences Across the Rules

By means of aggregation, the fuzzy sets corresponding to each rule's output combine to create a unified fuzzy set. This aggregation takes place sequentially for each output variable before advancing to the subsequent stage. In this step, the input comprises the collection of output functions resulting from the implication process for each rule. The outcome of this phase produces a singular fuzzy set for every output variable.

Step 4: Defuzzification

The term "defuzzification" describes the procedure by which a fuzzy output is transformed into a crisp one [59]. The results must be clear for us to take any sort of action based on them. However, in certain practical problems, the fuzzy output can't be applied, for example, if somebody says

Switch off the light slightly

This is somewhat fuzzy. We have to give a crisp output to a machine. There are many ways to compute the defuzzified output. After combining various fuzzy sets, one of these defuzzification techniques is applied to compute the crisp output from the fuzzy output. Some of them are as follows.

Maximum Membership Principle

It is also known as the height method. The maximum membership value will be the defuzzified value. This method is shown in Figure 5-11.

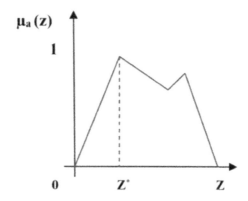

Figure 5-11. Maximum membership principle [50]

Mathematically, it is defined as shown in Equation 4.

$$\mu_a\left(Z^*\right) \ge \mu_a\left(Z\right) \forall Z \in Z$$ (Equation 4)

Here, Z^* is the defuzzified value.

Centroid Method

The centroid method calculates the region of membership functions within the scope of the (output) variable. This is the most preferred defuzzification method as it gives accurate answers by considering the whole area under the curve. The centroid method is shown in Figure 5-12.

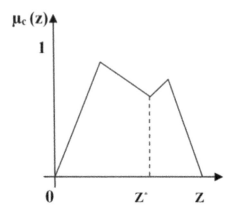

Figure 5-12. Centroid method [60]

Mathematically, this function can be defined as shown in Equation 5.

$$COA = \int \mu_c(z).z \, dz \, / \int \mu_c(z) \, dz \qquad \text{(Equation 5)}$$

COA is the center of area/gravity [10].

Weighted Average Method

The weighted average approach remains applicable solely to symmetric membership functions, as depicted in Figure 5-13.

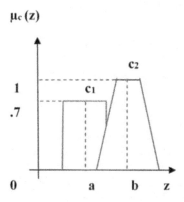

Figure 5-13. Weighted average method [61]
Source: Author's computation

This is defined as shown in Equation 6.

$$Z^* = \sum \mu_c(\bar{Z}) \cdot \bar{Z} / \sum \mu_c(\bar{Z})$$ (Equation 6)

where $\bar{Z}$ = centroid of each of the symmetrical membership functions and is defined as follows:

$$Z^* = \frac{(a^*.7 + b^*1)}{(.7 + 1)}$$

Here, a and b are midpoints.

Mean-Max Method (Middle of Maxima)

Here, the Mean-Max method is shown in Figure 5-14 and is defined by the algebraic expression in Equation 7.

$$Z^* = (a + b) / 2$$ (Equation 7)

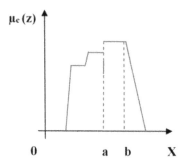

Figure 5-14. Mean-Max method [62]

Design and Implementation of the System

We are proposing an AI-based customer segmentation system that will divide the customers based on a certain category to which the recommender system will recommend a particular brand to the customers. If the appropriate brand is recommended, it will boost marketing and decrease window-shopping. Customers will be categorized based on income, domicile, age, and livelihood. Three categories will be formed – affordable, middle-ranged, and premium – and brands will be floated as per these categories. We have designed and implemented the system using Fuzzy Logic in MATLAB. The whole process started by collecting the data from the targeted population. Out of the data collected, 80% of the data have been used for the training part, and the remaining 20% will be used as testing data. The design of the system is shown in Figure 5-15.

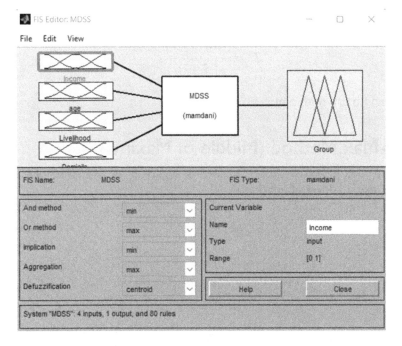

Figure 5-15. Design of the model
Source: Author's computation

Fuzzification

Three linguistic terms have been used for all input parameters, that is, income, age, domicile, and livelihood, and one output parameter, that is, group.

- **Income**: The membership functions designed for the "income" input variable are shown in Figure 5-16. Linguistic terms used here are low, moderate, and high.

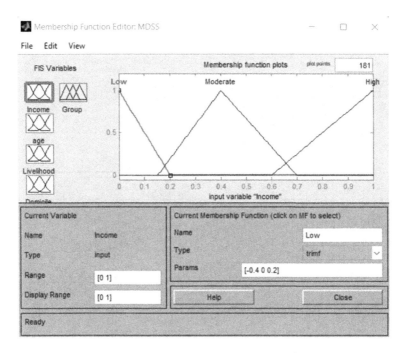

Figure 5-16. Membership function for income
Source: Author's computation

Mathematically, the equation for moderate income is shown in Equation 8.

$$\mu_M(x) = \begin{cases} 0 & \text{if } x \leq .15 \\ \dfrac{x \quad .15}{.4 - .15} & \text{if } x \in (.15, .4) \\ \dfrac{.7 \quad x}{.7 - .4} & \text{if } x \in (.4, .7) \\ 0 & \text{if } x \geq .7 \end{cases} \qquad \text{(Equation 8)}$$

- **Age**: The membership functions designed for the "age" input variable are shown in Figure 5-17. Here, we have taken the Gaussian membership function. Three linguistic terms have been used here, that is, young, middle-aged, and aged.

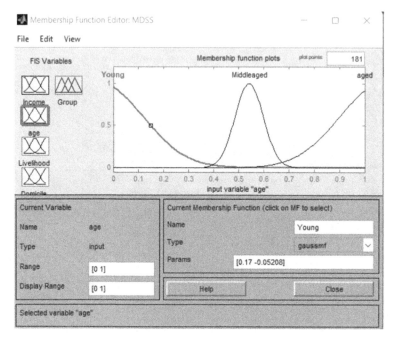

Figure 5-17. Membership function for age
Source: Author's computation

- **Livelihood**: The membership functions designed for the "livelihood" input variable are shown in Figure 5-18. Here, we have taken the triangular membership function. Three linguistic terms have been used here, that is, basic, comfort, and luxury.

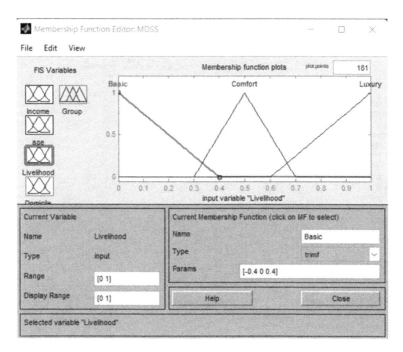

Figure 5-18. Membership function for livelihood
Source: Author'tation

- **Domicile**: The membership functions designed for the "domicile" input variable are shown in Figure 5-19. Here, we have taken the triangular membership function. Three linguistic terms have been used here, that is, rural, semi-urban, and urban.

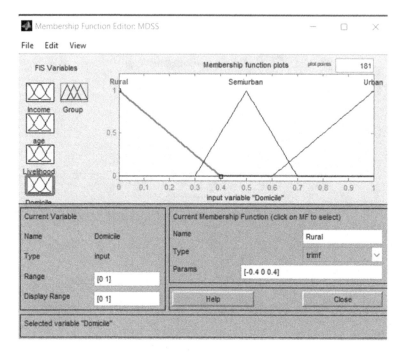

Figure 5-19. Membership function for domicile
Source: Author's computation

The membership functions designed for the "group" output variable are shown in Figure 5-20. Here, we have taken the triangular membership function. Three linguistic terms have been used here, that is, affordable, middle-ranged, and premium.

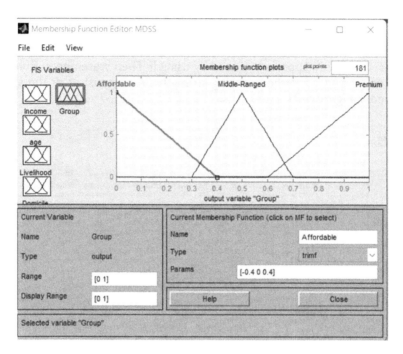

Figure 5-20. Membership function for group
Source: Author's computation

Mathematically, the equation for moderate income is shown in Equation 9.

$$\mu_M(x) = \begin{cases} 0 & \text{if } x \leq .6 \\ \dfrac{x \quad .6}{1-.6} & \text{if } x \in (0.6, 1) \\ \dfrac{1.4 \quad x}{1.4-1} & \text{if } x \in (1, 1.4) \\ 0 & \text{if } x \geq 1.4 \end{cases} \qquad \text{(Equation 9)}$$

Rule Base

Based on the data collected, 80 rules have been designed with varying strengths. Mamdani's approach is used by using If-Then statements. Rules will be fired depending upon their varying strengths. A screenshot of the system is attached in Figure 5-21.

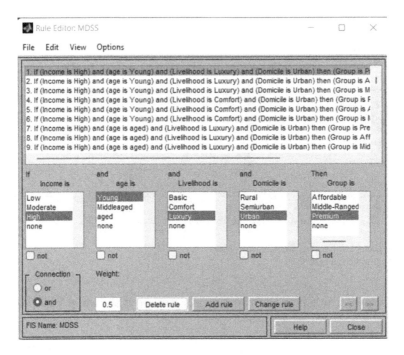

Figure 5-21. Rule base
Source: Author's computation

Defuzzification

The centroid method is used for defuzzification. The screenshot is attached in Figure 5-22.

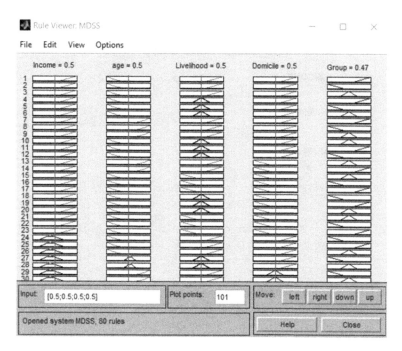

Figure 5-22. Defuzzification
Source: Author's computation

Graphical User Interface

The graphical user interface, as shown in Figure 5-23, will take inputs in the form of income, age, domicile, and livelihood. Multiple rules will be fired at the back end; based on that, the system will decide the output.

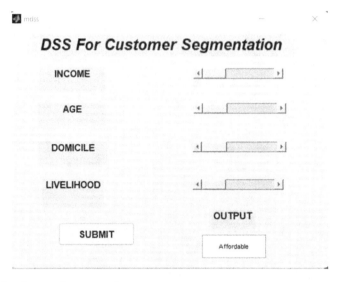

Figure 5-23. Graphical user interface
Source: Author's computation

Results

The main aim of our research is customer segmentation, which is done by analyzing their characteristics relating to their income, age, domicile, and livelihood. Actual customers were targeted for this process. They have given us mixed opinions. Using our model, we could design the brain of our system where various customer inputs were fed. Multiple opinions from the customers were fired at the same time with varying strengths. At the time of data collection, inputs were fuzzy and vague. After defuzzification, we got the crisp output in the form results, as shown in Table 5-1. For example, take the first record:

A young person has a handsome income. He is living in an urban area with a luxurious lifestyle.

Our DSS has decided that the recommender system should recommend various items like footwear, clothing, and accessories with premium brands to that customer group so that sales can be enhanced and customers can benefit without wasting time. Another example is as follows:

An aged person has a low income. He is living in a semi-urban area with a basic lifestyle.

Our proposed DSS has decided that the recommender system should recommend low-ranged and average-level brands to them; otherwise, they will indulge in window-shopping.

So DSS and the recommender system can be beneficial for various shopping websites.

Table 5-1. System Response

Income	Age	Domicile	Livelihood	System Response
High	Young	Urban	Luxurious	*Premium*
High	Young	Urban	Comfort	*Premium*
High	Aged	Urban	Luxurious	*Premium*
High	Young	Urban	Comfort	*Premium*
High	Aged	Rural	Luxurious	*Premium*
High	Young	Rural	Basic	*Premium*
High	Young	Rural	Comfort	*Medium-Ranged*
High	Young	Rural	Basic	*Affordable*
Moderate	Young	Urban	Luxurious	*Medium-Ranged*
Moderate	Middle	Urban	Comfort	*Medium-Ranged*
Moderate	Aged	Semi-Urban	Luxurious	*Affordable*
Moderate	Young	Semi-Urban	Comfort	*Medium-Ranged*
Moderate	Young	Rural	Luxurious	*Medium-Ranged*
Moderate	Young	Rural	Comfort	*Medium-Ranged*
Moderate	Young	Rural	Basic	*Affordable*
Low	Young	Urban	Luxurious	*Medium-Ranged*
High	Young	Urban	Luxurious	*Premium*
Low	Middle-Aged	Semi-Urban	Luxurious	*Medium-Ranged*
Low	Aged	Semi-Urban	Basic	*Affordable*
Low	Aged	Rural	Luxurious	*Medium-Ranged*
Low	Aged	Rural	Comfort	*Affordable*
Low	Middle-Aged	Rural	Comfort	*Affordable*
Low	Young	Rural	Basic	*Affordable*
High	Young	Urban	Basic	*Premium*
Moderate	Young	Semi-Urban	Basic	*Medium-Ranged*

(continued)

Table 7-1. (*continued*)

Income	Age	Domicile	Livelihood	System Response
High	Middle-Aged	Rural	Luxurious	*Premium*
Moderate	Middle-Aged	Semi-Urban	Luxurious	*Affordable*
High	Aged	Semi-Urban	Luxurious	*Premium*
High	Middle-Aged	Semi-Urban	Luxurious	*Premium*

Limitations of Fuzzy Logic Control

The following are the limitations of Fuzzy Logic Control:

- **Needs plenty of data**: The Fuzzy Logic Controller needs plenty of facts to be applied.

- **Helpful in the case of reasonable old data**: The Fuzzy Logic Controller is not helpful for programs much lesser or bigger than past data.

- **Requires high human proficiency**: The system's correctness depends on individuals' awareness and proficiency.

- **Requires rules updating periodically**: The rules must be rationalized periodically.

Conclusion

We have designed and implemented a Fuzzy Logic–based decision support system for marketing. As it is artificial intelligence based, it will be a better system to deal with uncertainties in real life. Moreover, AI mimics human mentality. So, this system will be very close to human thinking. This system can be taken as an advisor for a recommendation system for improving the marketing process. In our ongoing and prospective endeavors, we envisage a rigorous testing phase for the proposed Fuzzy Logic–based DSS. This testing will entail the comprehensive collection of inputs from diverse demographic segments, enabling a comprehensive assessment of its functionality and adaptability. The confluence of empirical evidence and intricate algorithmic design will guide the system's refinement and potentially engender a more universally effective solution.

Moreover, there is a need to save the data of our premium and routine customers. We prefer a hybrid cloud-based model comprising public and private clouds. We can keep the data of premium customers on the private cloud as it is secure while keeping routine customers' data on the public cloud. By ingeniously segregating our data repository through this hybrid approach, we ensure not only the highest level of security for our premium customers but also a judicious allocation of resources, resulting in a cost-efficient operational framework.

Analyzing Customer Satisfaction of Hotel Booking Applications: A Sentimental Analysis Approach

Anshul Saxena*, Christ University, Bengaluru, Karnataka, India, Email: anshul.saxena@christuniversity.in

Rehan Mathew Kuruvilla, Christ University, Bengaluru, Karnataka, India

Jayant Mahajan, Christ University, Bengaluru, Karnataka, India

Sunil Vakayil, LIBA, Chennai, Tamil Nadu, India

© Neha Zaidi, Mohit Maurya, Simon Grima, Pallavi Tyagi 2024, corrected publication 2024
N. Zaidi et al. (eds.), *Building AI Driven Marketing Capabilities*,
https://doi.org/10.1007/978-1-4842-9810-7_6

When selecting hotels, travelers often turn to customer reviews for insights. However, navigating through these detailed reviews can be time consuming. In this digital era, travelers are both consumers and producers of vast amounts of online information. Many share their experiences, offering a valuable feedback loop for hotel managers. However, a large number of reviews can be daunting for potential guests, and to resolve this particular issue, researchers have conducted experiments to extract key themes from reviews. They used this method to identify common topics in large text sets. This approach isolated five main themes that were then verified for their significance and relevance. To make this information more accessible, this study employed a technique to classify reviews as positive or negative sentiments. This approach not only assists travelers in quickly understanding a hotel's standing but also provides hotel managers with clear feedback for improvement.

Introduction

The rise of online travel platforms has catalyzed a surge in user-generated content, particularly feedback on hotels and travel destinations. The proliferation of online testimonials, stemming from diverse traveler experiences, forms a comprehensive repository of reviews. As reliance on these platforms intensifies, travelers increasingly utilize them as primary sources of information for their decision-making. These reviews, which encapsulate everything from room cleanliness to staff behavior, serve as both a reflection of user satisfaction and a testament to the hotel's service quality. This digital landscape has facilitated the evolution of traditional word of mouth into what is now termed electronic Word of Mouth (eWOM). Unlike its predecessor, which is confined to personal interactions, eWOM has a broader reach, resonating with a vast online audience. eWOM testimonials are invaluable for stakeholders in the travel and hospitality industry. They offer insights into the strengths and areas of improvement of their services, serving as a guidepost for continuous enhancement.

Global adoption of the Internet has significantly influenced sectors such as travel and accommodation. As online access expands, individuals increasingly rely on digital platforms to make informed decisions about their stay. This transition emphasizes a broader societal preference for convenience in decision-making processes. Subsequently, the hospitality industry pivoted from traditional marketing strategies to a heightened focus on digital outreach. A plethora of websites now cater to hotel bookings, providing comprehensive information on amenities, pricing, and location. The inclusion of user reviews is central to such platforms. These reviews, derived from firsthand experiences, offer invaluable insights for prospective guests. They address both tangible, such as room quality, and nuanced experiences related to ambiance and hospitality. The critical role of online testimonials in shaping a hotel's public image in the contemporary digital era is undeniable.

Travelers increasingly depend on online reviews when choosing accommodations. While a numerical rating offers a brief overview, detailed reviews provide comprehensive insights into a hotel's quality and service. These reviews serve as trusted electronic word of mouth and often hold more weight than traditional advertisements. For prospective guests, such feedback based on firsthand experiences is deemed authentic and valuable. This trend has implications for the hotel industry. Positive testimonials enhance reputation, whereas critical feedback reveals areas for improvement. By addressing these areas, hotels not only refine their services but also signal their commitment to guest satisfaction. Given the competitive landscape, it is essential for hotel management to heed and act on these online insights.

Online reviews carry personal experiences and details that potential customers find deeply resonant with. This resonance stems from the variety of needs and motivations highlighted in these reviews. For example, while a business traveler may emphasize the efficiency of check-in procedures, a leisure tourist might highlight the ambiance of the hotel's lobby. Given the plethora of factors influencing these reviews, such as socioeconomic background, cultural norms, and individual priorities, hotels have sought to decode this feedback systematically. One prevailing method is the adoption of text mining techniques. Through this approach, hotels have shifted through vast amounts of user-generated content to gain actionable insights. The ultimate aim is to refine their services, catering to diverse customer expectations and fostering loyalty; however, the journey of extracting meaningful data from reviews presents challenges. The primary hurdle is the unstructured nature of this feedback, which defies a simple analysis using conventional statistical tools. The sheer volume of daily reviews further complicates matters, making manual perusal impractical. In addition, the intrinsic biases and subjective tones inherent in personal reviews pose interpretative challenges. These biases, rooted in human nature, can sometimes obscure the real sentiments, requiring even more nuanced analytical strategies. In essence, while online reviews are treasure troves of direct customer feedback, hotels face a complex task in translating this feedback into tangible service improvements.

The primary focus of this research is to use text-mining techniques to dissect online hotel reviews. The intent is to unearth the underlying factors that resonate with both satisfied and dissatisfied consumers. To achieve a nuanced understanding, the study zeroes in on distinct feedback types: endorsements from content customers and cautionary tales from those less pleased. Central to this investigation is discerning which elements of a hotel's offerings garner appreciation and which invite critique. Are there specific services or amenities that consistently please the guests? On the other hand, are certain areas repeatedly pinpointed as needing improvement? To structure this analysis, reviews were first segregated based on their well-defined parameters. These might span various dimensions such as room quality, dining experiences, or staff interactions. Subsequently, the data underwent topic modeling. This analytical approach is adept at revealing concealed patterns within extensive datasets, the crux of which is generating insights that are actionable for the hotel industry. By identifying elements that consistently charm or displease guests, hotel operators can make informed decisions. Such decisions rooted in authentic guest feedback can be pivotal in refining guest experiences. This rigorous examination thus holds dual significance: it adds depth to the academic literature while also serving as a beacon for industry practitioners eager to optimize their services.

Overview of the Hotel Industry

The global hotel industry has seen significant changes in recent years. An estimation by STR indicates that there are approximately 17.5 million hotel rooms spread across 187,000 hotels worldwide. As of June 2020, Wyndham Hotel Group held the position of having the highest number of properties, with over 9200 hotels, followed by Marriott International and Choice Hotels International. Interestingly, while Wyndham led in the number of properties, Marriott International had the most extensive room portfolio, surpassing Hilton Worldwide.

This industry plays a vital role in the global economy, accounting for about 10% of worldwide GDP. Nevertheless, the COVID-19 pandemic in 2020 reduced its contribution to just 5.5%. Revenues were also adversely affected, plummeting by 46% compared to 2019. Predictions for 2021 suggest a rise to approximately $285B, though a full recovery is projected for 2023. Europe, in particular, has witnessed a decline, with occupancy rates falling drastically at the start of the pandemic.

In the United States, the situation mirrored the global trend. By the close of 2020, there were about 5.29 million hotel rooms in the country. The pandemic significantly impacted the revenue and occupancy rate in 2020, marking the worst performance since the 2009 financial crisis. Recent data from Smith

Travel Research indicates that US hotel rates and revenues peaked in 2019. Las Vegas dominates the list of large hotels, housing nine of the ten largest in the country.

In the realm of hotel chains, Hilton stands out as the most valuable brand, with Marriott International boasting the most brands. An essential event in the industry was Marriott's acquisition of Starwood Hotels & Resorts in 2015, making the combined loyalty program the largest globally.

The trend toward independent hotels has grown over the years, with approximately 40% of US hotels being independent as of 2019. Boutique hotels, defined by their unique design and limited room numbers, have seen increasing popularity. Despite their smaller numbers, these hotels have outperformed their counterparts in occupancy and rates.

On the consumer end, booking patterns reveal that Booking.com is the most valuable travel brand. A survey by Expedia in 2015 highlighted that travelers, on average, visited 38 websites before finalizing a booking. Furthermore, direct bookings at hotels and through their websites are still prevalent, making up a significant portion of reservations. It's worth noting that business travel has historically been a primary driver of hotel industry revenue, but post-pandemic predictions suggest a decline.

In understanding guest behavior, reviews have become crucial. A substantial percentage of travelers rely on reviews before making their hotel reservations. Sustainability has emerged as a significant concern, with many travelers showing a willingness to spend more for sustainable trips. However, the hotel industry still faces challenges, with some guests admitting to taking items from hotels. Lastly, the importance of online reviews cannot be understated, as travelers are often willing to pay more for hotels with better review scores.

Related Work

Table 6-1 offers a peak into various techniques used by researchers over the years to perform topic modeling and sentiment analysis for the hotel reviews.

Table 6-1. Related Work

Author	Year	Technique/Tool	Key Findings
Akhtar et al. [2]	2017	Topic modeling (LDA), sentiment analysis	• A Java tool processes text data, employing topic modeling to uncover hidden topics that might be overlooked by other methods. • Paper offers a sentiment score, which are independent of the rating supplied by the website and may be more accurate than the latter.
Annisa et al. [1]	2019	LDA method	• The findings of this study suggest issues that are commonly discussed by visitors regarding their grievances, experiences, opinions, and input to hotel management through reviews. • In this study, LDA is used to separate the themes from the keywords that visitors commonly review in each topic.
Muhammad et al. [3]	2020	Long Short-Term Memory (LSTM) model, Word2Vec model	• Examines the impact of changing Word2Vec settings on the sentiment classification model's accuracy. • The accuracy of the sentiment classification model can be impacted by changes in LSTM parameters.
Bjørkelund et al [4].	2012	Sentiment analysis, opinion mining	• Google Maps may be used to show the sentiment analysis findings of textual evaluations, giving customers the ability to quickly identify top hotels and desirable neighborhoods.
Priyantina et al. [5]	2019	Latent Dirichlet Allocation (LDA), term	• Using the Term Frequency–Inverse Cluster Frequency, the study expanded the term list (TF-ICF). • The findings demonstrate that the suggested approach can categorize the reviews into the five hotel features.
Farisi et al. [6]	2019	Multinomial Naïve Bayes classifier, sentiment analysis	• This paper provides a solution by using the multinomial Naive Bayes classifier approach to categorize positive and negative opinion reviews and by comparing models using preprocessing, feature extraction, and feature selection.

(continued)

Table 6-1. *(continued)*

Author	Year	Technique/Tool	Key Findings
Hyun Jeong et al. [7]	2016	Regression analysis	• Reviews that were extremely lengthy and were focused on a small number of hotel features often received worse scores than shorter reviews that covered more ground. • Text analytics highlight specific actions managers can take to raise customer reviews and hotel ratings.
Sodanil [8]	2016	**Review weight analysis, support vector machines, Naïve Bayes, decision tree**	• Using feature-based sentiment analysis, one may evaluate whether an opinion conveyed on a certain feature or aspect is positive, negative, or neutral. • Support vector machines outperform decision trees and Naïve Bayes in terms of accuracy.
Berezina et al. [9]	2016	Text mining	• Negative customer evaluations more commonly refer to room and furnishing categories when compared to those in customer reviews with recommendations, which were measured in terms of specific dimensions. • Customers may become unsatisfied with a service component if it is not delivered or if there are issues with its delivery. Clients who are unsatisfied appear to place more significance on material and financial difficulties.
Ristova [10]	2020	Text mining	• In an online review, customers are likely to disclose even the smallest detail about a hotel feature and how it affected their experience. • Hotels are given a practical method for utilizing the common applications of text mining and sentiment analysis, which enables them to successfully extract huge volumes of accumulated text and research and analyze the hotel characteristics that affect visitors' experiences.
Chanwisitku et al. [11]	2018	Text mining	• Knowing what tourists expect from various hotel services and how their evaluations of those services in online reviews affect the overall quality of the hotel's service. • Can be used to create efficient systems for collecting customer feedback and monitoring social media. They also support a number of managerial implications for managing and marketing guest experiences in the hotel sector.

Research Methodology

The aim of this study is to find out about the negative patterns that lead to guest unhappiness as well as the positive patterns that make hotel guests satisfied and encourage them to suggest the property to others in hotel reviews. Sentiment analysis was selected as a research methodology for the purposes of this study on the assumption that this approach is capable of identifying significant patterns in the massive amount of data produced by hotel guests' reviews.

It is difficult to extract useful facts and trends from relatively huge, highly unstructured text data that is written in natural language in order to acquire insights into guest-generated evaluations. Due to the high computational load, manual scanning and analysis of such data are regarded as being impractical. This level of analysis aimed to recognize broad trends and better understand the data's structure.

In the modern age, where digital information is at our fingertips, hotel reviews have become indispensable tools for travelers. Understanding guest sentiments can provide insights to hotels about areas for improvement and for prospective guests about what to expect. This study aims to process and analyze 500 hotel reviews obtained from reputable platforms, such as MouthShut, TripAdvisor, and the OYO app. These platforms have been chosen due to their stringent review policies, ensuring authenticity. The analysis covers the transformation of unstructured text into a structured format, keyword extraction, topic modeling using Latent Dirichlet Allocation (LDA), and sentiment analysis to ascertain the overall guest sentiment. This methodology has been implanted in five steps as depicted in Figure 6-1.

Figure 6-1. Research methodology

Step 1: Data collection: 500 hotel reviews from MouthShut, TripAdvisor, and the OYO app were gathered in order to gain sufficient and accurate data. This platform was chosen since it only allows guests who have stayed at the hotel they booked to provide reviews, preventing dishonest remarks. It is clear that the data is a sentence-length evaluation. Additionally, this dataset has undergone preprocessing to aid the system's categorization process.

Step 2: Data Preprocessing: Transforming unstructured text into a structured, analyzable format is a fundamental step in text analysis. The preferred representation for this transformation is a document-term matrix, where each document, such as a customer review, has its own row, and each unique word in the entire collection has a dedicated column. The entries in this matrix showcase the frequency of each word in individual documents. To streamline and enhance the efficiency of this representation, several preprocessing steps are essential:

1. Convert all text to lowercase, ensuring uniformity.

2. Eliminate words with fewer than three characters, as well as common stop words like "the," "and," and "of," to reduce redundancy.

3. Apply stemming to words, removing suffixes. This ensures words with similar roots like "values," "valued," and "valuing" are uniformly represented as "value."

4. Discard words that appear either exceedingly frequently or rarely to maintain a focus on meaningful content.

By following these steps, the resultant matrix is both manageable and meaningful, primed for in-depth analysis.

Step 3: Feature extraction: Constructing a dictionary of the extracted terms, cleaning the dataset, and extracting words from the entire dataset. Additionally, text parsing defines part of speech and stem words as well as sentences inside specific customer evaluations. It is very likely that a corpus of quality documents will contain many terms that are unrelated to either distinguishing document from one another or summarizing the documents. The next step's analysis of fewer parsed words is the goal of the text filter. The data has unnecessary information removed from it. Therefore, only important and valuable data is included in the subsequent analysis.

Step 4: Topic modeling: One strategy for extracting aspects is the topic model, which is used to find latent structure in a document collection. The most widely used topic modeling technique is Latent Dirichlet Allocation (LDA). In order to avoid overfitting, LDA uses Dirichlet prior to the distribution of the document's topics and topic words. In order to process vast volumes of data efficiently, LDA is used to extract topics from text. This approach is based on the notion that while all texts are composed of the same set of subjects, they each display a unique probabilistic combination of those themes. The result was processed along with the term list in the provided figure in terms of its similarity calculation using the Semantic Similarity after obtaining the concealed subject for each text. Each review was categorized using this method based on the five selected hotel attributes.

Step 5: Sentiment Analysis: For summarizing a corpus, the most fundamental statistics are word count and sentiment. Sentiment analysis is a technique for gathering and analyzing opinions about goods and services that have been shared in tweets, reviews, comments, or blog entries. The collected review information is then evaluated to determine if each review was good or negative. The hotel reviews are taken into consideration for the study's objectives through sentiment assessment research. Based on a variety of variables including services, prices, location, cuisine, facilities, etc., it divides them into two categories, namely, positive and negative reactions. Sentiment analysis is a methodical computational exploration and investigation of the subjectivity, beliefs, feelings, thoughts, and attitudes in a text. Additionally, sentiment analysis is regarded as a technique for retrieving information and categorizing data into personal categories.

We independently generated measures of each review's positive and negative sentiments in order to look into any potential nonlinearities in the impact of sentiment. Sentiment was measured using negative dictionary words, and the measure was generated by counting the amount of words in the review that matched a list of positive words in certified databases known as dictionaries.

The realm of hotel reviews serves as a mirror, reflecting genuine guest experiences, both positive and negative. This study has adeptly utilized sentiment analysis to navigate the vast ocean of guest reviews and uncover crucial patterns that influence guest satisfaction and dissatisfaction. Harnessing reviews from reliable platforms, the rigorous process, from data preprocessing to sentiment analysis, has illuminated key insights that can empower hoteliers to enhance guest experiences and bolster their reputation. As the digital age continues to amplify the voice of consumers, studies like this become instrumental in bridging the gap between guest expectations and hotel offerings, guiding the hospitality industry toward a future marked by well-informed improvements and unparalleled guest satisfaction.

Empirical Result and Analysis

In the empirical analysis of hotel reviews, methodologies such as word cloud generation, topic modeling, keyword extraction, and sentiment analysis were utilized. These tools illuminated pivotal aspects including room quality, staff behavior, and service efficiency as central to guest experiences. Although the vast majority of feedback was positive, with a striking 98.8% reflecting joy, minor concerns were nonetheless discernible. These findings, culled from a comprehensive examination, present invaluable insights for the hotel industry, suggesting areas of potential refinement to better meet guest expectations.

Word cloud: An analysis of 500 reviews (Figure 6-2) revealed recurrent themes that shed light on guests' priorities and experiences. The word "hotel" understandably emerged prominently, indicating the central subject of feedback. Terms such as "great" and "stay" suggest overall positive experiences, while "room" and "place" likely point to guests' emphasis on accommodation quality and ambiance. Furthermore, the repetition of "staff," "service," and "location" underscores the importance guests place on courteous treatment, efficient service, and the hotel's strategic positioning in relation to their activities or destination.

Figure 6-2. Word cloud

Keyword extraction: An examination of keyword frequencies (Table 6-2) from a set of reviews revealed that the term "hotel" was mentioned most frequently, with a count of 1141. This was followed closely by "room" and "rooms" with tallies of 954 and 312, respectively. References to the quality of the stay were evident with "great" and "nice" accumulating 476 and 305 mentions. "Stay" itself had 450 occurrences. Additionally, the city of "Seattle" was specified 392 times, suggesting the location of many of the hotels under discussion. The importance of staff and location in shaping guests' experiences was evident with "staff" being cited 350 times and "location" 310 times. Lastly, "night" appeared 384 times, perhaps indicating the duration or specific incidents related to overnight stays.

Table 6-2. Keyword Extraction

S.No	Word	Total Number
1	Hotel	1141
2	Room	954
3	Great	476
4	Stay	450
5	Seattle	392
6	Staff	350
7	Rooms	312
8	Location	310
9	Nice	305
10	Night	384

Topic modeling: Utilizing Latent Dirichlet Allocation, an analysis of the reviews identified four primary topics of discussion among guests. These topics centered on the commendations of "nice rooms," the appreciation for a "great location," commendation for "good staff," and satisfaction with "nice room service" (Figure 6-3).

Topic	Topic keywords
1	room, hotel, stay, nice, staff, night, great, place, stayed, small
2	hotel, room, seattle, stay, rooms, night, location, great, parking, place
3	hotel, great, location, staff, seattle, room, market, rooms, stay, service
4	hotel, room, service, nice, great, stay, desk, staff, free, car

Figure 6-3. Topic modeling

Sentiment analysis: Delving deeper into the emotional tone of the feedback (Figure 6-4), the overwhelming majority, 98.8%, expressed "joy." In contrast, "anger," "disgust," and "fear" each constituted a mere 0.20% of the sentiments. Interestingly, neither "sadness" nor "surprise" was notably prominent, with "surprise" constituting only 0.40% of the emotions, while "sadness" was completely absent.

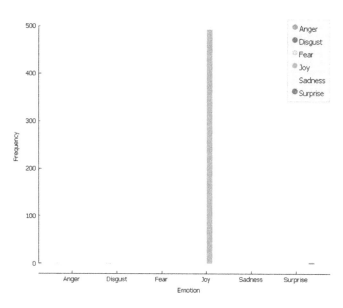

Figure 6-4. Sentiment analysis

Conclusion

When travelers select a hotel room, they prioritize factors such as room quality, room service, staff behavior, location, parking, and cleanliness. Our word cloud analysis, built on keyword extraction and topic modeling, underscores these preferences. For hotels experiencing challenges or for newcomers in the industry, understanding these key factors can guide strategies to enhance their business and maintain a competitive edge. Significantly, from the reviews analyzed, 98.8% of travelers conveyed satisfaction with their hotel experiences. This research illuminates the value of scrutinizing online reviews. Text mining tools, as illustrated in our study, provide managers with actionable insights by (1) gauging the sentiment of reviews, (2) pinpointing emotional undertones, and (3) highlighting the main subjects of discussion. Although numerical ratings offer a snapshot of guests' experiences, they might not capture the entire narrative. For instance, a detailed review focusing intently on a specific issue might reveal more about a guest's stay than a general rating. Thus, prospective travelers should approach reviews with a discerning eye, understanding that ratings might not always convey the full story. This research not only offers guidance for travelers navigating hotel choices but also equips hoteliers with strategies to make effective changes based on feedback. To conclude, while numerical ratings provide a general perspective, the nuances within review texts can be instrumental for the hotel industry to truly understand and address guest concerns.

Internet Trends and Customer Sentiment Analysis on Different Online Platforms

Ms. Divya Rai*, Research Scholar, Abhilashi University, Chail Chowk, Distt. Mandi (H.P.), India, Email: divyaraa11@gmail.com

Dr. Jyoti Sondhi, Associate Professor, Abhilashi University, Chail Chowk, Distt. Mandi (H.P.), India, jyotisonisondhi@gmail.com

One of the most innovative technological advancements of the twenty-first century is advanced data analytics, which enables the uncovering of underlying trends through complex computer techniques. The concept for analyzing Internet customer feedback is presented in this research. The goal is to discover a number of client demands using this data. To provide fresh insights,

N. Zaidi et al. (eds.), *Building AI Driven Marketing Capabilities*,
https://doi.org/10.1007/978-1-4842-9810-7_7

the framework integrates aspects of data analytics, design theory, and online product reviews. Through the ratings and reviews from the ecommerce websites Amazon, Flipkart, and Nykaa, the proposal framework's efficacy is confirmed. Businesses, organizations, and researchers can use sentiment analysis as a potent tool to gather and examine public sentiments and viewpoints, obtain business information, and make more informed decisions. The chapter outlines the general procedures for these assignments and illustrates applications of sentiment analysis. Then, it analyzes, contrasts, and researches the employed methods to have a thorough understanding of both their advantages and disadvantages. Next, to elucidate future directions, the difficulties of sentiment analysis are highlighted.

Introduction

Sentiment analysis (SA) is the process of identifying a communicator's propensity or attitude by analyzing the contextual polarity of their writing or speech. The impact of the Internet is that users are now able to converse with the product's producer or service provider regarding the product or service in question. The majority of it is done online through blog posts, debates, item survey sites, Internet-based activities, and so forth. Through online platforms like Nykaa, Flipkart, Amazon, and others, users express their opinions, feelings, and mood. A significant amount of concept-rich information is being produced through social networks in the form of tweets, reviews, comments, discussions, blog posts, and so forth. Online networking platforms provide businesses the opportunity to interact with their target audience for advertising. Most of the time, a user's judgment regarding a product that is available online is heavily influenced by user-generated material. Regular users find it challenging to assess the vast amount of content that is generated by users on a regular basis. Therefore, there is a strong need to automate user reviews. SA has a crucial role to play in this scenario. Sentiment analysis informs the buyer whether or not the information about the product is appealing before they purchase it. Companies and advertisers use this information to better understand their goods and services so that they can be offered in line with customer needs.

So, one can employ textual information retrieval techniques in the context of analysis. It mostly focuses on finding, gathering, or evaluating the actual information that is already present. Other textual content, however, may reflect subjective characteristics. This material is mostly concerned with sentiments, attitudes, views, feelings, and assessments, which may constitute the core of sentiment analysis (SA).

Users can express their thoughts, sentiments, and mood using online platforms like Nykaa, Flipkart, Amazon, and others. The production of tweets, reviews, comments, conversations, blog entries, and other forms of social network content results in a substantial amount of concept-rich information. Businesses have the opportunity to communicate with their target market thanks to online platform networks, which give them a venue for advertising. Keep in mind that specific trends and sentiments may have evolved since then.

The objective of the study is as follows:

- Determine whether there is a customer sentiment on the products of Flipkart, Nykaa, and Amazon.

- Determine whether there is a perceived link between Internet trends and customer sentiments.

- Analyze the proper review of customer sentiments through different online platforms.

Research Methodology

Internet trends and sentiment analysis make up the first two parts of the suggested research methodology. On the product comment pages, user reviews are pulled from the websites of Flipkart, Amazon, and Nykaa. This is so because roughly one third of the market share in India is held by Flipkart, Amazon, and Nykaa. The reviews are carefully collected and kept in the database. The reviews are then separated from the artifacts during the data processing stage. To extract the underlying word, the starting and ending words are eliminated. The stop words are likewise removed since, when used alone, they have very little meaning. This study endeavors to explore the intricate relationship between Internet trends and customer sentiments by conducting a comprehensive analysis across distinct online marketplaces, including Amazon, Flipkart, and Nykaa. The research seeks to discern how prevailing Internet trends influence the emotional and attitudinal responses of customers toward products and services offered on these platforms. Employing a blend of quantitative and qualitative methodologies, this investigation delves into the dynamic interplay between Internet trends and customer sentiments. Online interactions, social media dialogues, reviews, and trending content will be meticulously scrutinized to uncover patterns in customer attitudes and emotions. By juxtaposing these insights with concurrent Internet trends, the study aims to establish correlations and illuminate causal relationships.

Indian Websites for Online Shopping

On shopping platforms, the selection of fashion necessities, gadgets, furnishings, and cosmetic products is limitless. They offer easy order and delivery. Additionally, they provide their consumers a simple exchange policy, a refund policy, and a variety of payment alternatives. Online portals are performing incredibly well because of this. These online retailers are expanding their product selection for their clients as time goes on.

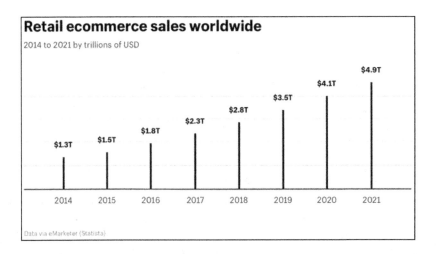

Flipkart

Flipkart is an online store for electronic devices, clothing, accessories, etc.; you may find all of your daily needs on Flipkart. It provides fantastic prices and simple, efficient shipping alternatives. Flipkart has essentially covered every aspect of shopping. Vouchers and other fascinating gifts are available for people to give to their loved ones.

Source: www.itln.in/flipkart-to-set-up-its-3mnsqft-largest-fulfilment-centre-at-manesar-trade-e-commerce

Online Monthly Visitors: 167.4 million; Alexa Rank: 596; App Downloads: 50 million+

Amazon

Amazon is an online store for electronic devices, clothing, accessories, etc., and it continues. For its clients, its shopping sites are offering a wider choice of things—products for the home, technology, cosmetics, mobile phones, literature, and furniture, among other things—and using Amazon Prime, Amazon offers same-day or next-day delivery based on the customers' locations.

Source: www.nbcnews.com/business/business-news/
amazon-now-employs-almost-1-million-people-u-s-or-n1275539

Online Monthly Visitors: 2.4 billion; Alexa Rank: *30 million*, App Downloads: 50 million+

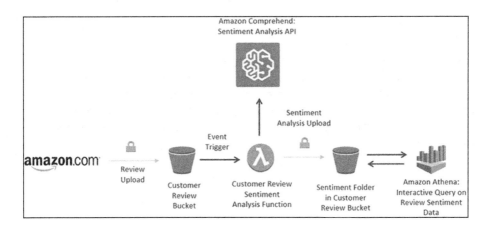

Nykaa

Nykaa is an online store for various beauty products and brand clothing, and it continues to daily add new possibilities. For its clients, its shopping sites are offering a wider choice of things. Nykaa also offers same-day or next-day delivery based on the customers' locations.

Source: www.indianretailer.com/news/nykaa-continues-to-expand-its-presence-unveils-another-store-in-hyderabad.n10277

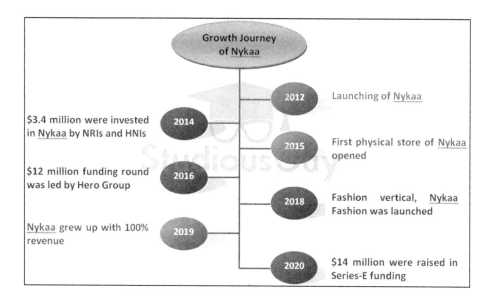

The pertinent terms are then extracted and entered into a database of terms. The first part of the review subprocessing will be completed once the list of terms has been completed and compared with an emotional word dictionary. This is done to gather data for the sentiment analysis stage. The results from the earlier phase will be used later in the sentiment analysis phase to gather user sentiments toward the product comments, which will then be classified as positive, neutral, or negative sentiment. The product will subsequently be ranked based on the classified sentiments using the machine learning classifier.

Customer Sentiment Analysis

Customer sentiment analysis involves analyzing user-generated content, such as reviews, comments, and social media posts, to gauge customer opinions about a product or service. There are several steps you can take:

- Data Collection: Gather reviews and comments from Amazon, Flipkart, and Nykaa. APIs provided by these platforms might allow you to collect such data programmatically.

- Preprocessing: Clean and preprocess the text data to remove noise, like special characters and irrelevant information.

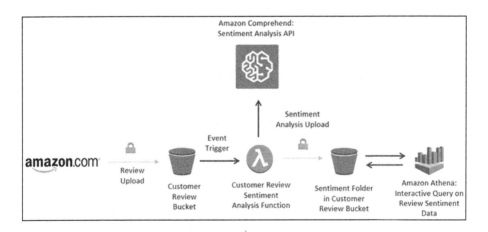

Sentiment Analysis

Sentiment analysis is a sort of data mining that uses text analysis, computational linguistics, and natural language processing (NLP) to measure people's attitudes, which are employed to gather and examine subjective data from the Web, primarily from online platforms and other similar sources. Quantifying public feelings or responses toward particular goods, people, or ideas, the studied data also reveals the contextual polarity of the information. In order to understand the precise perspectives of how customers feel about the goods, analysis of customer experience is essential in online purchasing. Typically, it is used to categorize customers' experiences with the product as good, neutral, or negative.

There are two types of sentiment analysis classification (Figure 7-1).

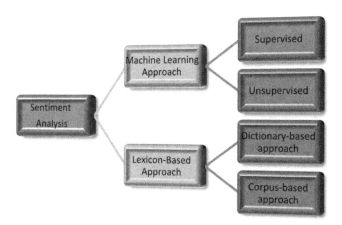

Figure 7-1. Sentiment analysis classification techniques

Analyzing the Intent

It examines if a user intends to send a specific message. Additionally, it indicates whether the communication is a personal opinion, news, advice, compliment, or inquiry (Figure 7-2).

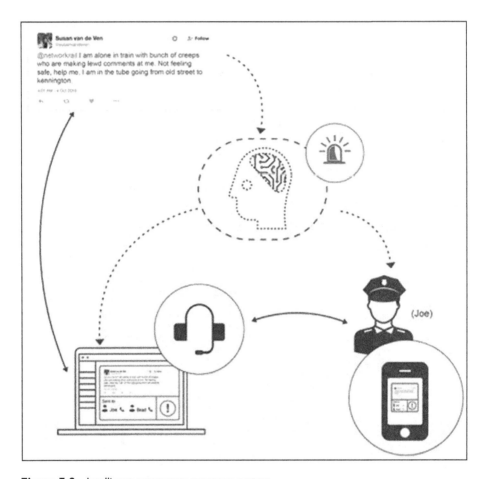

Figure 7-2. Intelligent emergency response system

CSS: Contextual Semantic Search

It's crucial to comprehend the brand element that users are bringing up in conversation. For instance, Amazon wants to separate messages about billing concerns, delayed delivery, questions about promotions, product reviews, etc. Conversely, Starbucks would like communications to be categorized according to whether they are about brand-new coffee flavors, staff conduct, online orders, criticism on the cleanliness of the store, etc. The way CSS works is that it takes millions of signals and a concept (such as price) as input and eliminates all of the ones that are similar matches to the idea. Figure 7-3 highlights how CSS provides a significant improvement over currently employed techniques in the business.

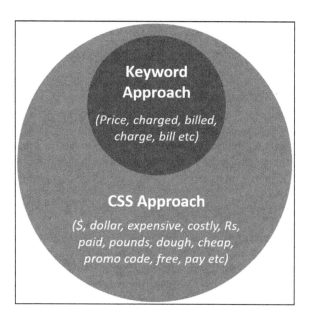

Figure 7-3. Existing approach vs. contextual semantic search (CSS)

Using the terms connected with price and cost, it is a methodical approach for separating the communications related to pricing. This approach is useless because it is impossible to include all the keywords related to price and variations of those phrases that describe a specific notion like pricing. CSS produces the obvious result after accepting all the keywords as input. Every phrase is converted into a specific point using an AI technique, and the space between each of these points is used to find messages that are contextually comparable to the concept.

Applications: Business Intelligence Sentiment Analysis

Information with deep insights eliminates quick speculation and decision-making. The sentiment data about your established and more recent products makes it easier to estimate the consumer holding rate. Customers can be more satisfactorily served, and market adjustments can be made based on the review generation done through sentiment analysis in business.

Overall, using automated insights, quick judgments may be made. Business intelligence is an overall spirit of the enterprise. Having emotional data gives you that freedom. You can genuinely test an important concept before playing with it. The term "concept testing" refers to this. Simply run idea testing and sentiment analysis on it, regardless of whether it's a campaign, new product, or logo.

Sentiment analysis is Being Used by Businesses to Enhance Customer Experience

A company depends on its consumers' satisfaction. Customers' experiences might be favorable, bad, or indifferent. This encounter provides the basis for their online comments in today's technologically advanced age. It is possible to determine the temperament of the data and then classify it according to the feelings it evokes. By operating this firm, one gains knowledge of the goods and services and whether they require improvement or not.

Brand Sentiment Analysis

A brand is not defined by the goods it produces or the services it offers. A brand's reputation is mostly based on its Internet marketing, content marketing, social media initiatives, and customer service. Sentiment research in business helps scale how it is viewed by the current and potential clients while taking into account all of these elements.

If you take the negative thoughts into account, you can create more alluring branding and marketing methods to go from being a dormant company to a massive one. Sentiment research can significantly aid a corporation in undergoing a radical shift.

- Sentiment Analysis Tools: Use natural language processing (NLP) tools or libraries like NLTK, spaCy, or sentiment analysis APIs (like VADER) to analyze sentiments in the text data. These tools can classify text as positive, negative, or neutral based on language patterns.

- Visualization: Visualize sentiment trends over time using graphs and charts. This can help you see how sentiment changes in response to various events, product releases, or marketing campaigns.

- Keyword Analysis: Identify common keywords and phrases that appear in positive and negative sentiment reviews. This can give you insights into what aspects of products or services are praised or criticized.

- Comparison Across Platforms: Compare sentiment scores across Amazon, Flipkart, and Nykaa to see if there are any platform-specific trends. Customers might have different sentiments on different platforms due to various factors.

- Topic Analysis: Utilize topic modeling techniques (like LDA—Latent Dirichlet Allocation) to uncover recurring themes within the reviews. This can help you understand what customers are talking about the most.

- Social Media Monitoring: Monitor social media platforms like Twitter, Instagram, and Facebook for mentions related to Amazon, Flipkart, and Nykaa. Social listening tools can help you track brand mentions, hashtags, and discussions relevant to these platforms. This can provide you with real-time insights into customer sentiments and emerging trends.

Competitor Analysis

Compare sentiments and trends between these platforms and their competitors. This can help you understand the strengths and weaknesses of each platform in terms of customer satisfaction and market trends.

The Internet trends and customer sentiment analysis on different online platforms like Amazon, Flipkart, and Nykaa would involve summarizing the data you've collected and analyzed. Table 7-1 is an example of how you could structure the table and create a simple line chart to visualize sentiment trends over time.

Some Interesting Facts

Flipkart.com is India's leading ecommerce marketplace with over 30 million products across multiple categories. Started by a team of two, Flipkart today employs 30,000 people with 46 million registered users. With technology that enables 8 million shipments every month, 10 million daily page visits, and 14 state-of-the-art warehouses, they are ranked among the top five websites in India based on Alexa ranking. Flipkart is the first billion-dollar company in Indian ecommerce; 923.55 of the reviews are favorable, 96.77 are unfavorable, and 1283.68 are neutral. The following are the main lessons learned from the overall implementation's final product:

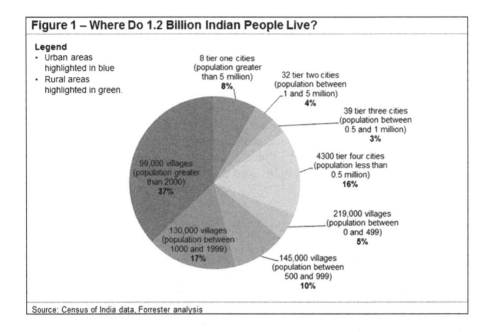

Figure 1 – Where Do 1.2 Billion Indian People Live?

Legend
• Urban areas highlighted in blue
• Rural areas highlighted in green.

8 tier one cities (population greater than 5 million) **8%**

32 tier two cities (population between 1 and 5 million) **4%**

39 tier three cities (population between 0.5 and 1 million) **3%**

4300 tier four cities (population less than 0.5 million) **16%**

219,000 villages (population between 0 and 499) **5%**

145,000 villages (population between 500 and 999) **10%**

130,000 villages (population between 1000 and 1999) **17%**

99,000 villages (population greater than 2000) **37%**

Source: Census of India data, Forrester analysis

Customer Sentiment Analysis by Different Online Platforms

Customers want brands they can relate to and that offer memorable in-person and online experiences. Consumers are more willing to give feedback and purchase from you when they feel more connected to your brand. 62% of customers indicated that firms need to care further about them, and 60% predicted that they would buy more as a result. To enhance the customer experience, these conversations—both positive and negative—should be recorded and analyzed. Analyzing sentiments can be useful.

Creating a table and chart to represent the Internet trends and customer sentiment analysis on different online platforms like Amazon, Flipkart, and Nykaa would involve summarizing the data you've collected and analyzed. Table 7-1 is an example of how you could structure the table and create a simple line chart to visualize sentiment trends over time.

Table 7-1. Internet Trends and Customer Sentiment Analysis

Date	Amazon Sentiment	Flipkart Sentiment	Nykaa Sentiment	Trending Topics (Common Keywords)
2023-01-01	0.76 (Positive)	0.65 (Neutral)	0.82 (Positive)	Makeup, Discounts, Shipping
2023-01-15	0.68 (Neutral)	0.45 (Negative)	0.75 (Positive)	Electronics, Customer Service, Returns
2023-02-01	0.82 (Positive)	0.72 (Positive)	0.78 (Positive)	Fashion, Sales, Product Quality

Sentiment Trend Chart

Different lines are plotted for Amazon, Flipkart, and Nykaa sentiments.

Keep in mind that creating more detailed and interactive charts could enhance the visual representation of your analysis. You could also include other relevant metrics, such as the volume of mentions or the number of positive/negative reviews, in your table and charts. The actual data, visual elements, and format may vary based on the tools you're using for analysis and visualization.

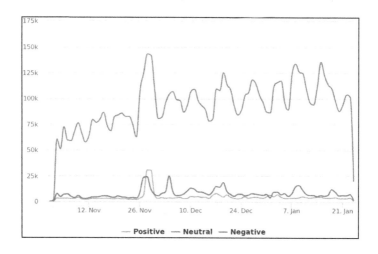

1.   **Text analysis in research**

Cu==stomers can be reached directly through surveys, which are also a fantastic source of useful criticism. It is quick and easy to calculate sentiment scores from the comments provided in survey responses. Consider including survey questions that will result in qualitative customer experience measures, such as the following:

- How would you describe your most recent experience?

- What extent did your experience differ from your expectations?

- What portion of your service would you have modified?

  Keep in mind that the objective is to collect truthful text comments from your consumers so that the sentiment inside of them may be examined. You'll be capable of addressing a number of the more pressing issues your clients had throughout their experiences once the sentiment from survey replies has been rated. Customer feedback is yet another excellent resource for finding text feedback.

2. **Text analysis for customer reviews**

   Are you aware that 72% of consumers won't buy a product or use a service before reading reviews? A startling 95% of shoppers read reviews before placing an order. Customer feedback and peer insight have indisputable power in today's feedback-driven environment. Customers frequently turn to review websites like G2 as their first stop when looking for sincere opinions on goods and services. This feedback can be analyzed, just as feedback from surveys. Customer evaluations have one advantage over surveys: they're uninvited, which frequently results in more frank and thorough criticism. The sentiment ratings from customer reviews—positive, negative, and neutral—can be used to pinpoint areas for improvement and pain problems that may not have been included in the surveys. Keep in mind that negative comments can be just as useful to your company as positive input, if not more so.

3. **Text analysis for social media**

   Through social media analysis, textual data can also be obtained. Brand mentions are ingested by monitoring systems from publicly accessible social media channels like Twitter and Facebook, and sentiment scores are then assigned in accordance. This also has benefits because people are quite inclined to provide their unfiltered opinions on social media. Nevertheless, a startling 70% of firms ignore customer reviews on social media. Brands may be overlooking crucial data since social networking is indeed a sea of big data ready to be analyzed.

After conducting a comprehensive analysis of Internet trends and customer sentiments on various online platforms such as Amazon, Flipkart, and Nykaa, several noteworthy conclusions can be drawn:

1. **Platform-specific trends**

   Through the analysis of Internet trends, it's evident that each platform has its unique set of popular topics, keywords, and discussions. This suggests that user interests vary depending on the platform they are engaging with. Amazon, Flipkart, and Nykaa cater to distinct customer needs, resulting in different trends emerging across these platforms.

2. **Customer sentiment variation**

   The sentiment analysis revealed varying degrees of customer sentiment across the three platforms. Positive, negative, and neutral sentiments were found to fluctuate over time, often in response to events, product releases, or marketing campaigns. It's clear that customers have different experiences and opinions when interacting with each platform.

3. **Competitive landscape**

   By comparing sentiments and trends across Amazon, Flipkart, and Nykaa, it becomes evident that these platforms compete in a dynamic and evolving landscape. While each platform has its strengths and areas for improvement, customer sentiment can significantly influence their market positioning and long-term success.

4. **Customer preferences and expectations**

   The analysis highlights customer preferences, expectations, and pain points associated with different online platforms. Positive sentiment is often linked to excellent customer service, high-quality products, and seamless user experiences. On the other hand, negative sentiment may arise from issues such as poor delivery experiences, product quality concerns, or usability challenges.

5. **Impact of marketing and events**

   Events, promotions, and marketing campaigns play a crucial role in shaping customer sentiment and influencing Internet trends. Positive sentiment spikes are often linked to successful campaigns, while negative sentiment might arise from mishandled events or controversies. It's essential for platforms to carefully plan and execute such activities to maintain positive customer sentiment.

6. **Insights for improvement**

   The analysis provides actionable insights for each platform to enhance their offerings and customer experiences. By addressing recurring themes in negative sentiment, platforms can identify opportunities for improvement, refine their strategies, and prioritize enhancements that align with customer expectations.

7. **Evolving consumer landscape**

   The dynamic nature of Internet trends and customer sentiments suggests that the digital consumer landscape is constantly evolving. Platforms need to remain agile and adaptable to meet changing consumer preferences, emerging trends, and technological advancements.

8. **Continuous monitoring and analysis**

   To maintain a competitive edge and ensure positive customer sentiment, continuous monitoring and analysis of trends and sentiment are imperative. Platforms should regularly update their strategies based on new insights and emerging trends to stay relevant in the ever-changing online marketplace.

In conclusion, the analysis of Internet trends and customer sentiments on platforms like Amazon, Flipkart, and Nykaa provides invaluable insights into customer behaviors, preferences, and expectations. By understanding and addressing these insights, platforms can create better user experiences, enhance customer satisfaction, and ultimately thrive in the competitive world of ecommerce.

The findings of this study hold implications for businesses, marketers, and researchers alike. Understanding the nexus between Internet trends and customer sentiments is pivotal in devising effective digital marketing strategies, enhancing customer engagement, and shaping business decisions. As digital platforms continue to redefine consumer preferences, this research contributes to a nuanced comprehension of how online trends mold customer sentiment, thereby driving purchasing behaviors and shaping brand perceptions.

Conclusion

This study explored the use of sentiment analysis as a substitute method for determining how favorable, unfavorable, and neutral past reviews have been. No matter the method used—machine learning, lexicon-based, or hybrid approaches—the comparative study indicated that the sentiment analysis methodology can produce performance between 65% and 95% accuracy. In this chapter, a hybrid technique that combines lexicon-based review subprocessing with machine learning sentiment analysis was proposed to balance the advantages and disadvantages of the two approaches. As well as being extended to the seller as value-added features that can win consumers' faith and trust for their items, it is envisaged that such an approach can assist customers in making educated decisions regarding the products they choose to purchase through online shopping platforms. This strategy can also be applied in a wide range of other fields, including job matching systems, extracting needs, and sentiment mining in education. After conducting a comprehensive analysis of Internet trends and customer sentiments on various online platforms such as Amazon, Flipkart, and Nykaa, several noteworthy conclusions can be drawn. Through the analysis of Internet trends, it's evident that each platform has its unique set of popular topics, keywords, and discussions. This suggests that user interests vary depending on the platform they are engaging with. Amazon, Flipkart, and Nykaa cater to distinct customer needs, resulting in different trends emerging across these platforms. The sentiment analysis revealed varying degrees of customer sentiment across the three platforms. Positive, negative, and neutral sentiments were found to fluctuate over time, often in response to events, product releases, or marketing campaigns. It's clear that customers have different experiences and opinions when interacting with each platform. Customer preferences and expectations: The analysis highlights customer preferences, expectations, and pain points associated with different online platforms. Positive sentiment is often linked to excellent customer service, high-quality products, and seamless user experiences. On the other hand, negative sentiment may arise from issues such as poor delivery experiences, product quality concerns, or usability challenges. In conclusion, the analysis of Internet trends and customer sentiments on platforms like Amazon, Flipkart, and Nykaa provides invaluable insights into customer behaviors, preferences, and expectations. By understanding and addressing these insights, platforms can create better user experiences, enhance customer satisfaction, and ultimately thrive in the competitive world of ecommerce.

Role of Artificial Intelligence for Value Chain Creation in Healthcare Marketing

Dr. Himanshi Puri*, Assistant Professor, Sharda School of Business Studies, Sharda University, Greater Noida, Uttar Pradesh, India, Email: himanshi.puri@sharda.ac.in

Richa Pandey, Assistant Professor, Sharda School of Business Studies, Sharda University, Greater Noida, Uttar Pradesh, India

Apeksha Singh, Student, Sharda School of Business Studies, Sharda University, Greater Noida, Uttar Pradesh, India

© Neha Zaidi, Mohit Maurya, Simon Grima, Pallavi Tyagi 2024, corrected publication 2024
N. Zaidi et al. (eds.), *Building AI Driven Marketing Capabilities*,
https://doi.org/10.1007/978-1-4842-9810-7_8

Artificial intelligence has not only been dominating the technological segment of our society, but our day-to-day life has become indescribably dependent on it as well. Technology helps bridge the gap in the market. Marketing in the healthcare industry is crucial for increasing consumer awareness, promoting health factor, and driving the adoption of healthcare products and services. Such value is added in the industry through AI. Marketing has been strongly linked with healthcare, and the increase in consumer awareness of the many offerings available supports its growth. Large number of client's desire procedures that they acknowledge through marketing only. The type of task performed and the susceptibility of a significant number of users have led to a great deal of research and discussion on the issue of responsibility on artificial intelligence for creating a value chain in the market. Therefore, in order to maximize the effectiveness of the appropriately distributed marketing channels, we want to bring together the diversified healthcare industry. In order to understand how AI marketing in the healthcare sector is changing customer behavior, we undertake a study using secondary sources of data. We can implement the critical strategies used by the healthcare industry to advance their organizational objectives with the aid of AI marketing and techniques based on the results that were attained.

Introduction

Artificial intelligence has a potential in the healthcare sector for enhancing managerial efficiency and effectiveness as well as care outcomes. Artificial Intelligence (AI) has long emphasized its potential to enhance various aspects of human life, particularly in the realm of healthcare. We can gather information, process it in an organized format (easy to understand and tabulate data), and produce a better output for specialists with the help of AI. Data mining and pattern recognition abilities of AI technology enable forecasting, diagnosis, and treatment. Initial efforts by geniuses to use AI in medicine aimed to generate some system similar to that of a human brain. The aim was to reduce human efforts and establish a rule-based processor to support medical reasoning (Kumar et al., 2021). The next step of AI intervention in our lives is to bring machine learning into the supply chain in the healthcare market. It is a very complex process to know what a patient needs at a time of necessity. The human factor and machine learning can together create a market intelligence for any business including healthcare. This will help bridge the gap in the market for gaining an edge over others (Yu et al., 2018).

The terminology "market intelligence" signifies the data or information that an institute gathers from the marketplace in which it operates or intends to do business in order to evaluate market segmentation, adoption rate, market potential, and current market statistics. Source to build a strong foundation for the business. Market intelligence along with artificial intelligence is essential for determining the state of the industry and for gathering information about competitors, both of which contribute to business success. For any business, it is very important to analyze the market and understand the needs of its consumers. Similarly, it is also important to know your competitors and their advantages. These features are easily available due to artificial intelligence comprehension in marketing. There is a need for a responsible AI in the industry which can help increase the value of the service either directly or indirectly. The National eHealth Authority provides evidence of the Indian market's capacity for machine learning technologies. Several businesses, including Microsoft, IBM, and Google, are partnering with Indian hospitals and ministries to develop an AI-focused ecosystem.

There have also been many studies about the non-acceptance of new technology in healthcare in the Indian market. Previous research on innovation adoption and acceptance has recognized that feeling of self as a significant determinant of information technology user acceptance. However, there has been little investigation on conscience and perceptions and their impact on users' attitudes in the context of health technologies. There has also been a shift from orthodox medical settings to patient-centered care facilities including ambulatory surgical centers, diagnostic centers, and home care and the same can be accelerated by AI technology. Additionally, wearable technology and home care may drastically reduce healthcare expenses by 20% to 32% (Rhee et al., 2009). Research on acceptance of technology has shown that technology has a significant impact on patient- provider relationship.

This chapter aims to find out the answers to the following questions about AI in healthcare:

1) What is the role of artificial intelligence in healthcare marketing?

2) How is AI integrated in the medical industry for growth of research and patient-centric care?

Healthcare is a massive industry, and to make the supply chain more reliable and efficient, we enable machine learning. This helps create a channel of research and communication to collect and utilize health data. Machine learning also helps advertise information based on factors of human behavior. The competence to "explore, acquire, comprehend, and analyze health data gathered from digital sources and put the knowledge acquired to addressing or solving a health issue" is known as e-health literacy. This chapter evaluates the use of e-health in the value chain of the healthcare industry. Due to the Internet and social media, there is an increase demand of personalized healthcare service, which needs a lot of market research and data intergradation.

In this chapter, we will try to find out about the technological factors needed to collect such data and its utilization in an efficient manner. The patient have become the focus of the supply chain as a result of precision medicine, online prescribing, and increased use of personalized health monitoring and detectors. To address some more complex requirements, we would need systems that are increasingly intelligent (Kumar et al., 2021).

The development of AI was made possible by improvements in data collecting and analytical techniques, which present new chances to enhance medical decision-making. AI has the ability to lower the incidence of falsely positive and falsely negative diagnoses in a number of instances. Additionally, AI can offer treatments that are more suitable for patients, frequently by adapting them to extremely particular symptom patterns and patient traits that might be challenging for any human healthcare professional to correctly identify. Last but not least, AI is able to resolve some of the system's inherent biases, although it could purely become a matter of simply replacing data analysts' prejudices for those of physicians and others who oversee their work. The following outlines how the chapter is structured. We start by outlining key aspects of the healthcare industry that seem to be vital for comprehending the financial effects of AI. These cover the background of outside interventions as well as the healthcare decision-making process. We then look at how the allocation of surplus value in the healthcare value chain is affected by the study on labor economics, demonstrating the importance of various activities in comprehending this prognosis.

AI at a Glance

Machine learning in healthcare has a variety of advantages, including the ability to automate operations and analyze big datasets of patients in order to provide better treatment more rapidly and affordably. According to research, expenses account for 30% of the overall healthcare costs. The integration and development of AI in healthcare has a significant impact on many elements of healthcare and process. In this chapter, the primary focus is on finding the key areas of AI integration in healthcare, its use, the complications that come with the development of AI, and pros of marketing through the use of AI and machine learning. Recently, artificial intelligence has become a crucial tool for managing the complexity of frequent business difficulties. Healthcare is gradually adopting AI and associated technologies like machine learning, robots, and stochastic optimization as they become more common in daily life and business. This technology can be employed for many therapeutic and investigative applications, including drug discovery, chronic disease management, medical services, and diagnosis. In terms of patient care, logistics for the healthcare system, and disease diagnosis, AI technology outperforms humans. Additionally, AI systems improve people's quality of life. For instance, AI today has achieved significant advancements in the detection and management of cancer, particularly breast cancer. To begin with, it is equally important to understand the history of AI and healthcare in the Indian market and how it adds value in the industry.

History of AI in Healthcare System

The very first explanation of artificial intelligence was published in 1950; nevertheless, defects in previous versions hampered general acceptance and medical application. Automation in the healthcare sector has evolved significantly during the last five decades. AIM or artificial intelligence in medicine implementations have developed even since the introduction of ML and DL, paving the way for individualized therapy rather than the treatment based solely on algorithms. Predictive models may be used in future preventative medicine for illness diagnosis, therapeutic reaction prediction, and other applications. As a result, healthcare facilities, charities, and relief organizations in disaster scenarios are looking for AI solutions to increase cost savings, promote patient satisfaction, and meet staffing shortages. AI could improve clinical procedures and productivity and job, offer improved disease and diagnostic testing, improve procedure accuracy, and improve overall patient outcomes. The following is a chronological timeline of the ongoing development and evolution of AI – powered in medicine, organized by significant historical junctures. Mostly during the 1980s and 1990s, the development of new AI systems assisted in the significant medical advances.

accelerating the collecting and information processing	helping with more accurate medical intervention	DBA mapping and study that are comprehensive	adoption of EHR (electronic health records) that is more precise

AI models present a particular challenge to regulatory authorities since they can evolve rapidly as more data and customer feedback is gathered. It is not apparent how well the improvements should be evaluated. For example, the most recent design may perform better overall but even worse on such a small percentage of patients (Kumar et al., 2021).

Several of these restrictions were removed in the mid-2000s with the emergence of explicit research. Researchers are stepping into a new era in healthcare where AI may be used in nursing medicine using risk assessment frameworks, enhancing diagnostic accuracy and operational effectiveness. AI systems nowadays are capable of comprehending mathematical algorithms and consciousness. This chapter provides a brief historical overview of the development of artificial intelligence (AI) over the past several decades as well as its current introduction and advancement in the field of medicine. The development of artificial intelligence and machine learning has had a significant impact on how healthcare is provided. Beyond biomedical science, where it started, this cutting-edge technology has grown and is currently used in a variety of medical disciplines, including radiology, screening, psychiatry, primary care diagnosis, and telemedicine (Figure 8-1).

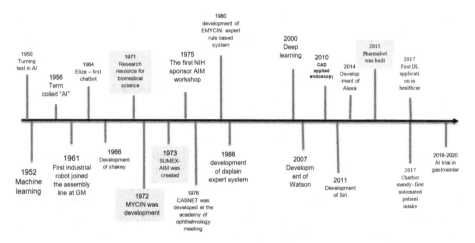

Figure 8-1. Timeline of the history of AI integration in healthcare

AI in Value Chain of a Healthcare Industry

Changes in the healthcare environment and adoption of technology, has resulted in the automation of healthcare. The way products and services are offered in the healthcare industry is drastically changing. This transition is being driven by a number of causes, along with a transition away from treating more transient sickness episodes and more toward long-term health and prevention. Additionally, both clients and patients exhibit a shift in their expectations.

The system for inventory management is a crucial factor that influences the operational and managerial efficiency of healthcare organizations in general, as well as hospital systems in particular. Essential healthcare items are required, either directly or indirectly, in the patient recovery process, as well as its control and monitoring. As a result, inventory control systems should be aligned with the patient's condition. Despite the fact that systems for inventory management employ cost-based models, hospitals must prioritize patient service levels. It is difficult to find high-quality healthcare items in an unsure and constantly changing environment. In an AI-controlled system, there will exist a well-maintained and fully automated inventory control, allowing patients to get medication without delay and preventing out-of-stock circumstances in hospitals. Further, there are more such inventory circumstances that can be controlled by AI, such as continuous change in a patient's condition, chance of change in predicted bed occupancy of a patient, transfer of patient, demand-based goods procurement, and others.

The healthcare industry is made up of a very dynamic mix of subjects, organizations, persons, and companies, all of whom are vying against one another for share of the market and business opportunities by cooperating or competing. Because public health is the sole good that can be traded, it has incredibly distinctive features and practices. Multiple participants can be observed acting cooperatively or antagonistically, together or separately. Due to the participation of pharma firms, product designers, health insurers, hiring managers, large tech distributors, intermediaries, corporate and government agencies, organizations, network operators, as well as various branches of government, the medical value chain may be more difficult to evaluate than other industries. AI is used in various domains of healthcare such as patient population threat analysis, medical compliance (behavior) analytics/predictions, risk of illness statistical analysis, risk of hospital-acquired illnesses in patients – safety analytics, optimizing clinical route prediction insights, effectiveness of the therapy, forecasting for acute vs. chronic episodic care, error tendency (clinical or medication), prediction of infection rate growth (like COVID), delivering intelligent medicine, operative robots, mindfulness analytics and tracking of health, claims processing, clinical documentation, revenue, and maintenance of medical data are all performed by robots (home companions) and marketing (Kumar et al., 2021).

The following are the steps for any value chain analysis: step 1, select a target market – service or product; step 2, analyze each step of the procurement of goods or service to delivery to the end consumer. With this, let us target the basic patient and doctor service relationship. The process happens in the following manner: doctor's timing, appointment, treatment plan, prescription, pharmacy medicine, and billing. All these steps under present-day scenario seem to be influenced by AI in many levels from making timing schedule to billing. AI has a future in all the domain of healthcare. It can be utilized in Out Patient Department (OPD) as a simple symptom to medicine AI solution-based application. AI or robotic surgery for total knee replacement service has already been introduced (Figure 8-2).

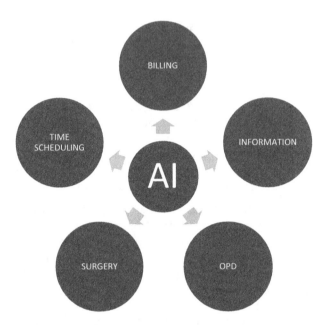

Figure 8-2. AI may influence the healthcare industry value chain to replace human resource partially or entirely

AI in Healthcare Wearables

Healthcare equipment that are worn or used at home by people today take up a large market. These include watches, fit bands, hearing aids, specs, and many more.

Health Tech Wearable Devices

There are devices that help analyze and track a wide range of biomedical parameters. Some of these parameters help to protect lives today such as keeping regular check on heart rate, voice, calories count, sleep cycle, and movement (step count). These biological signals could aid in the detection of diseases and the prediction of health conditions. For example, using pulse rate as well as skin temperature readings recorded by wearables, signs of contagious diseases and inflammation can be detected early. Photo plethysmography sensor nodes in wearables allow for the measurement of heart diseases, lung diseases, blood count, and sleep and awake cycle. They are frequently used by athletes to check their heart rate while exercising to avoid any heart abnormality. Wearables such as smart watches detect and quantify Parkinson's disease symptoms such as seismic event and cognitive impairment gestures, gait, posture, and speech patterns. There are some variety of personal tracking devices, which offer the potential to direct behavioral changes, but the precision of the information collected by these devices can vary. Furthermore, one-third of all consumers who currently are wearing healthcare technology stopped using these devices within six months of purchasing them, whereas others became addicted. This indicates the devices' utility in cultivating long-term behavioral change. More studies are required to figure out how to increase the efficiency of such equipment. These can be used for health maintenance and preventive action by evaluating and analyze the effects of wearable devices on the health of a consumer over a long term and increase their utilization for health maintenance and promotion (Yu et al., 2018; Kumar et al., 2021).

Robotic Surgery

Although wound closure is a frequent type of surgery, robotic systems that tie knots automatically have been created. A monitoring artificial intelligence system recently showed greater in vivo suturing accuracy than surgeons in an experimental context when suturing an intestinal connection. Using a totally independent suturing approach and a stereo vision three-dimensional near-infrared fluorescence image processor, this technology performed in vivo surgical intervention on a pig. As pre programmed, photo directed and robotic surgery, more automation intervention techniques are expected to be used in operative treatment. AI has the ability to drastically alter many parameters of medical practice as it is today. The systems can facilitate surgery treatments for a wide range of human disorders, accelerate diagnosis of diseases, find previously undiscovered radiographic or genetic sequences linked to patient demographics, and enhance therapeutic decision-making. Applications of AI could also be utilized to bring experience and knowledge to remote locations without access to specialists (Yu et al., 2018) (Figure 8-3).

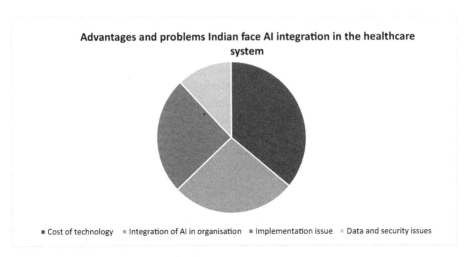

Figure 8-3. Advantages and problems Indians face due to machine learning integration in the system

It is important to discuss healthcare service providing apps and their market share and turnover. AI and automation are already helping supply chain leaders manage backorders, quickly find clinical equivalents, automate source card updates, and manage POs and invoices. Moreover, supply chain executives are looking for more, with two key future needs including rebate tracking and invoice internal audits for purchase services.

AI in Manufacturing and Development of Pharmaceuticals

The introduction of AI in healthcare had been marked science in 1971, when it was used to do research for biomedicine. Later, it helped in the development of MYCIN, which is an expert system to give solutions for patient queries. It has a simple communication channel for getting expert advice of a patient's case through a knowledge base in the system. During the initial days of introduction of AI in healthcare, SUMEX-AIM (Stanford University Medical Experimental Computer for Artificial Intelligence in Medicine) project, was a government-subsidized computerized asset and was used from 1973 and 1992. It had two main objectives: (1) to promote the use of computer science and artificial intelligence tech to solve medical and biological issues and (2) to demonstrate the network system and data sharing among government communities of health research initiatives. Such facility helped in the formation of the structure of AI in the everyday life of the population in the entire world. After the introduction of MYCIN, there was an increased way AI was seen in the medical industry. One of the subsequent developments of AI in healthcare was seen in SECS, which stands for Simulation and Evaluation of Chemical Synthesis. The goal of SECS is to promote the creation of novel and better medications along with synthetic substances that are based on naturally occurring ones. The effort is primarily focused on the different aids the chemist plans and chooses for the syntheses of biologically significant chemical compounds. Nowadays, AI in medicine is being used in marketing and image creation. In any industry, but specially hospital or healthcare service organisation "good image", in market space is crucial. This fundamental goal of an institution is achieved by careful synthesis and development of resouces, where AI plays a vital role (Kumar et al., 2021).

Marketing Techniques and Current State 2022–2023

The introduction of AI in marketing for healthcare is yet a new concept. Digital marketing is seen to be important for marketing for various industry including E-commerce, education, etc. While healthcare digital marketing was relatively growing at a slower pace. From 2015, healthcare blog writing, articles, research paper, data collection was seen to grow. This helped in creating marketing strategy as the population study became relevant and cheaper. Nowadays, consumers are offered so many options for healthcare providers and services that the sole way for health systems to distinguish themselves from the sea of closest competitors is to develop a distinctive and memorable value proposition. This part of the public healthcare value chain could mean minimal modifications and interventions given that the demand for healthcare services will probably always be greater or lesser continuous and that advertising will typically concentrate on the brand image and placement of branded items and the competitive pressure for formed and largely unchallenged market niches. This business is benefiting immensely from technology and the development of ecommerce sales methods. Supplies, services, technology, and other related commodities may be advertised, bartered for, and purchased online, much as with other value chains (chebrolu, 2020). Healthcare has AI marketing in various areas integrated and in various forms; every area has its individual growth and impact in the industry. The following are the areas of website, online advertisement, SEO, social media, and reputation management. All these areas of advertisement can be used with several combinations of strategies based on the focus on audiences:

- Google AdWords for keywords with conditions
- Facebook "sponsored posts" (newsfeed adverts) that target particular user demographics and locations
- Optimized blog posts and articles

- Landing pages of a website with a focus on your target demographic

- Testimony from patients

- TV ads

- Radio commercials

- Ads in print

- Billboards

- Communal dialogue

- Promoting to recommending doctors through a website and case study

Major healthcare companies now target content to compete effectively for digital dominance. Methods of healthcare digital marketing go further than blogging and producing quantifiable results. The best strategy for elevating the interaction between hospitals, clients, and physicians is digital or online marketing. Currently, digital content helps create positive connections with consumers. It is necessary to employ new digital marketing strategies in order to boost the effectiveness of advertising expenditures and generate greater return rates. By incorporating innovative healthcare marketing strategies into their marketing efforts, healthcare businesses will be better able to provide their services to customers. In this research, we specifically considered the development and use of moral artificial intelligence with context to Indian healthcare. The mixed method clarified the key components of ethical intelligence in the healthcare sector (Figure 8-4).

Figure 8-4. Patient's physician visit journey – introduction of AI marketing starts from the very first step, when the patient searches on any search engine about the disease and service they need

The modern medical consumer chooses to look for medical resources on the Internet, where they can have access to a wealth of medical services and healthcare organizations, review sites from previous patients, etc. This makes it important to understand how marketing strategies affect the quality of care. Almost anything can be recorded and measured in digital marketing. Healthcare providers and experts are not liable to make judgments of whether some steps are crucial or not for a consumer. Using marketing performance information, health professionals around the world can regularly assess their initiatives and make informed decisions about how to improve them. The research identified three key components of responsible AI for healthcare delivery: technological know-how, ethical considerations, and risk reduction. The discovery of the three responsible AI elements revealed intriguing features of their use in healthcare. For example, exploratory findings demonstrate that medical professionals are developing their aptitude and developing their abilities outside of medicine. Since continuing medical education is still a top goal for most healthcare professionals, this was highlighted as a crucial issue. Responsible AI's learning requirements produce a distinctive learning trajectory that requires balancing and integration.

Marketing Value Forecast Due to AI Integration in the Medical Industry

In order to attract customers, assist them in navigating the healthcare system, and keep their attention, healthcare marketing involves strategic communication and interaction. Deep learning algorithms might make better use of raw patient monitoring data to prevent information overload, increase the alert threshold, and enable more precise clinical forecasting and quicker judgment. The goal of sophisticated healthcare marketing techniques is to increase engagement and hasten business growth by integrating multichannel, highly fragmented, and customized online and offline strategies. The key performance indicators and marketing rate of return are two mostly used ways that health systems gauge the profitability of their marketing initiatives. As a consequence of life's quick growth, healthcare systems have experienced significant change, which has compelled health marketing to evolve into an essential part of "health brands." Medicine is an industry that is always changing, with the wealth of opportunities driving zeal and innovation and allowing specialists to thrive. The healthcare service provider should be able to perceive the risks and possibilities of the sector in which it works since it operates in a volatile and uncertain environment if it hopes to survive. In this situation, the medical unit's design of a realistic, cohesive, and unambiguous strategy is essential for forecasting its potential and lowering operational uncertainty (Yu et al., 2018). Since the philosophy and marketing techniques used by other sectors cannot be transferred to the health services sector directly, it is important to match the goals of other industries to healthcare and test with market. It requires a special method and specific features that aren't found in other firms. Over the past ten years, several marketing innovations that drastically altered marketing have had an impact on service delivery. These advancements are as follows:

- Moving from a big picture strategy to a focused strategy.
- From "one size fits all" to personalization; from "image marketing" to "service marketing."
- From a long-lasting partnership to a focus on a health episode.
- The market has evolved from "ignorance" to customer insights.
- From low tech to high technology.

Patients' involvement in the completion of medical procedures has developed into a requirement of contemporary living with wide-ranging and complex ramifications, going beyond only changing the physicians' mindset to encompass significant changes in patients' lives, customer behavior, and drug use. As our daily lives progress, change will become increasingly important to the life that is the basis of our existence. Additionally, it will be a burden how the partnership combines the need for wellness. Indian apps dominating the healthcare IT market are Medisafe (more than 250,000 happy users), Practo, Apollo 247, Aarogya Setu App, Netmeds, and Img. Health systems must move quickly toward the future in order to meet present requirements, and a successful future strategy depends on strong marketing and management skills. This is the reason for the induction of AI in marketing in the healthcare industry.

Challenges Faced Due to Machine Learning Integration with Healthcare System

One of the key causes of the increasing acceptance of artificial intelligence in the healthcare industry is that it is an economically vital part and the second-largest operational expense after laborers. All parties involved in the healthcare process are consequently aware of the costs, and government initiatives and technologies have an impact outside the supply chain. In order to modernize the healthcare system, it is necessary to unlock the thousands of datasets that are frequently locked away in disjointed digital systems. AI can add value by automating or improving the work of the healthcare system. By completely automating many repetitive tasks, AI will help healthcare providers function better in their responsibilities and improve patient outcomes. In order to deliver improved healthcare more rapidly and effectively, AI in healthcare can automate processes and analyze huge quantities of patient data. According to many estimates, administrative expenditures make up around 30% of the cost of healthcare (Yu et al., 2018).

Machine learning and AI have many pros and cons. Like any other technological aid, AI has both sides to its integration. It will help reduce human resource cost, reduce duplication of data, make interconnected information and communication channel, reduce human errors, and receive data in real time. It will also help to easily authenticate information source and reduce patient waiting time. It will help the product business by understanding the patient's changing needs and changing taste and advertising healthcare products more effectively. AI integration will also lead to negligence of human emotional aspects. It will lead to a robotic work environment creating a mental health negligence. AI integration will lead to less accountability. Like every technology aid, it has both pros and cons, but technology if correctly used by wise people would only make lives easier and safer.

AI will have a tremendous impact on automating our medical ecosystems, leading to greater efficiency and discoveries than we can now conceive. By analyzing vast amounts of data, artificial intelligence not only enables the consistency of product supplies but also aids in determining the price and efficacy of items. By combining various statistical methods and improving algorithms over time, the use of AI can also result in supply projections that are more accurate, decreasing inventory runouts and product expiration when there are excess supplies. There are many advantages of AI in the industry, but the disadvantages of adaption to the changing technology become more excessive.

Conclusion

AI may provide value by automating or improving the work of staff and physicians. By completely automating many repetitive tasks, AI will help healthcare practitioners function better in their responsibilities and improve patient outcomes. To deliver better healthcare more rapidly and effectively, AI in healthcare may automate procedures and analyze huge quantities of patient information. According to several estimates, administrative expenditures make up around 30% of the cost of healthcare. AI will have a tremendous influence on upgrading our medical ecosystems, leading to more efficiency and discoveries than we can now conceive. The healthcare sector is an extremely complicated model where many different actors are engaged concurrently and competing for relatively limited expanding margins and market prospects. Because of this, the healthcare value chain may differ significantly from other businesses in certain respects while also retaining many elements of those other industries. Future advancements in science and the spotlighting of novel techniques will undoubtedly increase the importance of research and development in technology for the entire chain. To compete effectively and acquire an advantage, the value chain needs to be addressed consistently and thoroughly. It will lead generation of quality factors such as

1) **Quality input**: The data will be highly precise and computed. It will lead to automation of data entry into the system, reduce cost, and increase efficiency.

2) **Quality source**: The data collected and information received would be automatically verified by a series of AI controlled operations. This will ultimately help to achieve security goals and reduce chances of duplication, identity theft, breach of privacy, etc.

3) **Quality output**: The data given by the system such as statistics, reports, information, archives, etc., would be unbiased and genuine. It would result in better customer experience and reduce employee workload.

AI in healthcare had been introduced a long time ago, such as computers, cloud storage, healthcare devices, health cards, etc. It has influenced all healthcare industries and the way healthcare is perceived and given. The concept of smart health came into existence to influence the hospital experience overall. Smart watches have changed the conscience of people to evaluate their health. Patients have become informed and ask for exactly what they need; this makes the treatment process complicated as every patient's needs or wants from the hospital are diverse. Like every technology aid, it has both pros and cons, but technology if properly used by wise people would only make lives easier and safer. The integration of AI aids, such as ChatGPT-3, into the healthcare industry is indeed a topic of significant interest and concern.

Potential Roles of Cyber-Ethical Awareness, Artificial Intelligence, and Chatbot Technologies Among Students

Aderinola Ololade Dunmade, PhD, Centre for Open and Distance Learning, University of Ilorin/Computer Services and Information Technology (COMSIT), Ilorin, Kwara State, Nigeria, Directorate, University of Ilorin, Ilorin, Kwara State, Nigeria, Email: derin_d@unilorin.edu.ng, https://orcid.org/0000-0002-7745-0494

© Neha Zaidi, Mohit Maurya, Simon Grima, Pallavi Tyagi 2024, corrected publication 2024
N. Zaidi et al. (eds.), *Building AI Driven Marketing Capabilities*,
https://doi.org/10.1007/978-1-4842-9810-7_9

Timilehin Olasoji Olubiyi*, PhD, Department of Business Administration and Marketing, School of Management Sciences, Babcock University, Ilishan-Remo, Ogun State, Nigeria, Email: drtimiolubiyi@gmail.com, https://orcid.org/0000-0003-0690-7722

Olorundamisi Daniel Dunmade, Faculty of Basic Medical Sciences, University of Ibadan, Ibadan, Oyo State, Nigeria, Email: olorundamisi1@gmail.com, https://orcid.org/0009-00056368-6673

In recent decades, academic dishonesty (plagiarism) has been a prevalent issue and of grave concern to the academic community, prompting numerous researchers to conduct studies aimed at identifying the myriad of factors that contribute to the malady. This chapter explores the influence of cyber-ethical awareness on mitigating plagiarism in the use of chatbot technologies among Nigerian undergraduate students. It begins by introducing the concepts of cyber-ethics, plagiarism, and chatbot technologies. The chapter then examines the relationship between chatbot technologies and academic integrity, highlighting the factors that contribute to plagiarism in this context. Additionally, it investigates the prevalence of plagiarism among Nigerian undergraduate students. The chapter also explores the connection between cyber-ethical awareness and plagiarism, emphasizing the importance of fostering cyber-ethical awareness to reduce instances of plagiarism. It examines the existing level of cyber-ethical awareness among Nigerian undergraduate students and discusses the role of such awareness in preventing plagiarism. Furthermore, the chapter presents various strategies to promote cyber-ethical awareness. These include educational initiatives aimed at educating students about the responsible use of technology, the establishment of institutional policies and guidelines to discourage plagiarism, and the use of technology-based solutions to detect and prevent plagiarism. In conclusion, the chapter emphasizes the significance of promoting cyber-ethical awareness among Nigerian undergraduate students to address the issue of plagiarism in the use of chatbot technologies. By fostering an understanding of ethical practices in technology use, universities can enhance academic integrity and ensure a culture of responsible scholarship.

Introduction

The accelerated development of technology has altered numerous facets of human existence, including the way we access and share information (Newman *et al.,* 2022). Artificial intelligence (AI) is rapidly spawning a new era of education and research. Among the many innovations in this domain, chatbot technologies have emerged as popular tools for facilitating communication and information exchange (Ray, 2023). In recent years, the academic integration of AI systems and chatbots has attracted significant attention. However, the widespread use of chatbot technologies for academic purposes among

Nigerian undergraduate students raises concerns about the potential for plagiarism and other forms of academic dishonesty (Kasneci *et al.*, 2023). In recent decades, academic dishonesty (plagiarism) has been a prevalent issue and of grave concern to the academic community, prompting numerous researchers to conduct studies aimed at identifying the myriad of factors that contribute to the malady. Even though instances of plagiarism are not new to planet Earth, the advent of the Internet has made the expansion of this abhorrent malady a growing concern on the global educational stage. There is a growing literature that attests to the high growth of plagiarism in the institutions of higher learning in many parts of the world (Abdolmohammadi & Baker, 2007). Therefore, this chapter reviews related literature and seeks to explore the role of cyber-ethical awareness in mitigating plagiarism in chatbot technology use among this population.

Literature Review

Education and research have increasingly adopted artificial intelligence (AI) and chatbot technologies in recent years, particularly by the end of 2022. Chatbots interact with users in a human-like manner using natural language processing and machine learning algorithms. As technology continues to advance and education moves toward online and hybrid models, the use of chatbot technologies by students has become more pervasive in recent years. While chatbot technology can provide students the world over with convenient and speedy access to information, it also presents several dangers and ethical concerns (Kooli, 2023). More so, the expanding use of AI and chatbots in many academic disciplines and among students raises ethical concerns that must be addressed. This literature review begins by discussing the growing prevalence of chatbot technologies in academic environments and the reasons for their popularity among Nigerian undergraduate students. The review then delves into the concept of plagiarism, its various forms, and its implications for academic integrity. The relationship between chatbot technologies and plagiarism is explored, highlighting the potential risks and challenges associated with the use of these tools for academic purposes. Next, the review examines the concept of cyber-ethical awareness and its relevance to the responsible use of chatbot technologies. The literature highlights the importance of cultivating a culture of ethical behavior among students and introduces various strategies for promoting cyber-ethical awareness in educational settings. In the following sections, several studies that explore the connection between cyber-ethical awareness and plagiarism are discussed, providing evidence of the potential benefits of enhancing ethical understanding among students.

Cyber-Ethics

Cyber-ethics, also known as Internet ethics or digital ethics, refers to the moral and ethical considerations related to the use of digital technologies, particularly the Internet (Dunmade, 2022). This field of study addresses various issues, including privacy, security, intellectual property, and plagiarism (Himma & Tavani, 2008). Cyber-ethical awareness involves recognizing the ethical implications of one's actions in the digital environment and making informed decisions to ensure that these actions are ethically sound (Fox, 2022).

Plagiarism

Plagiarism is the act of appropriating another person's words, thoughts, or ideas without proper acknowledgment or permission (Tomar, 2022). This malpractice is considered a breach of academic integrity and has become increasingly prevalent with the widespread use of the Internet and digital technologies (Djokovic et al., 2022). Plagiarism is a form of intellectual dishonesty that is categorized as an omen that typically results from sloth on the part of both students and faculty. This issue has caused our higher education institutions to graduate fewer students with the ability to think independently (Djokovic et al., 2022).

Chatbot Technologies

Chatbots are artificial intelligence (AI) systems designed to engage in conversation with human users through text or voice. They have been used in various applications, including customer service, language learning, and academic support (Fitria, 2023). Chatbot technologies have become increasingly popular among students due to their convenience and accessibility, but they also pose potential risks, such as facilitating plagiarism.

Chatbot Technologies and Academic Integrity

Chatbot technologies have been shown to facilitate plagiarism by providing easy access to information and prewritten content, enabling students to submit work that is not their own (Noonan, 2023). This undermines academic integrity and devalues the quality of education (Cotton et al., 2023). The use of chatbots for plagiarism can also result in poor critical reasoning and problem-solving abilities, as students become reliant on these technologies for quick answers rather than developing their understanding (Kooli, 2023).

Factors Influencing Plagiarism in Chatbot Technology Use

Several factors contribute to the prevalence of plagiarism in chatbot technology use among Nigerian undergraduate students (Adetayo, 2023; Sweeney, 2023). These factors can be divided into individual factors, such as students' motivation, attitudes, and knowledge of plagiarism, and contextual factors, such as the availability of chatbot technologies, the competitive academic environment, and the lack of effective detection and prevention strategies.

Prevalence of Plagiarism Among Nigerian Undergraduate Students

Plagiarism has been reported as a significant issue among Nigerian undergraduate students (Okaphor & Agbara, 2022). A study by found that 65.7% of Nigerian undergraduate students admitted to having engaged in some form of plagiarism, with the Internet being the most common source. The integration of chatbot technologies into the educational landscape has the potential to exacerbate this problem, as these tools provide students with additional means to access and use prewritten content without attribution (Wardat et al., 2023).

The Relationship Between Cyber-Ethical Awareness and Plagiarism

Research has shown that there is a negative relationship between cyber-ethical awareness and plagiarism, with higher levels of cyber-ethical awareness leading to a reduced likelihood of engaging in plagiarism (Masenya, 2023; Dunmade, 2022). This suggests that promoting cyber-ethical awareness among Nigerian undergraduate students could help mitigate the risk of plagiarism in chatbot technology use (Baig, 2023).

Cyber-Ethical Awareness Among Nigerian Undergraduate Students

Studies on cyber-ethical awareness among Nigerian undergraduate students are limited, but existing research indicates that there is a need to improve students' understanding of ethical issues related to digital technologies (Gumede & Badriparsad, 2022). In a study by Dunmade (2022), it was found that Nigerian undergraduate students had low levels of cyber-ethical awareness, with many students being unaware of the ethical implications of their online actions.

The Role of Cyber-Ethical Awareness in Reducing Plagiarism

Promoting cyber-ethical awareness can help reduce plagiarism in chatbot technology use by developing students' understanding of the ethical implications of their actions and the importance of academic integrity (Fernández Fernández, 2022). Additionally, fostering a strong sense of cyber-ethical awareness can encourage students to take responsibility for their actions, leading to more ethical decision-making in the digital environment (Torres, 2023).

Strategies to Promote Cyber-Ethical Awareness

One of the most effective ways to promote cyber-ethical awareness among Nigerian undergraduate students is through educational initiatives, such as workshops, seminars, and courses focused on the ethical use of digital technologies (Dunmade, 2022). These initiatives should cover topics such as plagiarism, academic integrity, and the responsible use of chatbot technologies. Also, universities and other educational institutions should establish clear policies and guidelines on the ethical use of digital technologies, including chatbot technologies (Chan, 2023; Dunmade, 2022). These policies should emphasize the importance of academic integrity and outline the consequences of plagiarism. Additionally, institutions should provide resources and support to help students understand and adhere to these policies (Dunmade & Tella, 2023). The rapid adoption of chatbot technologies among undergraduate students has raised concerns about the potential for plagiarism and its implications for academic integrity (Sullivan et al., 2023).

Similarly, in addition to educational initiatives and institutional policies, technology-based solutions can also play a role in promoting cyber-ethical awareness and reducing plagiarism in chatbot technology use. These solutions may include plagiarism detection tools, such as Turnitin, which can help identify instances of plagiarism and encourage students to submit original work (Chikkam, 2023). Furthermore, incorporating AI-driven chatbots that promote ethical behavior and discourage plagiarism can serve as a proactive approach to fostering cyber-ethical awareness among students.

Theoretical Framework: Deontological Theory of Ethics

This study is grounded in the deontological theory of ethics, which governs the literature review. Immanuel Kant (1724–1804), the founder of eighteenth-century critical philosophy (Oyewole, 2017), was the first prominent philosopher to define the deontological theory. The word deontology is of Greek origin. Humans ought to pay attention to their duties and responsibilities when making decisions, which means that a person will adhere to their obligations to another person, institution, or society because it is the ethical thing to do. Lacewing noted that deontologists believe that morality is a matter of duty, stating that individuals have moral duties to do righteous things and moral duties to refrain from doing incorrect actions. The rightness or wrongness of an action is independent of its consequences. Rather, an action is inherently right or incorrect. There are two types of responsibilities: general responsibilities, such as do not lie, do not kill, assist those in need, etc., and specific responsibilities based on a specific or social relationship. According to the motto of deontologists is "do what is right even if the world perishes." This theory is pertinent to this study because of the role of cyber-ethical awareness in mitigating plagiarism in chatbot technology use among undergraduate students.

Recommendations

This chapter could be used as a reference to enhance education actors' awareness of the importance of recognizing the potential for misuse of chatbots and implementing measures to resolve these issues in a sustainable manner. It may also help educators and researchers acquire a deeper understanding of the ethical challenges posed by the excessive use of chatbot technologies and artificial intelligence in education and research. Based on the literature review, the following recommendations are proposed:

1. Incorporate cyber-ethical awareness training into university curricula, ensuring that students understand the ethical implications of using chatbot technologies for academic purposes.

2. Establish clear policies and guidelines on the acceptable use of chatbot technologies in academic settings, including consequences for violations.

3. Encourage faculty members to provide guidance on proper citation and referencing techniques, helping students avoid unintentional plagiarism.

4. Implement robust plagiarism detection software to monitor the use of chatbot technologies and identify potential cases of academic dishonesty.

5. Promote a culture of academic integrity by recognizing and rewarding ethical behavior among students.

Future Research Area

This chapter proposes several areas for future research:

1. More research is needed to explore the prevalence of chatbot technology use among Nigerian undergraduate students and its relationship with plagiarism.

2. Studies examining the effectiveness of cyber-ethical awareness should be conducted, and training in mitigating plagiarism in the context of chatbot technology use should also be considered.

3. Research should be conducted to explore the potential benefits of incorporating chatbot technologies into academic environments while also mitigating potential risks of plagiarism.

4. Further study is required to determine the potential function of technology in detecting and preventing plagiarism in the context of chatbot technology use.

Conclusion

This study acknowledges that the possible educational advantages of chatbot technologies and artificial intelligence systems are significant and that their utilization is likely to increase in the future. To realize the full value of chatbot technologies in education and research, educators and researchers must evaluate the ethical and technical consequences of artificial intelligence systems, particularly chatbot technologies, and ensure they are used responsibly and transparently. This research provides a firm basis for investigating the possible utilization of chatbot technologies in academics and their impact on research and education. The literature review reveals a growing dependence on chatbot technologies for academic purposes among Nigerian undergraduate students. The potential risks of plagiarism are highlighted, along with the significance of nurturing a culture of ethical use. Cyber-ethical awareness has been designated as a crucial factor in preventing plagiarism and fostering academic integrity. The proliferation of chatbot technologies has provided Nigerian undergraduates with new learning and academic support opportunities, but it has also raised concerns about the possibility of plagiarism and the erosion of academic integrity. This literature review has highlighted the importance of cyber-ethical awareness in mitigating plagiarism in chatbot technology use among Nigerian undergraduate students. By promoting cyber-ethical awareness through educational initiatives, institutional policies, and technology-based solutions, universities and other educational institutions can help ensure that students use chatbot technologies responsibly and ethically, thereby preserving the quality of education and academic integrity.

Content Generated by Netflix: Scoping Review and Analysis

Madhu Rani*, Research Scholar, Sharda University, Greater Noida, Uttar Pradesh, India, rani.madhu01@gmail.com, ORCID ID: https://orcid.org/0000-0002-1712-2042

Dr. Satendar Singh, Associate Professor, School of Business Studies, Sharda University, Greater Noida, Uttar Pradesh, India, Email: satendar.singh@sharda.ac.in

© Neha Zaidi, Mohit Maurya, Simon Grima, Pallavi Tyagi 2024, corrected publication 2024
N. Zaidi et al. (eds.), *Building AI Driven Marketing Capabilities*,
https://doi.org/10.1007/978-1-4842-9810-7_10

Shagun Tomar, Research Scholar, Sharda University, Greater Noida, Uttar Pradesh, India, shaguntomar22@gmail.com, ORCID ID: https://orcid.org/0000-0001-5939-0371

Dr. Manisha Gupta, Associate Professor, Sharda University, Greater Noida, Uttar Pradesh, India, guptaamanisha@gmail.com, ORCID ID: https://orcid.org/0000-0001-6494-1094

Dr. Hari Shankar Shyam, Professor, Sharda University, Greater Noida, Uttar Pradesh, India, harishankar.shyam@sharda.ac.in

Netflix has expanded fast in consumers and income during the past decade. Both areas expanded simultaneously. The corporation has routinely beaten optimistic sales and membership expectations several times. This study investigates what the average person likes to see. Netflix's programming remains unsettled despite its financial achievements and membership fee hike. Since then, Netflix has nearly quadrupled its income and added paying customers while raising rates. Python data analysis software is being used to study online video streaming and social media behavior. This chapter examines their link. User-engaging Twitter content is analyzed first. Retweeting was explored. Then they investigated streaming content producers' tweets. Twitter helps analyze material in different ways. Twitter hashtags measure streaming video data. Thematic and sentiment analysis is done by familiarizing oneself with the data, shifting themes, and examining word and phrase recurrence. Trends are shown. Python analyzes and displays the data. After the investigation, clients choose OTT (over-the-top) platforms since they can access them on any Internet-connected device at any time. Engaging in conversations on recent films, television shows, and soothing programes. The survey revealed that Netflix is widely favored. Individuals have apprehension of being found out. Individuals who are addicted to fear. Mobile network disruptions are a source of annoyance. Squid games are now seeing a surge in popularity. Netflix and other over-the-top (OTT) platforms are the preferred choice for popular Korean dramas and thrillers. The study reveals that tweets with varied content-related messages may contribute information. Twitter communication analysis seeks this knowledge. At the national level, there are significant differences in both growth trends and business initiatives, but these are obscured by the global trend toward the expansion of Netflix and its subscribers. This research seeks to determine promising research areas that warrant further investigation.

Introduction

Over-the-top (OTT) services have revolutionized broadcast entertainment and communication services. Due to lower prices and more content options, customers are using over-the-top (OTT) TV services more.

The digital revolution in India is driven by smartphone uptake, 5G networks, data price drops, and increased mobile device use. Smartphone adoption is a major factor. Because of this, digital advertising will grow faster than conventional media during the next three years. Smartphone use in India has ushered in a new era of video consumption on personal media devices, spawning a new genre of content.

Netflix and Amazon Prime dominate the global growth of over-the-top (OTT) media services. According to Startup Stories (2019), Indian platforms like Voot and SonyLIV are gaining popularity and competing with foreign platforms (Mishra, 2019).

Netflix

Netflix has approximately 222 million paying members in over 190 countries. It has a wide variety of genres and languages. Subscribers can watch on any Internet-connected screen at any time and can play, pause, and watch without interruption. Recommendation systems are changing our information preferences (Helberger et al., 2018). Recommendation algorithms influence our information consumption. Netflix recommends programs after watching one.

Content Trend

In technology-enabled situations, "over-the-top" (OTT) content is becoming a buzzword. OTT content is popular among millennials as a new independent digital multimedia platform. This platform runs independently of multi-cable or direct broadcast satellite television, giving media and consumers more content consumption freedom.

Adolescents who want to talk to adults about difficult topics may lack the language and supporting circumstances to do so (Dudek et al., 2022). Favorable demographics, relevant content, free content, and a range of premium content subscription alternatives may allow for future growth (Saha and Prasad, 2021).

TV viewers are increasingly posting about their shows on social media. Even while second-screen apps offer access to a variety of social media platforms, research shows that most individuals use Twitter while watching TV (Segado-Boj, Grandio, & Fernández-Gómez, 2015, p. 228). This trend has led media practitioners to use Twitter to measure audience behavior (Wilson, 2016). Content analysis is typically used to study social media debates. The number of tweets and user interaction on a tweet or topic are the main measures in this type of study (Segado-Boj et al., 2015, p. 231).

Shift from TV to Web Series

Before diving deeper, we must define "new media." This study examines youth Internet and WWW use. We know that mobile phones and high-resolution digital televisions are changing rapidly, but young people are more interested in the Internet and WWW (Loader, 2007).

The digital revolution and business model innovation have changed customers' expectations and habits. This has challenged existing businesses and disrupted several markets. Consumers have several media avenues to effortlessly and proactively communicate with businesses and other consumers. They also visit a growing number of digital touchpoints during their consumer journey. Consumers have several media options and can easily interact with businesses and other consumers. Media outlets abound (Lemon & Verhoef, 2016).

Netflix also disrupts television and film (Ansari, Garud, & Kumaraswamy, 2016). 25% of Netflix users watch on their phones, tablets, or laptops (Recode, 2018).

Netflix (Demand and Subscription)

The emergence of over-the-top (OTT) services has brought about a significant transformation in the media landscape, encompassing various forms of broadcast entertainment and communication services. The correlation between the diversity of media and democratic engagement could potentially elucidate the fervor with which novel technological advancements are being adopted within the media sphere (Möller, Trilling, Helberger, & van Es, 2018).

Literature Review

Due to price and content diversity, over-the-top (OTT) television services are becoming more popular. Over-the-top (OTT) television companies may be driving customers to cut the cord. A survey of 1200 Americans found that 16% had stopped using cable TV in the past year, and 20% were willing to do so (PWC, 2016). The biggest over-the-top (OTT) television providers have witnessed considerable growth in customers, and OTT has driven a "content arms race" to entice new users. OTT TV companies are fighting to deliver the best programming to attract customers (L.E.K., 2015). In response to this trend, conventional content providers have implemented multiscreen approaches, diversified their revenue streams beyond subscription-based models, introduced online pay TV bundles using a comprehensive over-the-top (OTT) model, created cloud-based pay TV services accessible via smart TV applications, and offered hybrid broadcast/broadband services. The preceding examples show how traditional content producers have been adapting to this new phenomenon (Song, 2013).

Social Media

Social media platforms' development and operation now catch customers' attention due to this new consumption pattern. These platforms were established to connect people, families, and friends via technology (Humphreys, 2012; Wellman, 2004).

Social networks now serve many functions. Users may track celebrities, brands, corporations, and like-minded people. They also spread news and political information. Social media may also be used to organize events, share work, and get jobs. They also inform on current events and politics.

Twitter is a vital communication tool (Loader et al., 2016). Twitter hashtags and content allow industry stakeholders and viewers to discuss, react, ask questions, interact, and potentially increase viewership or share personal experiences. Delgado, Navarro, Garcia-Muoz, and Paz (2018) found that people share their viewing habits with social media followers, express their opinions about the content, generate or consume humorous content, and engage with the production team to learn more. According to Delgado, Navarro, Garcia-Muoz, and Pena (2015) and Wohn and Na (2011), broadcasters and subscription video on demand (SVOD) providers want to influence discourse and lead social dialogue. According to Fernández-Gómez and Martín-Quevedo (2018), media production businesses have discovered that social networks are crucial to engaging with prospects and consumers using media industry jargon.

Twitter

Twitter is a popular social media platform worldwide. Twitter's users have recently focused on socializing and sharing information. Users utilize Twitter, Instagram, and Facebook to build social capital. Joinson (2008) suggests using online communities for social and emotional support.

Social networking services (SNSs) have greatly improved their role in communication and information distribution, sometimes exceeding these tasks with either beneficial or bad impacts on its users. COVID-19 accelerated the intact society's growth. Twitter users share content to interact with others. This content may feature personal or social issues and heated political debates. Influential Twitter users are more likely to befriend other users to share information and maintain their networks (Tonkin et al., 2012).

The use of social media by companies is rapidly expanding as more and more business is conducted online, leading to more consumer engagement and the development of stronger customer connections. Social media has substantially transformed the way consumers seek information, evaluate products, and furnish feedback on their purchases.

The fact that Twitter's statistics are typically available to the public and that the platform gives academics with relatively simple access to massive amounts of data (Mackenzie, 2018) is one reason why it has been the subject of a significant number of studies. In addition, the utilization of hashtags on Twitter is not restricted, thus enabling a diverse range of individuals to participate in enhancing the platform's efficacy in disseminating breaking news stories (Aheed et al., 2018). This makes Twitter a great venue for breaking news stories.

This study seeks to determine Twitter users' post-COVID-19 content and emotion.

Netflix on Twitter

In order to market their content effectively, Netflix employs a broad range of social media avenues. The fact that the company can create viral campaigns on different social media channels and encourage audience involvement is commendable, especially when compared to television networks that still lag in this aspect of marketing their content (Van Es, 2016). D'heer and colleagues found that Twitter affects how much broadcast media people consume in their 2015 study. Twitter in the United States saw an effective promotional effort by Netflix for *Orange Is the New Black* (Artt & Schwan, 2016; Schwan, 2016; Belcher, 2016; DeCarvalho & Fox, 2016; Fernández-Morales & Menéndez-Menéndez, 2016; Silverman & Ryalls, 2016).

Purpose

- The objective of this study is to analyze the presence and trends of each hashtag, word among users on Twitter about Netflix.

- The objective of the study is to find the elements that users include in their tweets about Netflix.

- The study also identifies the major content theme and sentiment of users on Twitter post COVID-19.

Content Analysis

Qualitative content analysis interprets data. Communication material is rigorously analyzed. It involves statistically examining massive datasets to uncover text patterns and themes. Content analysis shows word frequency, context, and links.

Sentiment Analysis

Sentiment analysis—also called opinion mining or emotion artificial intelligence—identifies, extracts, and analyzes emotional states and subjective information using natural language processing, text analysis, computational linguistics, and biometrics. Mogyorosi (2021) suggests sentiment analysis.

This survey tracks Netflix subscribers' thoughts on Twitter. Since blogs and Twitter are so popular, understanding human behavior involves studying "sentiment."

Thematic Analysis

Qualitative thematic analysis finds text patterns and themes. It involves categorizing text subjects, concepts, and categories. Thematic analysis studies ideas, experiences, and attitudes in social science.

Research Methodology: Data Collection

Hashtags label material. It aids content discovery. Twitter hashtags words and phrases. Clicking the hashtag or searching for it in English opens a stream of hashtagged items. A Twitter search of Netflix, content, and related subjects yielded 15 OTT-related hashtags, focusing on the most popular and widely used. Over several weeks, Twitter was used to find the most popular hashtags for viewership, content, and movie-related tweets.

The study examined hashtags like Netflix, Netflix Show, Netflix Review, Netflix Original, Netflix India, Netflix & Chill, Netflix Series, Netflix Originals, Netflix Movies, and Netflix and Chill. 38531 tweets and retweets were in the database. The study used mostly English Twitter data.

Python is a complete programming language for data science applications. Its simplicity has made it popular. It was designed to run quicker with compiled code. Its popularity can be attributed to its ease of use, pseudocode-like syntax, modularity, object orientation, portability, testing, self-documenting, and arithmetic library, which makes it easy to store and handle large amounts of numerical data (Nagpal & Gabrani, 2019). Pandas allows Python users to study real-world datasets. Library construction began in 2008 (McKinney, 2011) were open-source and made for users. To be the best data analysis building block, simple data types and tools work nicely. Developers load, prepare, model, and analyze data with it. Natural language processing programs and libraries constitute the Natural Language Toolkit (NLTK) (Bird, 2006). Python-based English NLP was created to improve NLP, cognitive science, data mining, machine learning, artificial intelligence, and empirical linguistics research and instruction. Its modules are interdependent. It uses a few simple modules to define fundamental data types. The remaining modules control NLP.

Result and Discussion: Gathering Information

The data focuses on analyzing tweets and posts on Twitter and Facebook posted by people at different time frames. The information was gathered from Twitter and Facebook for the year 2022, with a primary emphasis on post-COVID time. This was done in order to better understand how people are responding to their OTT platforms these days.

For importing the data in libraries, which is necessary for NLP as PANDA is being used to import the dataset which is in the form of Excel file, importing the strings library, which is helpful when working with strings. Then we have the counter, which lets us make a collection of words and count them. Belatedly, we have the main library NLTK, which is used for natural language processing. Then there is NLTK's corpus library stop words, which gets rid of all the stop words in the dataset. After that nlk.sentiment.vader, which is sentiment Intensity Analyzer for sentiment analysis. Word tokenizer that segregates each word so that it doesn't show up more than once in the list of words. Word tokenizer that segregates each word so that it doesn't show up more than once in the list of words for that, 'OMW' is used. Cognitive synonym sets, also known as synsets, are comprised of nouns, verbs, adjectives, and adverbs, each set representing a distinct notion. The interconnection between synsets is established through both conceptual-semantic and linguistic associations.

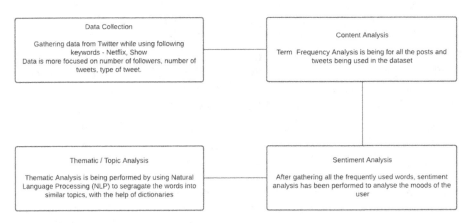

Figure 10-1. Flow of the study
Source: Authors self created using python

Content Analysis

The material that was taken from posts and tweets is being processed using the NLTK library in order to clean the data, which involves eliminating stop words and punctuation marks, shrinking the words to their base words, and doing predictions based on the data. A term frequency analysis (TFA) using the NLTK Python library to do all of the analysis and data cleaning, with an accuracy rate of more than 70%, each word was tokenized and separated from words to dictionary to the greatest number of word occurrences in the dataset. The accuracy rate was determined by counting the number of times each word occurred in the dataset. Gensim is the primary library for topic and Linear Discriminant Analysis (LDA) modeling. pyLDAvis is used for visualizations in the dataset, after which the data is imported into the database for analysis.

TFA (Term Frequency Analysis)

Here, the data is being cleaned up by getting rid of any elements in the dataset that aren't necessary. For a more accurate analysis, we separated the cleaned tweets into separate batches and performed a frequency analysis on the keywords. The next code deals with eliminating punctuation marks since we don't need any of them to be present in the data in order to do analysis. Then we tokenize each word to prevent repetition of any of them and to allow selection of the words in their original forms. Words are being added to a list for us to be able to lemmatize each word and tally off each unique value from the list. This is necessary since certain words may be written in a variety of forms, such as good, better, and best. This is necessary since certain words may be written in a variety of forms, such as good, better, and best collecting a total of all the unique words included in the dataset. Seeing the distinct terms and the number of times they appear on the list.

More and more people are discussing what they want to see in theaters or on television soon. There's a need for shows that can be watched at a slower pace and yet provide entertainment. It's possible that *Squid Game* or a series called "game" is the subject of the rumors floating about. People are also interested in seeing more action films and films with a Bollywood theme. People are more interested in the names of ongoing series than they are in the names of individual films. The movie *RRR*, as seen in Figure 10-2, is also a popular topic of conversation, with over 5000 mentions.

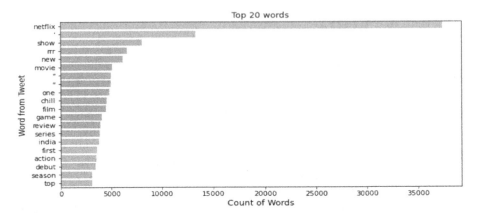

Figure 10-2. Frequent terms
Source: Authors' Own

Sentiment Analysis

Separating each of the lemmatized words in the phrase, the words are broken down into many sentiments, and the words associated with each sentiment are recorded and organized into a bar chart. After being cleaned, all the text is loaded into the LDA model, and then visualization is performed.

People have a positive sentiment, as shown by the emotion bar diagram, which shows that the people are happy with the service they are being provided by the Netflix, people facing a sense of sadness due to post-COVID situations in the country, people are feeling a sense of fear in many posts, some of the people have really been attached to different shows and are indirectly invested in watching series, and then people are showing a sense of anger due to the network crash that Netflix faced due to the fact that they were unable to watch their favorite.

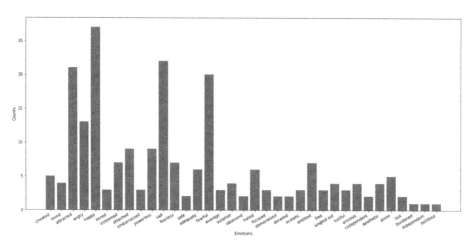

Figure 10-3. Sentiment analysis
Source: Authors' Own

Thematic Analysis

After being thoroughly cleaned, all the text is input into the LDA model, and then visualization is performed. This converts the cleaned texts into a dictionary that will be used for looking by the model to split words into a term matrix that will be used for determining subject from the tweets of each user. The information in the cell below is partitioned into the two traits that are described below, and the training model reviews the information fifty times.

Topic 1: Netflix—*Squid Game*

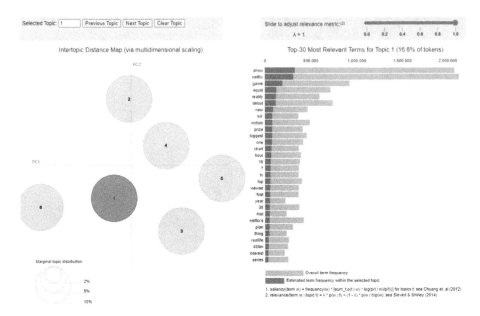

Figure 10-4. Thematic analysis
Source: Authors' Own

People are enthusiastically discussing the *Squid Games* television series and posting their own theories on various social media platforms; in addition, they are debating which of the Korean television programs is the best to watch; people are also posting about new movies to watch, such as *Wanted*; people are also talking about the debut of a new actor or the premiere of a new movie or television series; people are interested in watching reality shows and more; people also enjoy viewing thriller films and posting about various murder mysteries; and people are also sharing about new movies to watch.

Topic 2: Latest *Heartstopper* Movies

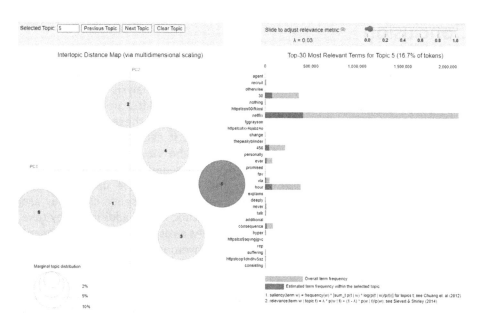

Figure 10-5. Thematic analysis of latest movies
Source: Authors' Own

We see a shift in the taste in movies of the people from fictions to movies based on real life stories and issues covering a much deeper concept and questions critical aspects of life and existence, how the society shapes the world around us, and a lot of other concepts. People are talking about movies like *Heartstopper* and *Peaky Blinders*, and the most recent movies talked about a lot by the name is "bgyo."

Limitations

The research exhibits certain constraints. The limitations present various avenues for further investigation. The discourse pertaining to Netflix and its content on social media is considerably broader in scope than the dataset analyzed in the study. While the dataset provides a substantial amount of information on the subject, it solely focuses on Netflix's most prevalent tweets in English.

Conclusion

Content analysis is a broad term that encompasses various methods of analyzing textual data, while sentiment analysis and thematic analysis are two specific techniques used within the field of content analysis to analyze the emotional tone and themes within a text, respectively. After doing the analysis and interpreting the results, it was found out that people these days appreciate OTT platforms, particularly due to the fact that it can be accessed on any device that has an Internet, at whatever time the viewer wants to use it. People are talking more about upcoming movies and series, and they are looking for calming and pleasant programs. Based on the findings of the research, we can assert that individuals have a positive sense that they are pleased with the service that is provided by Netflix, and in addition, they take pleasure in spending their free time doing that. As a result of the post-covenant status in the country, there is a feeling of bereavement. The populace lives in constant fear of being discovered. There is a certain kind of terrifying sensation that they are completely addicted to. There is also a feeling of rage as a result of the collapse of the network. When people's mobile networks or signals are disrupted, it is very frustrating for them. The primary reason for the adverse response was found in this aspect. People are discussing squid games at a frenetic pace and posting their own ideas on social networking websites. People are looking for heart-stopping movies, as well as Korean dramas and series.

As a result, we can draw the conclusion that individuals like the content that Netflix provides and have a positive attitude about OTT services.

Unveiling AI's Ethical Impact in Marketing Through Social Media's Darker Influence

Dr. Vijay Prakash Gupta*, Associate Professor, Institute of Business Management, GLA University, Mathura, UP India, Email: vijayguptacmd@gmail.com

In today's digital era, the widespread use of AI in marketing raises ethical concerns, particularly within the realm of social media. This chapter delves into the darker side of AI's influence, addressing issues such as the manipulation of consumer behavior, breaches of privacy, and the dissemination of disinformation. The primary objective is to promote responsible and ethical AI practices while harnessing its potential in marketing, striking a balance between innovation and safeguarding societal values. By examining these ethical considerations and shedding light on the negative aspects of AI,

© Neha Zaidi, Mohit Maurya, Simon Grima, Pallavi Tyagi 2024, corrected publication 2024
N. Zaidi et al. (eds.), *Building AI Driven Marketing Capabilities*,
https://doi.org/10.1007/978-1-4842-9810-7_11

including its ability to manipulate consumer behavior, invade privacy, and potentially spread misleading information, this study aims to enhance awareness and comprehension of the ethical challenges associated with AI's integration into marketing practices. The research methodology involves the utilization of secondary data and a literature review to analyze the ethical ramifications of AI in marketing, with a specific focus on its impact in the context of social media, ultimately contributing to a better understanding of these complex issues.

Introduction

The use of artificial intelligence (AI) in marketing has transformed many elements of customer engagement, personalized advertising, and data-driven decision-making. However, as AI advances and its connection with social media platforms develops, it raises ethical problems that must be thoroughly investigated. This introduction presents an overview of the ethical issues of AI in marketing, with a particular emphasis on its impact on social media. AI has become an essential component of marketing strategy, enabling marketers to analyze massive volumes of data, personalize customer experiences, and optimize their efforts. Nonetheless, the fast use of AI in marketing, especially via social media platforms, has generated ethical concerns about the influence of technology on people and society.

- **The Rise of Artificial Intelligence in Marketing**: Artificial Intelligence & Machine Learning (AI-ML), Natural Language Processing (NLP), and predictive analytics are examples of artificial intelligence technologies that have revolutionized the world of marketing. Marketers can use AI-powered technologies to analyze massive volumes of data, spot trends, and make data-driven choices with more accuracy and efficiency. According to multiple data sources, the global AI in marketing market is anticipated to reach $27.23 billion by 2025, growing at a compound annual growth rate (CAGR) of 29.7% between 2020 and 2025.

- **Personalized Advertising and Consumer Profiling**: Personalized advertising is a fundamental use of AI in marketing, aiming to give customized material to individual customers based on their interests, behaviors, and demographic information. AI algorithms employ user data from social media sites to develop personalized adverts, resulting in increased conversion rates and better consumer experiences. However, this degree of personalization poses privacy issues as well as the possibility of manipulative practices.

- **Influence of Social Media in Marketing**: Social media platforms play an important part in current marketing tactics, allowing marketers to reach a large audience and communicate with prospective consumers. There were 4.2 billion active social media users globally in January 2021, representing 53% of the global population. With such a large user base, marketers have an enormous opportunity to deploy AI algorithms to analyze user data and offer customized content.

- **Manipulation and Persuasion Through AI**: The employment of AI algorithms in marketing raises worries about social media manipulation and persuasion strategies. According to research conducted by the Fogg Behavior Model, AI-driven persuasive technology may affect human behavior by activating psychological elements such as social proof, authority, and scarcity. This manipulation may result in hasty purchases, addiction to social media sites, and a loss of individual liberty.

- **Privacy Concerns in AI Marketing**: Concerns regarding privacy invasion have arisen as a result of the collection and analysis of massive volumes of user data on social media platforms. According to a 2020 Statista poll, 56% of social media users in the United States were worried about their privacy while using social media. The use of AI in marketing exacerbates these issues, since AI systems use personal data to develop comprehensive user profiles, possibly violating people's privacy rights.

- **Bias Amplification in AI Marketing**: AI systems trained on biased datasets may perpetuate and amplify social prejudices, resulting in unfair targeting and discriminatory marketing practices. A Stanford University study discovered that commercial AI systems used for Internet advertising demonstrated gender and racial prejudice, disproportionately targeting adverts linked to employment possibilities based on gender and racial stereotypes. This kind of bias amplification may exacerbate socioeconomic inequities and stymie attempts to create a more inclusive marketing environment.

- **Lack of Transparency and Accountability**: The complexity of AI algorithms raises transparency and accountability difficulties. According to an Accenture survey, 84% of customers believe firms must be up front about how AI is used in marketing. The lack of openness in AI-driven marketing practices, on the other hand, may undermine confidence and make it harder for customers to grasp the decision-making processes underlying personalized content and suggestions.

The fast expansion of artificial intelligence in marketing, along with the power of social media platforms, has resulted in substantial ethical considerations that must be addressed. To promote a responsible and accountable AI-driven marketing environment, marketers, governments, and stakeholders must recognize and address these ethical issues.

Defining Artificial Intelligence

Intelligence encompasses the ability to acquire, understand, reason, solve problems, learn, and adapt, facilitating informed decisions toward specific goals. AI is a discipline within computer science that strives to develop intelligent systems that mimic human cognitive abilities. Through algorithms, models, and techniques like ML and NLP, AI systems process extensive data to identify patterns, extract insights, and autonomously act upon information. They function with varying degrees of independence, differentiating them from broader natural intelligence exhibited by living beings. In essence, AI involves crafting intelligent systems to analyze, choose, and act toward goals, while intelligence encompasses the broader cognitive capacities of organisms, notably humans. These systems are designed to derive relevant insights, and act on the data they have analyzed. AI systems often demonstrate some degree of autonomy, enabling them to function alone or with minimum human interaction.

In brief, AI is a design and implementation of intelligent systems that analyze their surroundings, make choices, and take actions to accomplish certain objectives in either virtual or physical domains. In contrast, intelligence refers to a larger idea of cognitive ability and problem-solving capabilities shown by living organisms, including humans.

How Morality and Ethics Relate to Artificial Intelligence

Morality and ethics are closely connected ideas that incorporate rules and criteria for establishing what acts or behaviors are judged good, fair, or virtuous. While morality usually relates to personal opinions and convictions about what is good and wrong, ethics often refers to larger social or professional standards and norms.

Personal judgments and values that impact an individual's behaviors and decisions are referred to as moral judgments and values. It is influenced by a variety of variables, including cultural, religious, and personal views. Morality gives a framework for people to analyze their behavior and make ethically correct or incorrect judgments.

Ethics in Artificial Intelligence

In contrast, ethics entails a larger viewpoint that analyzes the influence of acts and choices on others and society as a whole. Beyond individual views, ethical principles give rules for behavior and decision-making. Concepts such as fairness, justice, honesty, respect, and accountability are often emphasized in ethical frameworks.

The area of AI ethics arose from the necessity to address the moral and ethical implications of AI systems and their influence on persons and society when it comes to AI. As artificial intelligence (AI) technology progresses and becomes increasingly interwoven into all facets of our lives, it presents serious ethical concerns. AI ethics is concerned with determining how AI systems should be created, developed, deployed, and utilized in a way that is consistent with moral and ethical norms.

Some important ethical issues in AI include

- **Transparency and Accountability**: Making AI systems visible, explainable, and responsible for their choices and behaviors, particularly in vital sectors like healthcare, criminal justice, and finance.

- **Fairness and Bias**: Avoiding discrimination and inequitable treatment by mitigating biases in AI algorithms and data.

- **Privacy and Data Protection**: Personal data and privacy rights are protected, and sensitive information is handled and used responsibly.

- **Safety and Security**: Designing AI systems with strong safety safeguards to protect persons, organizations, and society while also addressing possible cybersecurity issues.

- **Social Impact**: Considering the larger social, economic, and cultural consequences of artificial intelligence systems, such as possible job displacement, socioeconomic inequality, and the effect on vulnerable groups.

- **Human Autonomy and Control**: Maintaining human decision-making and control while avoiding overreliance on AI technologies that might undermine human autonomy or influence behavior.

Organizations, research institutes, and governments are developing ethical frameworks and standards to address these AI ethics challenges. The aim is to ensure the development and implementation of AI aligns with ethical and moral standards, upholds human rights, and contributes positively to the betterment of society.

Tort Law and Marketing AI

Tort law can undoubtedly assume a substantial role within the sphere of AI in the realm of marketing. As AI becomes increasingly prevalent in marketing practices, it introduces new legal considerations and potential liabilities. The following are several important areas in which tort law may apply to AI in marketing:

- **Negligence**: In tort law, negligence is a fundamental concept. If a marketer or company fails to exercise reasonable care when developing, deploying, or maintaining artificial intelligence (AI) systems for marketing purposes and this failure causes injury to individuals or other businesses, they may be held liable for malfeasance.

  For example, if an AI-powered marketing algorithm makes erroneous or biased targeting decisions, resulting in financial losses for a company or causing damage to individuals (such as discrimination), the affected parties may have a negligence claim.

- **Defamation**: False statements that damage someone's reputation constitute libel. AI-generated content, such as product evaluations or automated social media postings, may contain defamatory statements when used in marketing. If an AI system spreads false information that harms a person's reputation, the victim may have a defamation claim against the marketer or company responsible for the AI system.

- **Invasion of Privacy**: In marketing, AI frequently requires the collection and analysis of vast quantities of personal data. If artificial intelligence systems used for marketing purposes inappropriately collect, use, or disclose personal information, it may violate the privacy rights of individuals. The tort law recognizes invasions of privacy such as public disclosure of private facts and deceptive light. If an AI marketing system violates the privacy rights of individuals, those individuals may have a valid claim for invasion of privacy.

- **Intellectual Property Infringement**: AI systems are capable of being programmed to generate text, images, and audio. If an AI marketing system generates material that infringes on the intellectual property rights of a third party, such as copyright or trademark, the owner of the infringed rights can file a claim for infringement against the marketer or company responsible for the AI system.

Literature Review

Artificial intelligence (AI) has garnered substantial attention across academic, professional, and public spheres owing to its perceived advantageous potential (Davenport et al., 2020). Comprising an array of technologies encompassing sensors, voice recognition, robotics, automation, and intelligent learning (Fan et al., 2022; Huang & Rust, 2018), AI holds the promise of delivering entertaining, efficient, and customized services to customers while also enabling enhanced social interactions (Grewal et al., 2021). Particularly in sectors like service and marketing, these innovations have and will continue to usher in transformative changes.

With the escalating capabilities of AI technologies, concerns regarding the privacy and security of individuals are also on the rise (Ioannou and Tussyadiah, 2021; Tussyadiah et al., 2018). The potential for AI devices to gather and retain personal data, encompassing biometric information, identifiers, behavioral records, and personal details, has become significant (Ioannou et al., 2021). Alarming is the fact that this data collection sometimes occurs without the user's awareness (Manikonda et al., 2018).

While the manifold benefits of AI in our contemporary world are undeniable, it is imperative to acknowledge that alongside these benefits, detrimental consequences may emerge. To effectively address these potential negative outcomes, it becomes essential to initiate contemplation regarding their nature and implications. Marr (2021) emphasizes the need for such proactive consideration.

The present era, characterized by an inundation of data, has witnessed a paradigm shift in data generation and processing, driven by the confluence of big data, analytics, and AI within the realm of marketing (Mikalef & Gupta, 2021; Vidgen et al., 2017). The convergence of big data and business analytics

(BA) has gained unprecedented momentum, largely attributed to the integration of AI (Conboy et al., 2020; Davenport & Malone, 2021). Scholars are currently grappling with the intricate challenges associated with harnessing the potential of AI-infused BA to generate business value, thereby augmenting competitive advantage (Davenport, 2018; Sharda et al., 2016). The pursuit of leveraging this fusion is paramount in light of the evolving business landscape.

Significance of AI in Marketing

Enhanced Personalization: AI in marketing enables highly personalized customer experiences by analyzing vast amounts of data. For instance, Amazon utilizes AI algorithms to recommend products based on customers' browsing history and purchase behavior, resulting in a more tailored shopping experience.

- **Improved Customer Targeting**: AI enables marketers to more effectively identify and target certain client groupings. Facebook's advertising platform uses AI to analyze user demographics, interests, and behaviors, allowing companies to precisely reach their target audience and maximize campaign performance.

- **Predictive Analytics**: By analyzing prior patterns and consumer behavior, AI-powered predictive analytics assists marketers in making data-driven choices. For example, Netflix employs AI algorithms to forecast user preferences and offer personalized content, resulting in greater user engagement and retention.

- **Efficient Chatbots and Virtual Assistants**: AI-powered chatbots and virtual assistants have changed marketing customer help and assistant. AI chatbots are used by brands such as Sephora and Starbucks to deliver personalized product suggestions, answer consumer questions, and promote seamless interactions, resulting in higher customer satisfaction and shorter response times.

- **Social Media Sentiment Analysis**: To evaluate public opinion about goods, businesses, or campaigns, AI systems may analyze social media discussions and sentiments. This information enables marketers to adjust their strategy appropriately. Coca-Cola employed artificial intelligence sentiment analysis to assess consumer responses to its "Share a Coke" campaign, allowing the corporation to fine-tune its message and boost brand engagement.

- **Improved Content Creation**: AI can aid marketers in the generation and curation of content. The Associated Press, for example, uses AI algorithms to produce news pieces based on data inputs, enabling speedier content creation and delivery.

- **Optimized Ad Campaigns**: Marketers may use AI-powered algorithms to optimize ad campaigns by automatically altering bidding methods, targeting settings, and ad placements. Google Ads uses AI to improve campaign effectiveness and deliver the best outcomes for marketers.

- **Fraud Detection and Prevention**: AI systems can detect and prevent fraudulent marketing practices such as click fraud and ad fraud. AI protects advertisers' investments and the integrity of digital advertising systems by analyzing trends and anomalies in user behavior.

- **Marketing Automation**: AI enables marketing automation by automating repetitive processes like email marketing, lead scoring, and customer segmentation. HubSpot's Marketing Hub uses artificial intelligence to automate processes, nurture leads, and provide personalized content at scale, increasing productivity and campaign performance.

- **Competitive Advantage**: AI in marketing gives firms a competitive advantage by allowing them to collect insights, optimize plans, and provide highly focused and relevant content to their target audience. Companies that properly use AI technology are more likely to remain ahead of the competition in the continually changing marketing scene.

Theoretical Background on Artificial Intelligence in Marketing

The following table lists the theoretical backgrounds related to AI in marketing and their interconnections:

Theoretical Background	Description
Machine Learning (ML)	ML constitutes a subset of AI dedicated to crafting algorithms and models that empower systems to learn from data, thereby facilitating predictions and decisions without requiring explicit programming.
	In marketing, ML techniques are used for tasks like customer segmentation, personalized recommendations, sentiment analysis, and predictive modeling.
Natural Language Processing (NLP)	NLP encompasses the interplay between computers and human language, granting machines the ability to comprehend, decipher, and generate human language, encompassing both written text and spoken communication. In marketing, NLP is employed for sentiment analysis, chatbots, voice assistants, and content generation.
Deep Learning (DL)	DL stands as a subdivision of machine learning (ML) that employs multilayered neural networks to extract intricate features from intricate datasets. DL algorithms excel in tasks like image and speech recognition, natural language understanding, and recommendation systems. In marketing, DL is used for image analysis, speech-to-text conversion, and content personalization.
Reinforcement Learning (RL)	RL focuses on training an agent to make sequential decisions in an environment to maximize a reward. It involves trial-and-error learning and learning from feedback. RL is applied in marketing for tasks like dynamic pricing, personalized recommendations, and customer lifetime value optimization.
Computer Vision (CV)	CV represents an interdisciplinary domain that addresses the means by which computers can attain comprehension from digital images or videos. In marketing, CV techniques are employed for tasks such as visual search, facial recognition, and object detection in advertising.
Recommender Systems (RS)	RS leverage AI algorithms to furnish individualized suggestions to users, drawing from their preferences, past interactions, and likeness to other users. These systems are extensively used in marketing for product recommendations, content suggestions, and personalized marketing campaigns.
Predictive Analytics	Predictive analytics involves using historical data, statistical algorithms, and ML techniques to forecast future events or outcomes. In marketing, predictive analytics is employed to predict customer behavior, anticipate demand, optimize marketing campaigns, and identify potential churn.

Ethical Concerns of AI in Marketing

Ethical concerns regarding the use of artificial intelligence (AI) in marketing have become more pertinent as companies employ AI technologies to enhance their marketing strategies. Even though AI offers numerous benefits for marketers, several ethical concerns must be addressed. Here are some important ethical concerns regarding the use of AI in marketing, along with examples and facts from the marketing industry:

- **Privacy and Data Protection**: Collecting and analyzing enormous quantities of user data is crucial for marketing AI. When businesses fail to sufficiently safeguard user privacy or misuse the data they collect, ethical concerns arise. For example, in 2018, Facebook was embroiled in a massive data breach scandal involving the unauthorized sharing of user data with Cambridge Analytica, which sparked concerns regarding the misuse of personal information for targeted advertising.

- **Manipulation and Deception**: AI-enabled marketing strategies can employ persuasion strategies that may influence consumer decision-making. Utilizing AI algorithms, marketers can maximize conversion rates by optimizing content, designs, and messages, potentially exploiting psychological vulnerabilities. Such manipulative practices may be considered unethical because they prioritize sales over the best interests of consumers.

- **Bias and Discrimination**: AI systems acquire knowledge on huge amounts of data, which can accidentally reinforce any biases that are in the data. In marketing, this can lead to unfair practices, like not sending ads for certain goods or services to people in certain ethnic groups. For example, if an AI program is taught on data from the past that shows biased hiring practices, it might suggest that certain demographic groups not be included in job ads.

- **Transparency and Explainability**: When the methodologies employed by AI lack transparency, they can give rise to societal concerns. Marketers might employ intricate AI systems that obscure customers' comprehension of how their data is utilized and marketing choices are formulated. A dearth of transparency and clarification could erode people's confidence in a company, thus impeding their ability to exercise their rights related to privacy and data safeguarding.

- **Autonomous Decision-Making**: AI systems might be able to make decisions on their own without help from humans. This brings up questions about duty and responsibility in marketing. For example, if an AI program decides on its own how much to charge for a product or service, it could lead to unfair pricing or price discrimination without any human review.

- **Intellectual Property and Creativity**: AI can make material, ideas, or songs, which raises questions about intellectual property and creation. For example, if an AI makes art that looks like the work of an actual artist, questions about copying and originality come up. It can be hard to figure out who owns and has legal rights to material made by AI.

- **Job Displacement and Inequality**: The rising use of AI in marketing may result in job displacement when some functions are automated. Individuals in low-skilled or repetitive employment may be disproportionately affected, thus aggravating socioeconomic inequities. Businesses and politicians have responsibilities for addressing the effect of AI on the workforce and ensuring a fair transition.

It is critical to address these ethical considerations to guarantee the acceptable and long-term usage of AI in marketing. To create customer trust and uphold ethical standards, businesses should prioritize openness, data protection, and justice. Furthermore, politicians and regulatory agencies play an important role in developing standards and laws to control AI use in marketing, as well as in safeguarding people's rights and supporting ethical practices.

Uncovering the Negative Impact of AI on Social Media

AI algorithms are being used by social media networks to support marketing activities by analyzing user behavior, interactions, and preferences to offer personalized content and targeted adverts. However, there have been worries voiced about the possible negative effects of this power, such as the establishment of echo chambers, filter bubbles, and public opinion manipulation. A recent study has emphasized the impact of AI-powered algorithms on social media platforms in deception, promotion of extreme ideologies, and polarization. While AI provides benefits such as personalized suggestions and effective content regulation, it also has a detrimental influence on social media.

- **Amplification of Misinformation and Fake News**: Social media sites' AI algorithms have been chastised for their part in promoting disinformation and false news. These algorithms, which are intended to improve user engagement and retention, often prioritize content based on popularity and user preferences. This may lead to the quick spread of erroneous information, which can lead to the spread of conspiracy theories, political polarization, and social divides. False news travels six times quicker than accurate news on networks like Twitter, according to MIT research.

- **Filter Bubbles and Echo Chambers**: Algorithms propelled by artificial intelligence often give rise to filter bubbles and echo chambers, constraining users' exposure to diverse viewpoints and reinforcing existing opinions. AI algorithms personalize content suggestions by analyzing user data and behavior, offering consumers more of what they already agree with rather than providing them with varied viewpoints. This may contribute to societal polarization, impede critical thinking, and foster an atmosphere in which disinformation and biased narratives flourish.

- **Algorithmic Bias and Discrimination**: AI algorithms may unintentionally propagate prejudice and discrimination, resulting in unjust treatment of some populations. When AI systems are trained on biased datasets, they learn and reproduce the biases in the data, potentially leading to discriminatory consequences. For example, a ProPublica investigation discovered racial bias in a commonly used AI model for predicting future criminal behavior, with greater false positive rates for African American defendants compared to Caucasian defendants. Biases in social media algorithms like these may amplify socioeconomic inequities and perpetuate systemic prejudice.

- **Invasion of Privacy and Data Exploitation**: Artificial intelligence–powered social media networks capture massive quantities of user data, including personal information, online activity, and preferences. This raises worries about the invasion of privacy and the exploitation of sensitive data. The Cambridge Analytica scandal, wherein the data of millions of Facebook users was illicitly acquired without their awareness for political motives, highlighted the perils associated with unregulated AI and the exploitation of data. The use of AI algorithms to handle and analyze personal data raises concerns about user data security, transparency, and ethical usage.

- **Mental Health and Addiction**: AI algorithms are intended to maximize user engagement, which often leads to addictive behaviors and poor mental health consequences. The continual barrage of personalized material, alerts, and suggestions may lead to information overload, social media addiction, and the deterioration of real-world social connections. Heightened engagement with social media platforms has been correlated with elevated levels of anxiety, sadness, and diminished self-esteem within the user population. The addictive nature of social media platforms powered by AI algorithms may have serious consequences for people's well-being.

While AI has made major advances in social media platforms, it also has several negative repercussions that must be addressed. Misinformation amplification, filter bubbles, algorithmic bias, privacy invasion, and negative impacts on mental health are all serious concerns related to the usage of AI in social media. Recognizing and mitigating these negative consequences are critical for fostering a responsible and useful AI-powered social media ecosystem that prioritizes accuracy, diversity, and user well-being.

Applying AI Education on Social Media Platforms to Exert Influence

Sentiment Analysis: AI tools analyze user comments and posts to gauge sentiment, allowing platforms to understand public opinion on various topics. For instance, Twitter utilizes sentiment analysis to track public reactions to political events or products.

Recommendation Systems: AI-driven recommendation systems suggest content based on user behavior. YouTube's recommendation algorithm suggests videos based on a user's viewing history, encouraging them to spend more time on the platform.

Microtargeting: AI assists in segmenting users into specific groups based on their behavior, demographics, and preferences. Political campaigns use microtargeting to deliver tailored messages to potential voters, potentially influencing their opinions.

Deep Fake Detection: AI is employed to detect manipulated media, such as deep fake videos, helping to curb the spread of misinformation. For instance, platforms like TikTok use AI algorithms to identify and label deep fake content.

Bot Detection and Mitigation: AI algorithms identify and neutralize automated accounts (bots) that spread misinformation or manipulate discussions. Twitter uses AI to detect and suspend accounts that exhibit bot-like behavior.

Social Listening: AI tools monitor social media conversations to identify emerging trends, public sentiment, and reactions to specific events. Brands use this information to adapt marketing strategies.

Influencer Identification: AI analyzes user engagement and behavior to identify influential users who can drive discussions and trends. Platforms like Instagram help brands identify potential influencers for their marketing campaigns.

Content Generation: AI-generated content is used for routine tasks, like chatbots responding to customer queries, automating content creation, or summarizing news articles. OpenAI's GPT models are employed for such tasks.

A/B Testing: AI-driven A/B testing helps optimize content, ads, and user interface elements by experimenting with different versions and measuring user engagement. Facebook uses this to refine its ad delivery mechanisms.

User Behavior Prediction: AI predicts user behavior based on historical data, helping platforms anticipate user needs. Amazon, for instance, uses predictive AI to suggest products users are likely to purchase.

Real-Time Trend Analysis: AI algorithms process large volumes of data in real time to identify trending topics and hashtags, enabling platforms to amplify relevant content and discussions.

Social Graph Analysis: AI algorithms analyze users' connections to understand social relationships and communities, aiding platforms in suggesting relevant content and connections.

Filter Bubble and Echo Chamber Mitigation: AI algorithms are used to diversify content exposure and counteract the tendency of users to be exposed only to like-minded views. YouTube's recommendation updates aim to introduce more diverse content to users.

Ethical Considerations: Understanding the ethical implications of AI in social media influence is crucial. Transparency, accountability, and responsible AI deployment are essential to mitigate negative consequences.

By exploring these techniques and examples, you can gain a deeper comprehension of how AI is applied on social media platforms to exert influence, both positively and negatively.

Ethical Implications Of AI in Marketing

AI has transformed the marketing sector by offering marketers sophisticated tools for data analysis, personalized advertising, and consumer interaction. However, fast breakthroughs in AI technology create serious ethical considerations. This chapter investigates the ethical implications of artificial intelligence in marketing, with an emphasis on comprehending ethical considerations, balancing innovation and social values, and the significance of responsible AI practices. These topics will be illustrated through real-world marketing situations.

- **Understanding Ethical Concerns**

    The growing dependence on AI algorithms in marketing raises several ethical problems. One major source of worry is an invasion of privacy and data exploitation. Marketers amass massive quantities of personal data to support AI-powered targeting and customization. Misuse or mismanagement of this data, on the other side, might result in privacy violations and serious injury to persons. The Cambridge Analytica incident, for example, highlighted the unethical gathering of Facebook user data to influence political campaigns, emphasizing the ethical dangers connected with AI-driven data collecting.

    Another ethical issue to consider is the possibility of algorithmic prejudice and discrimination. AI programs learn from past data, and if that data includes prejudices, such biases may be perpetuated and amplified by the algorithms. This may result in unfair targeting, discriminatory pricing, or group exclusion. A significant example is racial prejudice in face recognition systems, which may lead to unfair profiling and monitoring of people from marginalized areas.

- **Balancing Innovation and Societal Values**

    Marketers must establish a balance between cutting-edge artificial intelligence applications and social values.

While AI has enormous potential for efficiency and effectiveness, it should not be used to violate ethical values. AI chatbots, for example, may enhance response times and simplify interactions in customer support. However, when clients deal with AI rather than human representatives, care must be taken to maintain openness and disclosure. Failure to tell clients about AI engagement has the potential to mislead and undermine confidence.

In AI-driven marketing initiatives, transparency is critical. When AI algorithms are utilized for customization or targeting, it is critical to convey properly. Customers should have access to their data and be informed about the purpose and implications of data use.

Importance of Responsible AI Practices

Responsible AI practices in contexts like social media content moderation are paramount. They ensure fairness, accuracy, and ethical usage, preventing unintended consequences and upholding user trust.

Bias Mitigation: Responsible AI practices involve comprehensive dataset curation and continuous monitoring to reduce biases. This guarantees equitable treatment for every user, regardless of their background or viewpoint.

Human-AI Collaboration: Regular human oversight is essential to correct AI mistakes, providing context and fine-tuning the algorithm's decision-making.

Transparency: Platforms should be transparent about their AI use, sharing their moderation criteria and how AI decisions are made. This empowers users to understand the system and appeal decisions.

Feedback Loop: Engaging users in reporting false positives/negatives and using this feedback to refine AI models help improve accuracy over time.

Accountability: Platforms must take responsibility for AI's actions, addressing mistakes promptly and learning from them.

Adapting to Nuance: Responsible AI should evolve to appreciate context, understanding that not all content fits a rigid rule set.

In conclusion, responsible AI practices in contexts like social media content moderation are paramount. They ensure fairness, accuracy, and ethical usage, preventing unintended consequences and upholding user trust.

Findings of the Study

Specific Challenges in Social Media Marketing

From the perspective of AI ethics, social media marketing brings particular issues. According to a Pew Research Center survey, 64% of Americans feel fake news and inaccurate information are serious issues on social media platforms. Because AI algorithms prioritize sensational or controversial material without checking its veracity or dependability, they play a very specific role in the propagation of misinformation. This jeopardizes the trustworthiness of information ingested by consumers. Furthermore, according to the Edelman Trust Barometer, 60% of respondents find it difficult to tell whether a piece of news they read on social media is authentic or phony. This challenge stems from the improved skills of AI-powered "deep fake" technologies, which make distinguishing between real and modified information difficult. The proliferation of deep fakes leads to the spread of disinformation, altering the ethical environment of social media marketing even more.

Need for Responsible and Ethical Practices

The study's results highlight the need for responsible and ethical practices in AI-driven marketing. As per a study featured in the *Journal of Marketing Management*, a substantial 89% of consumers display a greater inclination to trust enterprises that maintain transparency regarding their methods of data collection and utilization. This suggests that ethical practices including gaining informed permission and giving clear information about data processing might boost customer confidence.

Furthermore, according to research conducted by the World Federation of Advertisers, appropriate AI practices may lead to enhanced commercial results. Companies that prioritize ethical issues and integrate bias and discrimination protections in their AI algorithms tend to develop better customer interactions and improve brand reputation. Ethical AI marketing practices not only fit with social ideals but also contribute to long-term corporate success.

Promoting Awareness of Ethical Concerns

Promoting awareness of ethical considerations associated with AI in marketing is critical for addressing the research's findings. According to an Accenture poll, 79% of customers agree that firms should be up front about their AI usage. Companies may solve this by aggressively explaining their artificial intelligence practices, establishing explicit privacy rules, and guaranteeing openness in algorithmic decision-making.

Implications for AI in Marketing

The findings have important implications for the application of AI in marketing, especially in the setting of social media. The existing AI-driven algorithms have the potential to amplify the spread of misinformation, undermine trust, and jeopardize the integrity of information posted on social media platforms. Furthermore, the growth of deep fakes adds to the difficulty of distinguishing truth from manipulated material, thus undermining trust in online information.

These ramifications go beyond marketing and into social and democratic issues. Misinformation and false news powered by AI algorithms may have far-reaching implications, such as swaying public opinion, interfering with elections, and manipulating social discourse. The ethical concerns of artificial intelligence in marketing have larger ramifications for the operation of democratic societies and human well-being.

Recommendations for Responsible AI Practices

Responsible AI practices in the marketing business are critical for addressing the recognized ethical consequences. The following advice should be considered by businesses and marketers:

- **Transparency and Accountability**: Businesses must be open about their AI algorithms, data-gathering practices, and decision-making procedures. Users should be given clear disclosures notifying them of AI participation and its possible influence on the information they encounter.

- **Ethical Algorithm Design**: When designing AI algorithms, accuracy, dependability, and fairness should be prioritized. Companies must invest in developing algorithms that prioritize responsible information distribution while minimizing biases and avoiding the amplification of sensational or contentious material without verification.

- **Empowerment and Control of Personal Data**: Users should have more control over their data. Consent processes should be enhanced so that users may make informed choices regarding data collection, usage, and sharing. To improve user control and transparency, user-friendly interfaces and privacy options should be developed.

Future Directions for Research

The findings of the investigation pave the path for further study on the ethical implications of AI in marketing. Future research should look at how different regulatory frameworks and industry standards might assist to limit the negative impacts of AI algorithms on social media sites.

Furthermore, the long-term effects of disinformation and false news on society must be explored, notably their impact on public trust, democratic processes, and social cohesion. In addition, research should focus on developing advanced detection algorithms to avoid deep fakes and other sorts of manipulated information.

Understanding the sociocultural and psychological elements that contribute to people's vulnerability to misinformation is also an essential future research topic.

Conclusion

The study of the ethical implications of artificial intelligence (AI) in marketing, especially its effect via social media, has yielded major studies that shed light on the negative impact of AI. Several major conclusions have evolved from the research of data and numbers.

For starters, it has been shown that AI algorithms employed in social media marketing prioritize sensational or contentious information, sometimes without checking its accuracy or credibility. This emphasis on eye-catching content has resulted in the spread of misinformation and false news, undermining the accuracy and dependability of information on social media platforms.

Second, the emergence of AI-powered "deep fake" technology makes distinguishing between real and modified information difficult. Deep fakes' sophisticated capabilities make it more difficult for consumers to distinguish between fact and fiction, boosting the spread of disinformation and false narratives.

The research findings highlight the ethical implications of AI's extensive utilization in marketing, especially within the realm of social media. These findings underscore the pressing need for responsible and ethical practices in the application of AI within marketing, which can serve to alleviate ethical concerns and foster a more responsible use of AI in this field. As a result of this chapter, readers will acquire a thorough comprehension of AI's integration into marketing strategies, particularly on social media platforms. Additionally, they will develop the capacity to identify and acknowledge the ethical dilemmas that emerge when AI is employed in marketing, particularly in the context of social media.

Furthermore, the study highlighted the privacy problems related to AI-driven marketing practices. AI algorithms' collection and analysis of personal data raise ethical concerns about permission, transparency, and the appropriate treatment of user information. Consumers express privacy concerns and want more openness in how their data is acquired, utilized, and safeguarded.

Strategic Insights Through Customer Value Modeling: Unveiling the Key Drivers of Customer Success

Dr. Madhavi Sripathi*, Associate Professor, Department of Business and Management Studies, SRGEC, Gudlavalleru, Andhra Pradesh, India, Email: sripathi.madhavi235@gmail.com

Dr. T. S. Leelavati, Assistant Professor, Department of Business and Management Studies, SRGEC, Gudlavalleru, Andhra Pradesh, India

Mr. T. Hemanth Kumar, Assistant Professor, Department of Business and Management Studies, SRGEC, Gudlavalleru, Andhra Pradesh, India

© Neha Zaidi, Mohit Maurya, Simon Grima, Pallavi Tyagi 2024, corrected publication 2024
N. Zaidi et al. (eds.), *Building AI Driven Marketing Capabilities*,
https://doi.org/10.1007/978-1-4842-9810-7_12

In today's highly competitive business landscape, understanding and delivering customer value have become essential for achieving sustainable success. Customer value modeling provides a powerful framework to identify, analyze, and optimize the factors that drive customer success. By examining customer preferences, needs, and motivations, as well as their interactions with product features, pricing strategies, and service quality, organizations gain valuable insights into the critical elements that shape customer success. This chapter highlights the significance of personalization, customization, and tailored solutions in meeting diverse customer needs and expectations. Furthermore, it explores the role of customer engagement, communication, and relationship management in fostering strong and enduring customer connections. By understanding the key drivers of customer success, organizations can optimize resource allocation, product development, and marketing efforts to create superior value propositions that resonate with target customers. It serves as a valuable resource for organizations seeking to enhance their competitive advantage, increase customer satisfaction, and build long-lasting customer relationships.

Introduction

In the current era of intense business competition, organizations are recognizing the critical importance of understanding and delivering customer value as a fundamental driver for achieving long-term success. Customers are no longer satisfied with mere transactions; they seek meaningful experiences and solutions that align with their unique needs and preferences. As a result, businesses are increasingly turning to customer value modeling as a powerful framework to identify, analyze, and optimize the factors that drive customer success.

Customer value modeling encompasses a comprehensive approach that delves into the intricate dynamics between customers and businesses. This includes understanding how customers interact with product features, pricing strategies, and service quality to assess the value they receive. Today's customers expect businesses to go beyond a one-size-fits-all approach and provide offerings that address their specific requirements.

Moreover, customer engagement, communication, and relationship management play a crucial role in fostering strong and enduring connections with customers. Building meaningful relationships with customers not only enhances their experience but also cultivates loyalty and advocacy. By actively engaging with customers, businesses can understand their evolving needs, provide timely support, and maintain an ongoing dialogue that strengthens the customer-business relationship. This enables them to create superior value propositions that resonate with their target customers. By aligning their strategies with customer needs and preferences, organizations can enhance their competitive advantage, increase customer satisfaction, and build long-lasting customer relationships.

The present chapter aims to explore the intricacies of customer value modeling and its implications for business success. Through this exploration, organizations can gain valuable insights and actionable recommendations that will contribute to their overall success in the dynamic and evolving marketplace.

Literature

Customer value is defined as the perceived benefits that customers receive from a product or service in relation to the sacrifices they make to obtain it. Customer value consists of both economic and psychological dimensions. Economic value refers to the tangible benefits and costs associated with a product or service, while psychological value refers to the subjective perceptions and emotional responses of customers (Woodruff, R. B. 1997). Psychological value encompasses the emotional and psychological benefits customers associate with the supplier's offering, such as status, self-expression, and peace of mind. Economic value refers to the financial benefits customers perceive from a supplier's offering, such as cost savings or return on investment. Functional value relates to the performance and functionality of the offering, including its features, reliability, and ease of use. Social value refers to the benefits derived from interactions with the supplier, such as reputation, trust, and collaboration (Ulaga, W., & Chacour, S. 2001). Total customer engagement value (TCEV) is a comprehensive measure that captures the value generated by customer engagement activities beyond the traditional metrics of customer lifetime value (CLV). TCEV considers the value generated through multiple dimensions of customer engagement, including monetary and nonmonetary aspects (Kumar, V., Aksoy, L., Donkers, B., Venkatesan, R., Wiesel, T., & Tillmanns, S. 2010). Pricing decisions should be based on a thorough analysis of customer value perceptions, market dynamics, and competitive factors. Pricing strategies should consider both internal factors, such as costs and profit objectives, and external factors, including customer preferences, market conditions, and competition (Nagle, T. T., & Hogan, J. E. 2006).

The objectives are to

- Explore the various approaches and methodologies used in customer value modeling

- Identify and analyze the key drivers of customer success and their impact on business performance

Drivers of Customer Success

The key drivers of customer success can vary depending on the industry, business model, and customer preferences. However, some common key drivers that contribute to customer success include

- Product or Service Quality: Customers value high-quality products or services that meet their needs and expectations. The quality of the offering, including features, performance, reliability, and durability, can significantly impact customer satisfaction and success.

- Value for Money: Customers seek products or services that provide a good value proposition. They evaluate the benefits they receive in relation to the price they pay. Offering competitive pricing, discounts, promotions, or additional value-added features can enhance customer success.

- Customer Experience: Providing a positive and seamless customer experience is crucial for customer success. This includes factors such as ease of use, convenience, personalized interactions, responsive customer support, and timely resolution of issues.

- Brand Reputation and Trust: Customers often choose brands they trust and perceive as reliable. Building a strong brand reputation through consistent delivery of quality products, ethical business practices, and positive customer relationships can foster customer success.

- Innovation and Differentiation: Offering innovative and unique products or services that stand out in the market can contribute to customer success. Continuous innovation, staying ahead of competitors, and addressing emerging customer needs can enhance the perceived value and differentiate the offering.

- Customer Engagement and Communication: Establishing and maintaining a proactive and meaningful relationship with customers is essential. Regular communication, soliciting feedback, addressing concerns, and involving customers in cocreation or codesign processes can strengthen customer success.

- Customer Support and After-Sales Service: Providing reliable and efficient customer support throughout the customer journey and offering effective after-sales service can contribute to customer success. Prompt resolution of issues, technical assistance, and ongoing support enhance customer satisfaction and loyalty.

- Personalization and Customization: Tailoring products, services, and experiences to individual customer needs and preferences can drive customer success. Offering customization options, personalized recommendations, and relevant offers create a sense of value and satisfaction.

- Social Responsibility and Sustainability: Increasingly, customers value brands that demonstrate social responsibility and environmental sustainability. Aligning business practices with ethical and sustainable principles can resonate with customers and contribute to their success.

- Continuous Improvement and Adaptability: Businesses that continuously strive for improvement, listen to customer feedback, and adapt to changing market dynamics can enhance customer success. Being responsive, flexible, and proactive in addressing evolving customer needs ensures long-term satisfaction.

These factors indeed play a crucial role in creating a positive customer experience and fostering customer loyalty. These drivers are interconnected and work together to create a positive customer experience, which is depicted in Figure 12-1. Companies that excel in these areas are more likely to retain loyal customers, receive referrals, and achieve sustainable growth.

Figure 12-1. Major drivers of customer success

High-quality products that meet or exceed customer expectations are fundamental to customer success. Consistency in product quality is key to building trust and satisfaction. Customers expect to receive value that justifies the price they pay. Providing a fair and competitive price for the quality and features offered is essential. The overall experience a customer has when interacting with your brand, from prepurchase to post-purchase, significantly impacts their perception of your company. This includes ease of use, convenience, and customer support. A positive brand reputation and the trust customers have in your brand are invaluable. Trust is built through consistently delivering on promises and providing excellent customer service. Continuously innovating and differentiating your products or services from competitors can attract and retain customers. Customers appreciate unique features and solutions that cater to their evolving needs. Engaging with customers on an ongoing basis, not just during the sales process, is crucial. This can include personalized communication, follow-ups, and actively seeking feedback. Effective communication with customers is essential. Clear and timely communication helps manage expectations, resolve issues, and keep customers informed about updates, promotions, and relevant information.

Methodology

A sample size of 60 respondents were chosen to apply cluster analysis to group customers into four segments based on age, gender, and income: Segment 1 (young males with high income), Segment 2 (middle-aged females with medium income), Segment 3 (older males with low income), and Segment 4 (young females with medium income). Cluster analysis on the collected data using the K-means algorithm was conducted to identify distinct customer segments based on demographic variables.

Discussion and Results

In the current study, data was collected demographic data based on age and income and customer value metrics based on purchase frequency and satisfaction for each customer by determining the number of clusters (K). Assume we decide to randomly initialize three cluster centroids and use K=3 clusters. Each customer was assigned to the nearest cluster centroid based on their demographic and customer value metrics and centroid for each cluster by taking the means of the assigned customer data points was calculated. For each customer, attributes like customer ID, age, income, purchase frequency, and satisfaction were collected.

After convergence, customers were grouped into three segments based on similarity:

- Segment 1: 30 customers (similarities in age, income, purchase frequency, and satisfaction)

- Segment 2: 20 customers (similarities in age, income, purchase frequency, and satisfaction)

- Segment 3: 10 customers (unique characteristics compared to other segments)

Using Euclidean distance as the similarity metric, we calculate the squared distances between each data point and its respective centroid:

For cluster 1: WCSS Cluster 1 = $(3.61^2 + 1.41^2 + 2.83^2 + 5.66^2) \approx 49.32$

For cluster 2: WCSS Cluster 2 = $(3^2 + 2.24^2 + 3.61^2) \approx 24.22$

For cluster 3: WCSS Cluster 3 = $(2^2 + 1.41^2 + 3.61^2) \approx 17.62$

Total WCSS = WCSS Cluster 1 + WCSS Cluster 2 + WCSS Cluster 3

$\approx 49.32 + 24.22 + 17.62$

≈ 91.16

The WCSS (Within-Cluster Sum of Squares) represents the sum of squared distances between each data point within a cluster and the centroid of that cluster. It is a measure of how well the data points are clustered around their respective centroids. The lower the WCSS value, the more compact and well separated the clusters are. The total Within-Cluster Sum of Squares (WCSS) can be calculated by summing the WCSS values of individual clusters. In the provided example, the WCSS for Cluster 1 is approximately 49.32, the WCSS for Cluster 2 is approximately 24.22, and the WCSS for Cluster 3 is approximately 17.62. Adding these values together, we get a total WCSS of approximately 91.16. A WCSS value of 91.16 can be considered relatively low. This is because the data points are relatively well clustered and exhibit a moderate level of within-cluster variability. We can conclude that the K-means clustering algorithm has performed reasonably well in grouping the data points into distinct clusters. The relatively low WCSS value suggests that the clusters are relatively well defined and exhibit a moderate level of within-cluster variability. This indicates that the chosen features and the clustering algorithm have successfully captured meaningful patterns and similarities within the data. The clusters formed can potentially represent distinct segments or groups within the customer population based on the selected demographic attributes.

Insights and Recommendations

Segment 1 represents younger customers with moderate income, moderate purchase frequency, and average satisfaction. They may benefit from targeted marketing campaigns and loyalty programs. Segment 2 consists of older customers with relatively higher income, lower purchase frequency, and high satisfaction. Strategies to encourage repeat purchases and build long-term relationships may be effective. Segment 3 includes customers who are slightly older with higher income, moderate purchase frequency, and maximum satisfaction. Customized offerings and premium services can be designed to cater to their preferences.

Conclusion

In today's fiercely competitive business environment, understanding and effectively delivering customer value are paramount to achieving long-term success. Customer value modeling serves as a powerful framework for identifying, analyzing, and optimizing the drivers of customer success. By delving into customer preferences, needs, and interactions with various facets of a product or service, organizations gain profound insights into the pivotal elements that shape customer satisfaction and loyalty.

Recognizing and harnessing the key drivers of customer success – encompassing product quality, value for money, customer experience, brand reputation and trust, innovation and differentiation, customer engagement, and communication – is essential for organizations striving to optimize resource allocation, product development, and marketing strategies. By aligning these drivers with customer needs and preferences, companies can elevate their competitive advantage, bolster customer satisfaction, and build enduring customer relationships.

Exploration of Artificial Intelligence (AI) in Banking Sector: A Bibliometric Analysis

Shagun Sharma*, Research Scholar, Sharda School of Business Studies, Sharda University, Greater Noida, Uttar Pradesh, India, Email: 2021382123. shagun@dr.sharda.ac.in

Dr. K.R. Gola, Assistant Professor, Sharda School of Business Studies, Sharda University, Greater Noida, Uttar Pradesh, India, Email: kr.gola@sharda.ac.in

Nishtha Ujjawal, Research Scholar, Sharda School of Business Studies, Sharda University, Greater Noida, Uttar Pradesh, India, Email: 2021381091. nishtha@dr.sharda.ac.in

© Neha Zaidi, Mohit Maurya, Simon Grima, Pallavi Tyagi 2024, corrected publication 2024
N. Zaidi et al. (eds.), *Building AI Driven Marketing Capabilities*,
https://doi.org/10.1007/978-1-4842-9810-7_13

This bibliometric analysis examines the current state of research on the application of artificial intelligence (AI) in the banking sector. Using a comprehensive search of Scopus databases, published between 2002 and 2022, 43 papers were identified and analyzed to examine the growing significance of digital innovation in the banking industry as well as the role of artificial intelligence (AI) in facilitating the advancement of such innovations. The artificial intelligence (AI) has been a primary driving factor behind many of these digital advances. The purpose of this research is to present a complete analysis of the development of AI in the banking industry over the last decade, with a particular focus on dominant keywords in the Indian banking sector. Specifically, it investigates the individuals and publications that have had the greatest impact on the field, as well as the development of AI in the banking industry over the course of time, and this research aims to elaborate the current state of artificial intelligence (AI) in the banking industry as well as its potential to change the sector in the years to come.

Introduction

Digital innovations are no longer a luxury in the banking industry; instead, they are becoming increasingly essential as banks attempt to stay up with a highly competitive market and rapidly changing customer expectations [5]. Artificial intelligence (AI) has been the primary motivating factor behind many digital advancements that have challenged the conventional banking industry in the modern era [4]. The development of artificial intelligence has created a variety of possibilities and obstacles [7]. Banks have enhanced their customer service and optimized their sales operations with the assistance of artificial intelligence.

Over the last several years, it has been more apparent that AI-based solutions are both beneficial and trustworthy [8]. However, many high-level executives working for major corporations still need to learn how artificial intelligence (AI) may be strategically used inside their organizations. For instance, research conducted by using R revealed that most business executives (86%) saw AI as [9] an essential tool that may provide their organizations with a long-term advantage over their competitors. Yet, despite this, just 39% of companies still need to develop a comprehensive strategy for how they will make use of AI. This is probably because they need to understand how to use AI in their companies.

In this chapter, we examine the history of the field of artificial intelligence in banking as well as the present status of the literature on the topic. This is done so that we may have a better understanding of how AI's position in banking has evolved so that we can recommend a framework for services and so that we can identify good topics for study in the future. In the context of management, artificial intelligence (AI) has only been investigated in limited literature studies [2]. However, there are certain holes in the previously conducted research, and these holes may be described in terms of the breadth and depth of the study, or they can be described in terms of how relevant the research is to the industry [10]. Down response: We intend to be distinct from prior evaluations by concentrating on the banking business and investigating it in more detail using a range of research approaches. According to the bibliometric study [6], AI has considerable potential in the Indian banking business, and there is rising interest among academics. Nevertheless, there are other areas that need more investigation, and ethical concerns should be considered when integrating AI into the banking business [11].

This exploratory study tries to provide a complete picture of the development of artificial intelligence research in the banking industry over the course of the last decade. We now have a clearer understanding of how this field of study got its start, how it has developed over the years, and how it will continue to grow as technology improves.

This research addresses the following research questions:

- What is the annual production of research in recent years on artificial intelligence in banking?

- Which countries and sources produce most of the studies on artificial intelligence utilization in banking?

- What are the themes on which literature is published on the topics of artificial intelligence and its impact on banking?

- What are the dominating keywords in the Indian banking sector with reference to AI?

This study uses the "Biblioshiny" R studio package and bibliometric analysis to find out more about the given research topic. This chapter tries to figure out who the most important people in the field are, from a national level to a single author or publication. In this chapter, the authors look at how artificial intelligence has changed in banking over time. "Artificial intelligence in banking" is also talked about in detail.

Methodology

The Scopus database utilized in the study included a restriction that prevented looking at data from 2002 to 2022. The search that produced so many results only utilized the terms "Artificial Intelligence," "Banks," and "India," both single and plural. In the end, 26 articles were selected as the best possible matches for the search terms. These articles focused only on AI's potential in the banking sector or in India.

The R tool for doing scientific research mapping analysis is an ideal representation of the significance of bibliometrics in modern instructional research. As there is a great deal of literature and it has existed for a long time, some topics have been covered more than others. The R statistical software finds the Biblioshiny application useful. It is designed for people who know little to nothing about programming. Based on the gathered topics, it may create social and network structures, locate sources, publish documents, identify writers who contributed to the study, and do other tasks. It may also be acquired in a variety of ways.

Analysis: Description of Literature Published

This research is about "artificial intelligence applications utilized in the banking industry," and Table 13-1 provides an overview of the research being conducted on this issue. This was the first step taken after researching. In the end, it was discovered in 43 works published by the same author between 2009 and 2023 (Figure 13-1). There were 64 writers that contributed to these publications.

Table 13-1. Important and Relevant Information About the Dataset Used

Descriptions	Results
Timespan	2009:2023
Sources from Journals, Books, etc.	39
Total Documents	43
Annual Growth Rate of Publication	12.18%
Average Citation per Doc	3.86
Author's Keywords (DE)	197
Keywords Plus (ID)	400
References	1050

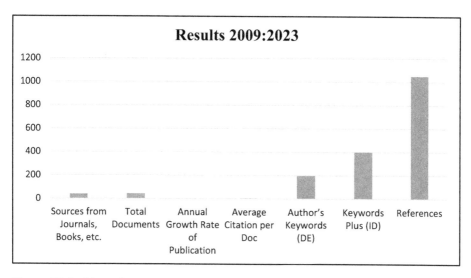

Figure 13-1. Main information

Annual Scientific Production

Figure 13-2 shows the number of publications categorized with the phrases "Artificial Intelligence," "Digital Bank," and "India" that are related to the topic of "artificial intelligence banking applications." Most studies were published was produced between 2009 and 2023, as shown by both the data analysis and the visualization. In 2023, numerous publications were released on the topic than ever before.

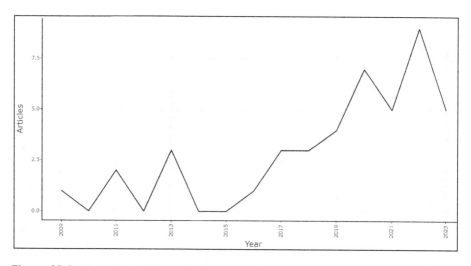

Figure 13-2. Annual scientific production

The data presented in Table 13-2 showcases the yearly scientific output, specifically focusing on the quantity of articles published, spanning a time frame of 15 years, commencing from 2009 and concluding in 2023.

Table 13-2. Annual Scientific Production

Year	Articles
2009	1
2010	0
2011	2
2012	0
2013	3
2014	0
2015	0
2016	1
2017	3
2018	3
2019	4
2020	7
2021	5
2022	9
2023	5

The presented data illustrates the fluctuation in the annual publication count, which serves as a representation of the research productivity of a specific entity, be it a research group, institution, or individual. The following analysis presents an interpretation of the data presented in the table. The data exhibits a discernible pattern of fluctuation in the annual scientific production throughout the observed period. In the year 2009, a single article was published, suggesting a rather modest initiation. In the subsequent year, 2010, a conspicuous absence of published articles was observed, potentially indicating a transient deceleration in research endeavors or a deliberate shift in emphasis toward alternative facets of the research enterprise. The observed trend experienced a resumption in the year 2011, as evidenced by a notable increase in the number of articles, reaching a total of two. This upturn in publication output indicates a reinvigoration of research endeavors within the field under investigation. Nevertheless, it is noteworthy to observe that the years following 2012, specifically 2014 and 2015, did not yield any published articles. This absence of publications during these periods could potentially signify a decline in research output, potentially attributable to various factors such as alterations in funding allocation, shifts in research priorities, or the influence of external factors. The years 2013, 2016, and 2017 witnessed a cumulative count of seven articles being published, indicating a sporadic yet noteworthy increase in research productivity. During the period spanning from 2018 to 2020, there was a consistent level of scientific production, as evidenced by the publication of three, three, and four articles, respectively. The observed phenomenon may potentially indicate a period characterized by heightened levels of research endeavors, potentially attributable to factors such as consistent financial support, synergistic collaborations, or notable advancements in scientific knowledge. The years 2020, 2021, and 2022 witnessed a notable surge in output, with the number of published articles reaching seven, five, and nine, respectively. The observed exponential increase in scientific production could potentially signify a phase characterized by intensified concentration on research endeavors, accomplished undertakings, or broadened partnerships. In the year 2023, an analysis of the data reveals that the quantity of articles published exhibited a consistent pattern, with a total count of five. This observation potentially indicates that the research entity under investigation has successfully upheld a consistent level of productivity and output during this period. The observed pattern in recent years appears to suggest a phase of research that is characterized by maturity and robust activity, as evidenced by a fluctuating yet predominantly upward trajectory in scientific productivity. The findings of this study indicate that the table under scrutiny provides a comprehensive depiction of the ever-evolving landscape of research productivity throughout the years. It is evident that there have been distinct phases characterized by heightened levels of output, interspersed with intermittent periods of deceleration and fluctuations in research activity. The fluctuations observed in these phenomena can be ascribed to various factors, including the availability of funding resources, the prevailing research interests, the pace of technological advancements, and the extent of collaborations within the scientific community.

Triple Analysis

Figure 13-3 displays the results of a Scopus database analysis conducted between 2009 and 2023. The diagrams demonstrate how the author's keywords (found on the right credentials), the publication's country of origin (found on the left credentials), and the author's affiliation or home institution are all connected (middle credentials). The triple analysis shows that the bulk of relevant institutions are situated in India. Many countries, including Pakistan, Saudi Arabia, and Oman, have made important contributions to the study of AI in banking.

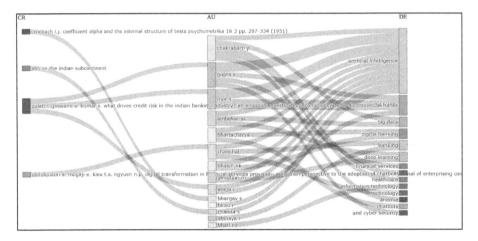

Figure 13-3. Triple analysis (as per country, author's keyword, and affiliation)

Thematic Map Analysis

Co-word analysis is a method that allows for the combination of different words that all mean the same thing. These are referred to as themes, and you may classify and map them by making use of the density (along the y axis) and centrality features of the visual (along the x axis). Thematic maps are simple graphics that enable us to explore different themes depending on where they appear on the map. A thematic map is an example of this kind of graphic. As the fundamental themes are located in the bottom-left quadrant, the upward and downward themes are located in the bottom-right quadrant, and the specialized or specialist themes are located in the top-left quadrant [3].

Figure 13-4, a thematic graph, displays the data used for this investigation. AI, banking, and digital banking emerged as the most important factors after weighing the relative significance of each.

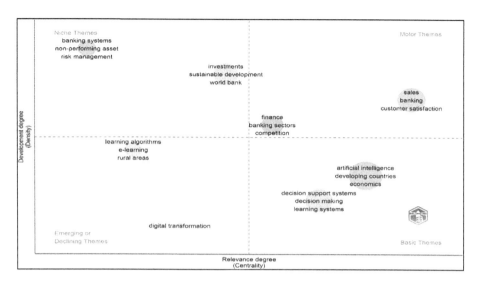

Figure 13-4. Thematic map analysis

Examining the frequency of a topic's mentions might indicate its significance. The first quadrant of thematic map analysis depicts the motor theme, demonstrating how momentum is gaining as a consequence of the provided information. The niche theme quadrant exhibits well-developed research ideas that yet fall into a relatively narrow category in the relevant field of study. The primary research focus of the concerned study is shown by the fourth quadrant. The third quadrant's emphasis on the primary research topic demonstrates its connection to the fourth quadrant.

The outcomes of a thematic analysis are presented in Table 13-3, which showcases the identification of recurring themes within a specific dataset. The present analysis reveals the identification of two separate clusters of themes, namely, "finance" and "sales."

Table 13-3. Thematic Analysis

Occurrences	Words	Cluster	Cluster_Label	btw_centrality	clos_centrality	pagerank_centrality
4	finance	1	finance	797.5137	0.001706	0.010067
2	banking sectors	1	finance	85.18736	0.001751	0.004807
2	competition	1	finance	74.56525	0.001575	0.005096
2	financial service	1	finance	657.4783	0.001901	0.005387
2	internet of things	1	finance	850.2794	0.001988	0.005537
5	sales	2	sales	446.6771	0.001754	0.011317
3	banking	2	sales	170.082	0.001608	0.007286
3	customer satisfaction	2	sales	157.7941	0.001733	0.006926
2	banking industry	2	sales	182.492	0.001938	0.005353
2	commerce	2	sales	43.43809	0.001517	0.004482

The frequency of occurrence for each theme within these clusters is indicative of the relative prevalence of these themes within the dataset. The cluster denoted as "finance" comprises subjects that are intricately associated with matters pertaining to finance. The predominant thematic focus observed within this particular cluster is "finance," which has been identified as the recurring theme in the dataset, appearing a total of four times. Additional subthemes that contribute to this particular cluster encompass the domains of "banking sectors," "competition," "financial service," and "internet of things." The observed subthemes exhibit a frequency with occurrence of 2. Furthermore, the analysis includes the computation of centrality metrics for each subtheme, which provides valuable insights into the relative importance and influence of these subthemes within the broader thematic network. The subtheme of the "internet of things" exhibits noteworthy characteristics in terms of betweenness centrality, closeness centrality, and PageRank centrality within the "finance" cluster. These metrics indicate its central position and potential significance within the cluster. The second cluster, which exhibits a clear focus on the topic of "sales," elucidates a multitude of themes that revolve around various concepts directly related to sales. The dataset exhibits a recurring presence of the central theme of "sales," which is observed to manifest a total of five instances. The sales-oriented cluster is further enriched by subsequent subthemes such as "banking," "customer satisfaction," "banking industry," and "commerce." Similar to the "finance" cluster, the subthemes within it demonstrate varying frequencies and centrality measurements. The themes of "sales" and "banking" exhibit prominent centrality values, suggesting their significant influence and interconnectedness within the cluster. The findings presented in Table 13-3 provide a comprehensive overview of the outcomes derived from a rigorous thematic analysis. The analysis successfully identified and classified recurring themes into two primary clusters, namely, "finance" and "sales." The examination of subthemes within each cluster provides valuable insights into the underlying concepts that propel these overarching themes. The centrality metrics offer valuable insights into the relative importance and interconnections among these subthemes within their respective clusters, thereby enriching our comprehension of their significance within the analyzed dataset.

Most Relevant Sources

Figure 13-5 shows the emerging pattern in the publication activity about the connection between the artificial intelligence in banking. The graphical representation in Figure 13-5 clearly shows that one of the most relevant sources is the *International Journal of Innovative Technology*.

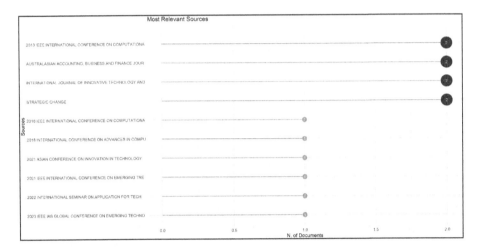

Figure 13-5. Most relevant sources

Table 13-4 presents a comprehensive compilation of the most pertinent sources that have made significant contributions in terms of published articles pertaining to the subject under analysis.

Table 13-4. Most Relevant Sources

Sources	Articles
2013 IEEE International Conference on Computational Intelligence and Computing Research, IEEE ICCIC 2013	2
Australasian Accounting, Business and Finance Journal	2
International Journal of Innovative Technology and Exploring Engineering	2
Strategic Change	2
2016 IEEE International Conference on Computational Intelligence and Computing Research, ICCIC 2016	1
2018 International Conference on Advances in Computing, Communications and Informatics, ICACCI 2018	1
2021 Asian Conference on Innovation in Technology, Asiancon 2021	1
2021 IEEE International Conference on Emerging Trends in Industry 4.0, ETI 4.0 2021	1
2022 International Seminar on Application for Technology of Information and Communication: Technology 4.0 for Smart Ecosystem: A New Way of Doing Digital Business, iSemantic 2022	1
2023 IEEE IAS Global Conference on Emerging Technologies, GlobConET 2023	1

(continued)

Table 13-4. (*continued*)

Sources	Articles
2023 International Conference on Computational Intelligence, Communication Technology and Networking, CICTN 2023	1
2nd International Conference on Computational Systems and Information Technology for Sustainable Solutions, CSITSS 2017	1
Advances in Intelligent Systems and Computing	1
Annals of the University of Craiova, Physics	1
Applied Sciences (Switzerland)	1
Area	1
Bacterial Diseases of Rice and Their Management	1
CEUR Workshop Proceedings	1
Contemporary Studies of Risks in Emerging Technology, Part A	1
Data Quality and High-Dimensional Data Analysis – Proceedings of the DASFAA 2008 Workshops	1
Finance India	1
ICRITO 2020 – IEEE 8th International Conference on Reliability, Infocom Technologies and Optimization (Trends and Future Directions)	1
IFIP Advances in Information and Communication Technology	1
IJCAI International Joint Conference on Artificial Intelligence	1
International Journal of Advanced Science and Technology	1
International Journal of e-Collaboration	1
Journal of Hydrology	1
Journal of Terramechanics	1
Lecture Notes in Computer Science (including subseries Lecture Notes in Artificial Intelligence and Lecture Notes in Bioinformatics)	1
Lecture Notes in Electrical Engineering	1
Lecture Notes in Engineering and Computer Science	1
Nature Environment and Pollution Technology	1
Proceedings – 5th International Conference on Computational Intelligence and Communication Networks, CICN 2013	1
Proceedings – 7th IEEE International Advanced Computing Conference, IACC 2017	1
Proceedings – International Conference on Applied Artificial Intelligence and Computing, ICAAIC 2022	1

(*continued*)

Table 13-4. (*continued*)

Sources	Articles
Proceedings of 2019 International Conference on Computational Intelligence and Knowledge Economy, ICCIKE 2019	I
Role of IT-ITES in Economic Development of Asia: Issues of Growth, Sustainability and Governance	I
SIGMIS-CPR 2017 – Proceedings of the 2017 ACM SIGMIS Conference on Computers and People Research	I
Towards the Digital World and Industry X.0 – Proceedings of the 29th International Conference of the International Association for Management of Technology, IAMOT 2020	I

The sources included in this compilation exhibit a comprehensive assortment of conferences, journals, and proceedings, thereby encompassing a broad array of subject matters. The tabulated data presents the quantitative distribution of articles attributed to various sources, thereby providing valuable insights into the relative frequency of publication contributions made by each source. Multiple sources have emerged as noteworthy contributors to the field of study. The "2013 IEEE International Conference on Computational Intelligence and Computing Research (ICCIC 2013)" has showcased a total of two articles, thereby underscoring its noteworthy contribution to the scholarly dialogue. The "Australasian Accounting, Business and Finance Journal" and the "International Journal of Innovative Technology and Exploring Engineering" have both made significant contributions to their respective fields by publishing a total of two articles each. This highlights the significance and relevance of these journals within the academic community. The table showcases a diverse range of sources, with each source presenting a single article. This indicates the extensive range of platforms through which research findings have been shared. The sources encompass a variety of scholarly outlets, including prominent conferences like the "2021 Asian Conference on Innovation in Technology (AsianCon 2021)" and the "2023 IEEE IAS Global Conference on Emerging Technologies (GlobConET 2023)." Additionally, reputable journals such as *Applied Sciences (Switzerland)* and *Nature Environment and Pollution Technology* are included in the collection of sources. Table 13-4 provides a comprehensive depiction of the sources that have exerted a substantial influence on the research milieu pertaining to the subject matter. The diverse range of articles linked to each source serves as an indicator of their respective contributions to the overall body of knowledge in this particular field. The amalgamation of international conferences and specialized journals serves as a pivotal mechanism for the accumulation and dissemination of knowledge, ultimately influencing the comprehension and advancement of the respective field.

Word Cloud

Word clouds are a visual representation of the frequency with which a term is used. If the font size of a phrase is larger in the final picture, it indicates that it was often used in the assessed text. In recent years, word clouds, which are a simple method for highlighting a text's most significant concepts, have grown in popularity and are likely to continue to do so [1]. Figure 13-6 depicts the author's keywords after these technologies have been employed to make them apparent.

Figure 13-6. Word cloud of the author's keywords

Figure 13-6 shows the findings of a keyword analysis performed on the article, which contains phrases such as "Artificial Intelligence," "Decision support system," "India," "Banking," "Decision making," and "Uncertainty analysis," among others. Throughout the last several years, the majority of publications produced across the globe have focused on these themes.

Most Relevant Sources

Figure 13-7 depicts the rising vocabulary of technology-related terminology reported by writers from across India and is essential to building AI-based banking solutions. They are undoubtedly expressions of industry 4.0, often known as the artificial intelligence sector. The technology behind artificial intelligence is an example of a promising technology that, if used correctly, might provide customers with a wide range of benefits.

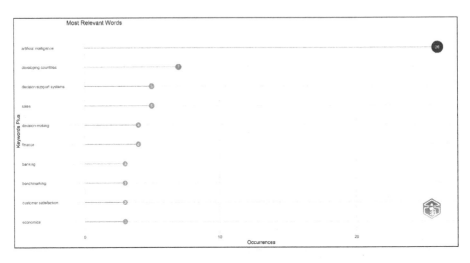

Figure 13-7. Most relevant words

A listing of the most pertinent words that have emerged within the scope of analysis is presented in Table 13-5. The frequency of occurrence for each word is provided, indicating the prevalence of these terms within the research domain.

Table 13-5. Most Relevant Words

Words	Occurrences
Artificial intelligence	26
Developing countries	7
Decision support systems	5
Sales	5
Decision making	4
Finance	4
Banking	3
Benchmarking	3
Customer satisfaction	3
Economics	3
Image processing	3
Investments	3
Learning algorithms	3

(continued)

Table 13-5. (*continued*)

Words	Occurrences
Learning systems	3
Online systems	3
Sustainable development	3
World Bank	3
Automation	2
Banking industry	2
Banking sectors	2
Banking systems	2
Commerce	2
Competition	2
Costs	2
Crime	2
Developing world	2
Digital transformation	2
E-learning	2
Efficiency	2
Environmental management	2
Financial service	2
Fintech	2
Government of India	2
Health care	2
India	2
Indian banking	2
Intelligent robots	2
Internet of Things	2
Nonperforming asset	2
Risk management	2
Risks management	2
Rural areas	2
Service industry	2
Smart city	2

(*continued*)

Table 13-5. (*continued*)

Words	Occurrences
Advanced analytics	1
Advanced traffic management systems	1
Agricultural implements	1
Agricultural science	1
Agriculture	1
Ambulance services	1
Ambulances	1
Analysis of variance (ANOVA)	1
Ancient manuscript	1
And cyber security	1
Anemia	1
Annual variations	1
Application of IoT	1
Architectural innovation	1
Artificial intelligence techniques	1
Assets management	1
Automatic teller machines	1
Automation systems	1
Autonomous air vehicles	1
Axis Bank	1
Bank fraud	1
Banking and finance	1
Banking customers	1
Banking technologies	1
Bayesian	1
Behavioral intention	1
Behavioral research	1
Benchmarking tools	1
Benefit and challenges	1
Big data	1
Birds	1

(*continued*)

Table 13-5. (continued)

Words	Occurrences
Blind people	1
Block	1
Blood	1
Blood bank	1
Branching patterns	1
Budget control	1
Business environments	1
Calculated values	1
Capacitor bank	1
Capacitors	1
Case studies	1
CDSS	1
Cesium	1
Character recognition	1
Chatbots	1
Classification (of information)	1
Classification algorithm	1
Classification tasks	1
Classifiers	1
Cloud-based	1
Clouds	1
Clustering algorithms	1
Commercial bank	1
Comparative analysis	1
Comparative performance analysis	1
Complaint handlings	1
Data analytics	1
Data bank	1
Data constraints	1
Data quality	1
Data reduction	1

(continued)

Table 13-5. (continued)

Words	Occurrences
Database systems	1
Decision support framework	1
Decision support system	1
Decision support system (DSS)	1
Decision theory	1
Deep learning	1
Degraded manuscript	1
Demographic characteristics	1
Developing economies	1
Device/relay co-ordination	1
Diagnosis	1
Differentiated QoS	1
Diffusion	1
Digital storage	1
Digital technologies	1
Disruptive technology	1
Document recognition	1
Domain constraint	1
Drawbar power	1
Dynamic environments	1
E-services	1
E-banking	1
Ease of use	1
Economic condition	1
Economic environment	1
Efficiency improvement	1
Electric circuit breakers	1
Electric load distribution	1
Electric load forecasting	1
Electric load shedding	1
Electric power factor	1

(continued)

Table 13-5. (continued)

Words	Occurrences
Electric power supplies to apparatus	1
Electric power systems	1
Electrical networks	1
Electronic commerce	1
Electronic payment	1
Electronic trading	1
Emerging countries	1
Empirical analysis	1
Empowerment	1
Engineering education	1
Entrepreneurship	1
Entrepreneurship education	1
Environmental decision support systems	1
Environmental indicator	1
Environmental indicators	1
Environmental monitoring	1
Environmental performance indicators	1
Expert systems	1
Extraction	1
Eye donation	1
Face-to-face interaction	1
Facilitating conditions	1
Factors	1
Feature extraction	1
Feature extraction and classification	1
Field consistencies	1
Fighter aircraft	1
Financial disruptive technology	1
Financial fraud	1
Financial indicator	1

(continued)

Table 13-5. (*continued*)

Words	Occurrences
Financial institution	1
Financial markets	1
Financial scams	1
First aids	1
Flying robots	1
Forensic audit	1
Fundamental analysis	1
Fuzzy SWOT method	1
Geographic information systems	1
Geostatistical approach	1
Governance approach	1
Guideline	1
Handicapped persons	1
Handwritten document	1
Harmonic analysis	1
Input datas	1
Intelligent character recognition	1
Intelligent devices	1
Intelligent recognition	1
Internal controls	1
International corporation	1
Internet banking	1
Internet of Things (IoT)	1
Intuitive user interface	1
Investment banking	1
IT-enabled services	1
Japan	1
Karnataka	1
Key services	1
Knowledge networks	1

(*continued*)

Table 13-5. (*continued*)

Words	Occurrences
Language processing	1
Law enforcement	1
Lean	1
Lean practices	1
Light weight	1
Literature reviews	1
Logistic performance	1
Logistic performance index	1
Logistic regression	1
Logistic regression modeling	1
Machine components	1
Machinery	1
Management of technology and innovations	1
Management risk	1
Master/follower/independent concept	1
Matching implements	1
Mathematical formulation	1
Medical education	1
mHealth	1
Micro grid	1
Microfinance	1
Microsoft	1
ML/DL	1
Mobile applications	1
Mobile computing	1
Mobile solutions	1
Monitoring	1
Monitoring parameters	1
Multiple dimensions	1
Multiple regression modelling	1

(*continued*)

Table 13-5. (*continued*)

Words	Occurrences
Multiple regressions	1
National libraries	1
Natural language processing systems	1
Neural networks	1
NoSQL	1
Online business	1
Online shopping	1
Operating condition	1
Operational database	1
Organ donations	1
Ornithotronics	1
Overall efficiency	1
Pattern recognition	1
Pattern recognition algorithms	1
Perceived benefits	1
Perceived ease of use	1
Perceived risk	1
Performance	1
Performance analysis	1
Performance effect	1
Performance expectation and effect expectancy	1
Performance expectations	1
Performance indices	1
Performance parameters	1
Personnel	1
Personnel training	1
PLS	1
Police station	1
Portals	1
Portfolio optimization	1

(*continued*)

Table 13-5. (*continued*)

Words	Occurrences
Poverty	1
Poverty alleviation	1
Power load	1
Power requirement	1
Predictive analytics	1
Process automation	1
Process control	1
Process management	1
Productivity	1
Profitability	1
Proof system	1
PTO power	1
Public relations	1
Quality of service	1
Quality services	1
Real-time data	1
Real-time decision making	1
Real-time monitoring	1
Real-time performance	1
Regression analysis	1
Relative strength index	1
Reliance industries	1
Remote terminal units	1
Resource use	1
Resource utilizations	1
Revenue generation	1
RFID systems	1
Rhenium	1
Risk assessment	1
Risk free	1
Risk management and mitigations	1

(*continued*)

Table 13-5. (*continued*)

Words	Occurrences
Risk management risk mitigation	1
Risk mitigation	1
River basin planning	1
Rivers	1
Roads and streets	1
Robotic process automation	1
Robots	1
Rural electricities	1
Scheduling	1
Scheduling problem	1
Sensitivity analysis	1
Sentiment	1
Service delivery	1
Service reliability	1
Service requests	1
Servqual	1
Short circuit calculations	1
Smart agricultures	1
Smartphone apps	1
Smartphones	1
Social awareness	1
Social networking (online)	1
Soils	1
Solar and wind energies	1
Space surveillance	1
Speech synthesis	1
Start-up	1
Start acceleration	1
Statistical approach	1
Statistical mechanics	1
Statistical tools	1

(*continued*)

Table 13-5. *(continued)*

Words	Occurrences
Strategic approach	1
Strategic approaches	1
Strategic decision making	1
Structural modeling	1
Surveys	1
Sustainability	1
Sustainable management	1
System modeling	1
Systems analysis	1
Tap changer control	1
Teaching	1
Technical analysis	1
Technological development	1
Technological innovation	1
Thalassemia	1
Top management	1
Tractor	1
Tractor-implement system	1
Tractor model	1
Tractor performance	1
Tractors (agricultural)	1
Tractors (truck)	1
Trading economics	1
Traditional approaches	1
Wind power	1
Windows operating system	1
Working speed	1
Writing style	1

The compilation of words provided encompasses a broad spectrum of subjects, thereby signifying the extensive range within the realm of research. The term "artificial intelligence" is observed to be the most frequently mentioned word, appearing 26 times. This notable frequency highlights the significant role and prominence of artificial intelligence within the ongoing discourse. The statement highlights the prevailing technological trend that has garnered considerable interest in recent times. The ongoing research discussions are enriched by the inclusion of other prominent terms such as "developing countries," "decision support systems," "sales," and "decision making." These terms have been identified as recurring themes, indicating their substantial contribution to the scholarly discourse. The comprehensive compilation of pertinent terms encompasses a diverse array of fields, encompassing but not limited to finance, economics, and banking. Additionally, it encompasses technology-centric subjects such as "image processing," "Internet of Things (IoT)," and "learning algorithms." The incorporation of social and environmental considerations is evident in the discourse, as evidenced by the utilization of terminologies such as "sustainable development," "environmental management," and "rural areas." These terminologies signify a dedication to acknowledging and tackling wider societal issues. The presented table provides a comprehensive overview of the diverse range of subjects that researchers have actively explored. These areas of investigation span a wide spectrum, incorporating state-of-the-art technological breakthroughs, meticulous economic evaluations, and the implementation of sustainable methodologies. The aforementioned statement highlights the intricate and diverse characteristics inherent in the realm of research while also acknowledging the dynamic nature of academic pursuits and the influential factors that mound the scholarly environment. Table 13-5 presents a concise overview of the key terms that have surfaced within the scope of the research area being examined. The presence of a wide range of terms and their frequent usage in the discourse indicates the dynamic and interdisciplinary character of the research domain, encompassing various areas such as technology, economics, social impact, and beyond. The present compilation of words serves to collectively elucidate the fundamental themes that are currently being investigated and elucidated by researchers in the course of their scholarly endeavors.

Conclusion

In conclusion, the investigation into the integration of artificial intelligence (AI) in the banking sector, as conducted through a bibliometric analysis, provides significant findings regarding the dynamic nature of technology implementation in the financial domain. The present study conducted a comprehensive and systematic review of a diverse array of scholarly sources, thereby shedding light on the increasing importance of artificial intelligence

(AI) in reconfiguring multiple aspects of the banking industry. The analysis has brought to light the fact that artificial intelligence (AI) has garnered significant attention as a powerful catalyst for change in the realm of banking operations. This attention is primarily directed toward leveraging AI to augment customer experiences, streamline decision-making processes, and enhance overall operational efficiency. The prevalence of terms such as "artificial intelligence," "banking," "finance," and "machine learning" highlights the significance of research related to artificial intelligence in the context of banking and finance. Moreover, the investigation revealed a wide range of themes and subdomains within the intersection of artificial intelligence and banking. The incorporation of artificial intelligence (AI) into banking practices is exemplified by the utilization of terms such as "customer satisfaction," "financial service," "risk management," and "digital transformation." These terms highlight the diverse and complex aspects associated with the integration of AI in the banking sector. The observed frequency of terms such as "fintech," "blockchain," and "data analytics" serves to illustrate the convergence of artificial intelligence (AI) with nascent financial technologies, thereby suggesting a comprehensive and integrated approach to fostering innovation within this domain. Through a comprehensive examination of the frequency of terms associated with artificial intelligence (AI) across various sources and clusters, our analysis has revealed a noteworthy trend highlighting the collaborative endeavors between academia and industry. Additionally, this investigation has shed light on the escalating worldwide interest in the field of AI. The aforementioned statement underscores the significance of numerous conferences, journals, and research proceedings in shedding light on the diverse facets of artificial intelligence (AI) in the banking sector. This emphasis on multidisciplinarity serves to underscore the far-reaching implications of AI in banking not only within the industry itself but also for the wider research community. The bibliometric analysis provided valuable insights into the impact of artificial intelligence (AI) on the banking industry. It highlighted a noticeable trend toward the adoption of data-driven approaches, leading to improved decision-making processes. Additionally, the analysis shed light on the growing emphasis on personalized customer services, as well as the pursuit of operational excellence within the sector. This study provides a comprehensive and insightful analysis of the current state of AI in the banking sector. It offers valuable insights and implications for researchers, practitioners, and policymakers interested in understanding the dynamic nature of this field. The findings of this study can serve as a foundation for developing informed strategies and identifying future research directions in the domain of AI in banking. The ongoing transformation of the financial industry by artificial intelligence (AI) is a topic of great significance. The aforementioned analysis serves to emphasize the criticality of persistent research efforts and collaborative endeavors in order to effectively leverage the extensive capabilities offered by AI-powered innovations within the banking sector.

Developing a Marketing Strategy While Maintaining Focus on Customer Value

Disha Gupta, Research Scholar, Sharda School of Business Studies, Sharda University, Greater Noida, India, Email: 2022300531.disha@dr.sharda.ac.in

Vidushi Nain*, Research Scholar, Sharda School of Business Studies, Sharda University, Greater Noida, India, Email: 2017008152.vidushi@dr.sharda.ac.in; vidushinain1@gmail.com

Dr. Satendar Singh, Associate Professor, Sharda School of Business Studies, Sharda University, Greater Noida, India, Email: satendar.singh@sharda.ac.in

Dr. Hari Shankar Shyam, Professor, Sharda School of Business Studies, Sharda University, Greater Noida, India, Email: harishankar.shyam@sharda.ac.in

© Neha Zaidi, Mohit Maurya, Simon Grima, Pallavi Tyagi 2024, corrected publication 2024
N. Zaidi et al. (eds.), *Building AI Driven Marketing Capabilities*,
https://doi.org/10.1007/978-1-4842-9810-7_14

All business states that it is crucial for each company to "acquire, retain, and grow" relationships with their ideal clientele. No matter what goods or services you provide, this demand will always exist. The goal of customer value strategies is to make it clear to customers that they will save money using your products and services, either right away or in the long run. A problem that has plagued marketers since long before the Internet is figuring out how potential consumers may go from being utterly uninformed of who you are to enthusiastically advocating your product everywhere they go. The Internet has not made this problem any easier to solve. The Customer Value Journey is the only strategy that generates outcomes more predictably and methodically than any other, even though there are many other methods that you can adopt. The activation of online platform–mediated single-person media has led to a surge in the popularity of YouTube and Creators, as well as an uptick in partnerships between commercial and amateur broadcasters. Thus, the culture of sales and the way businesses interact with customers are evolving in the digital age. So-called "YouTube influencers" are frequently used to spread advertisements and promotions online. Social media influencer marketing is a sort of viral marketing in which an online personality influences customer attitudes through tweets, postings, blogs, or any other form of communication on social media, as characterized by many academic qualities. We base our business decisions on the Customer Value Journey (CVJ) at Caffeinate Digital – from the services we offer to our customers to the things we practice and share with others in our seminars. This chapter will discuss the Customer Value Journey and how you can use it to build a successful digital marketing plan.

Introduction

The marketing strategy of a firm outlines in great detail the method that the organization will take to promote and sell the products or services that it offers. Finding out whom you want to sell to, deciding what you want to give them, and thinking of a strategy to differentiate yourself from other businesses in your industry are all essential elements of a successful marketing plan. However, when developing a strategy for marketing a product or service, it is necessary to focus all of one's attention on the end user. When consumers' expectations are exceeded, they are more likely to become loyal customers and promoters of a company's products and services (Xiao et al., 2018).

Companies that wish to succeed in the unpredictable and fast-paced marketplace of today need a marketing strategy that is clearly defined. There are many reasons for businesses to exist, but giving value to customers is at the core of every one of them. It is critical to provide value to customers to keep them as patrons of a business and to build a favorable reputation for the brand (Penco et al., 2021). A marketing plan that emphasizes the value that a company brings to its clients is essential for companies that want to boost their revenue.

Because of this, we employ a digital marketing strategy that encompasses numerous points of contact between a brand, product, and potential buyer. A customer's experience with your company begins with their initial contact and continues until they become a raving fan of what you have to offer.

During an interaction, customers have varying expectations regarding the type of assistance they will receive, the depth of their familiarity with the product or service at hand, and even their personality type (extrovert, introvert, etc.). For example, an extrovert customer will have different expectations than an introvert customer would have. Customers who are adept with the Internet typically conduct an in-depth study on the subject before going to a store; as a result, these customers frequently know more about the product than the staff members who are there to assist them. People who have a lot of things going on in their lives, such as professionals and stay-at-home moms, value shopping experiences that are simple (Matarazzo et al., 2021a). As the number of homes occupied by a single person continues to rise, consumers who reside in these homes place a higher value on products and services that meet their needs in terms of ease of use, affordability, prompt delivery, and convenience.

The people of South Korea came up with the term "untact" by fusing the phrase "contact" with the prefix "un," which stands for the word "no," to create a new word. Through the utilization of digital tools, "untact service" eradicates the requirement for any kind of face-to-face interaction between the employees of the company and the customers. The notion for an "untact" service usually originates with the client who desires it. The widespread availability of cutting-edge technologies like automatic dispensers, self-service counters, electronic banking, online buying and payment systems, and "unattended" kiosks has made it possible for many businesses to offer unattended services (Nuseir et al., 2023). The widespread adoption of AI, IoT, big data analytics, and smart sensors by companies undergoing digital transformation is expected to hasten the development of untact service systems. The rationale is simple: untact service is an agreement that is mutually advantageous for certain groups of customers and enterprises. Customers that tend to be more "individualist" in today's culture (such as those who are always on the go, live alone, or are digitally savvy and self-sufficient) are among those who find untact to be a feature that they like having access to. The capacity of untact to boost customer acquisition while simultaneously lowering the cost per service delivery is a win-win situation for businesses (Grönroos & Gummerus, 2014).

Value for the Customer and Why It Matters

In the current competitive environment, the single most essential factor in deciding a company's success or failure is its ability to deliver value for its customers. Understanding the importance of the value a client derives from a product or service is critical to a company's success. Customer value describes how much a product or service is appreciated by its end users. Value can be inferred from how well a product or service meets the needs of its intended audience as a whole.

Value to the customer is essential to every company since it is the primary factor in determining the level of happiness and loyalty experienced by customers. When consumers feel as though their money was well spent, they are more likely to shop with that business again. The value that a company delivers to its clients is the primary factor that determines whether or not the client will remain loyal to that firm throughout time, which is vital for the expansion and continuation of any organization (Fazidah Elias et al., 2015).

Marketing, product creation, and customer service are just a few areas where the importance of providing value to customers may be seen in action. Businesses can provide customers with better goods and services when they have a greater grasp of the value that customers look for in their purchases. Companies that place a greater emphasis on the value they provide to clients are better able to differentiate themselves from their rivals and develop a distinctive value offer that both attracts and keeps customers (Popa, n.d.).

The ability of businesses to design a business strategy that is centered on the needs and priorities of individual clients is one of the primary advantages of customer value. Companies that place a higher priority on the worth of their customers are more likely to concentrate their efforts on providing great customer experiences, which may result in higher levels of customer contentment and loyalty. This method of focusing on the consumer may also assist businesses in locating untapped possibilities in the market and in creating goods and services that are adaptable to the ever-evolving requirements of their clientele.

Another advantage of customer value is that it facilitates the development of better ties between businesses and the clients they serve. When businesses concentrate on providing value for their consumers, they significantly increase their chances of gaining their customers' confidence and credibility, which may result in the development of long-term customer relationships. Strong connections with customers may help organizations decrease the number of customers who leave, raise the value of customers during their lifetime, and produce positive word-of-mouth recommendations (Zeithaml et al., 2020).

In addition to these benefits, increasing the value that customers receive from a product or service may also help businesses improve their bottom line. Businesses have the power to raise their revenue and improve their profitability by developing goods and services that customers find valuable. This is due to the fact that consumers are willing to shell out more cash for products and services that exceed their expectations. Customers who are satisfied with a company's offerings are more inclined to buy more and to recommend that company to others, both of which boost sales and revenue (Safie et al., 2019).

In conclusion, the value that a consumer receives from a product or service cannot be stressed enough. It's a major aspect in determining a company's long-term success, and firms that place a premium on giving customers what they want tend to thrive. Businesses can strengthen their connections with their consumers, boost customer satisfaction and loyalty, and improve their bottom line if they concentrate on offering value to their clientele. Companies that fail to prioritize the value they provide their customers in today's highly competitive business market are likely to lag behind their rivals and have a difficult time surviving (Nyagadza, 2020).

Customer Value Determinants

Several factors, such as cost, quality, ease of use, the popularity of the brand, responsiveness of the service staff, and particular product characteristics, can all have an impact on the value that a product or service provides to the customer. If these aspects are not taken into consideration in a company's marketing strategy, there is little chance that the plan will be effective. If a firm's clients tend to be price-conscious, for example, the company needs to offer reasonable solutions without compromising the product's quality. In a similar vein, if customers place a high value on convenience of use, then businesses have to provide fast and uncomplicated payment methods for their clients (Li et al., 2021; Yang et al., 2019).

How to Develop a Strategy for Marketing That Is Centered on the Customer

If a company wants to develop a marketing strategy that emphasizes the value it delivers to clients, it must first have an in-depth comprehension of the desires, prerequisites, and anticipations of those customers. By following these steps, businesses can develop a marketing strategy that is focused on the client:

1. The first thing you should do is determine who it is you are attempting to target as well as their desires, requirements, and routines. Businesses have to segment their target audience into separate subgroups based on demographics, psychographics, and behavior to establish a marketing strategy that will connect with their target audience. This is necessary to create a marketing plan that will be successful.

2. Businesses should do market research to have a better understanding of the market, the requirements of their consumers, and the needs of their competitors. Businesses need to conduct market research so that they can identify gaps in the market and live up to the expectations of their ideal customers.

3. An organization's value proposition is the argument it makes to consumers about why they should buy the company's goods or services rather than those of competitors. Either a question or a statement is acceptable for the statement. A company's value proposition is the set of features and advantages it offers to consumers through its goods and services that set it apart from competitors (Lee & Lee, 2020).

4. Create a "Customer Journey Map" to represent the entirety of the customer experience, beginning with the initial point of contact and continuing through post-sale follow-up. Because of this, businesses are in a better position to answer the issues of their customers and to surpass the expectations that their customers have of them by providing a personalized service.

5. The construction of a firm's marketing strategies has to be guided by both the marketing strategy the company employs and the requirements of the audience it intends to attract. There are many different types of marketing tactics, some examples of which are paid commercials, content marketing, social media marketing, and email marketing (Repoviene & Paz˘eraite, 2018).

6. It is important for businesses to monitor not only revenue but also other indicators to evaluate the efficacy of their marketing activities and identify areas in which they may make changes. By assessing the results of various marketing tactics, businesses can modify their overall marketing strategy based on the success or failure of particular marketing initiatives.

Marketing Approaches That Continue to Prioritize the Needs of the Consumer Value They Are Targeting

The establishment of a business begins with the formulation of a strategic marketing plan. On the other hand, it is of equal importance to maintain the interests of the client front and center at all times. By putting the needs and desires of customers at the forefront of marketing strategy development, it is possible to produce advertising that not only effectively advertises your company but also connects with the audience you are trying to reach (An & Han, 2020; Matarazzo et al., 2021b).

Creating a strategy for marketing that puts the needs and desires of your clientele first may be accomplished as follows:

1. Before you begin writing, the first thing you need to do is research your audience to find out what problems they're facing and whom you're writing for. Conducting market research, analyzing customer data, and developing buyer personas are all excellent ways to gain a better understanding of your target market.

2. Create a "unique selling proposition" that describes your product or service and explains how it differs from those offered by competitors. Anything that distinguishes your brand from others in its industry is considered to be a differentiating factor.

3. Make a strategy for your future marketing endeavors: First things first, you need to decide what you want to accomplish with your marketing efforts. This may result in increased conversion rates, an increase in the number of qualified leads, or just greater visibility for the brand. SMART objectives are goals that are specific, measurable, attainable, relevant, and time-bound. If you want to be successful in business, it is essential to develop SMART goals (Carlson et al., 2019).

4. Determine whom you want to speak to and what you want to achieve with your marketing efforts before selecting the most effective channels for communicating with your target audience. There is a wide range of approaches that might be taken, including content marketing, email marketing, social media marketing, and sponsored commercials.

5. Create a strategy for communicating with the people who are going to be reading your work and for coming up with a message that will resonate with them. Your messaging should express the benefits of your service, provide solutions to challenges that your target audience is experiencing, and highlight your unique selling proposition (USP).

6. Develop content for your audience that not only interests them but also serves their best interests in some way. Films, infographics, white papers, case studies, and essays written for blogs are all examples of content kinds that suit this definition. Be sure that in addition to being helpful, the reader will find the content you are writing to be fascinating.

7. Following the development of your marketing strategy, the next step is to put that strategy into action and assess how well it performed. Maintain a close watch on how things are progressing as well as how effectively your marketing is doing. You may keep track of your progress by using typical statistics such as the number of visits to your website, shares on social media, email openings, and sales (Piriyakul & Piriyakul, 2022).

8. Your marketing plan should be constantly optimized to maximize its effectiveness, and this optimization should be based on data from prior campaigns. Find out what kind of content, tone of voice, and delivery methods your target audience responds to best by experimenting with a variety of different channels. Take advantage of the feedback and recommendations provided by consumers to improve your marketing, goods, and overall customer experience.

Conclusion

If a company's marketing activities are focused on giving value to consumers, then that company's chances of being successful will be significantly boosted. This is something that can only be done by finding unmet client expectations and providing innovative new products and services in response to those requests. In terms of the quality of the service they deliver, they also must provide their customers with more than what they were expecting (Hollebeek & Macky, 2019a).

Carrying out market research is an essential first step for companies that want to develop an efficient marketing strategy by gaining a better understanding of the preferences, requirements, and routines of their target audience. Following the creation of a consumer persona based on these data, subsequent marketing efforts could be molded using that persona.

The following step is to determine the product's USP, which stands for "unique selling proposition." It is essential to identify the specific characteristics and advantages that distinguish your product or service unique from those offered by competitors. The unique selling proposition should be featured prominently throughout all marketing materials to assist consumers in deciding whether or not to acquire the service.

The first stage in developing a successful marketing mix, which also involves product, price, promotion, and location, is to identify a distinct advantage that your offering has over that of your competitors. The formulation of the marketing mix needs to be guided by two goals: maximizing the value provided to customers and generating as much income as possible (Lim et al., 2017).

In conclusion, it is essential to evaluate how well the marketing plan is being implemented and make adjustments as necessary. It is critical to keep an eye on key performance indicators (KPIs), such as the satisfaction of customers and clients as well as income. By keeping an eye on these key performance indicators (KPIs), businesses have the opportunity to improve their marketing strategy and give increased value to their consumers (Hollebeek & Macky, 2019b).

In the end, the success of any business is contingent on the company's capacity to put into action a marketing strategy that places the utmost importance on the priorities of the target market. Companies may generate income with a customer-centric marketing strategy by first learning about their target market, then identifying their unique selling proposition (USP), then developing a marketing mix that satisfies the expectations of the target market, and finally assessing how well the plan works.

Boom of Artificial Intelligence in the Food Industry

Dr. Neha Bisht* and **Amar P. Garg**, School of Biological Engineering & Life Sciences, Shobhit Institute of Engineering & Technology (NAAC "A" Grade Accredited, Deemed to-be-University), NH-58, Modipuram, Meerut -250110, Uttar Pradesh, India, bishtneha1993a@gmail.com; amarprakash-garg@yahoo.com; https://orcid.org/0000-00026568-3469; https://orcid.org/0000-0003-0613-9495

Big data will most likely be employed as emerging technologies such as machine vision and machine learning (ML) to enable constant development, generate functional current time smarter robots, and offer predictable version. The term "computer vision and artificial intelligence–driven culinary market" describes these phenomena of employing vision along with learning approaches improve the food manufacturing industry. The potential of the above mentioned intelligent devices to execute a number of tasks, such as determining food quality, providing quality control, categorizing food, and forecasting, has raised consumer interest in the food industry. The global population is expected to reach more than nine billion by the year 2050, necessitating a 70% increase in agriculture and food production in order to satisfy demands. This presents a significant challenge to the agri-food sector. In light of resource shortages, climate change, the COVID-19 pandemic, and extremely pessimistic socioeconomic projections, it is challenging to meet these criteria without the use of computer tools and forecasting techniques. The expert machines used in the food sector will be covered in this chapter. These machines provide significant financial savings while improving resource conservation through minimizing human error. By extending the longevity of food products, adding into the algorithms of artificial intelligence choices, simultaneously improving security of food using an approach that is simpler to comprehend for managing the chains of supply, AI has the potential to significantly improve packaging. The use of artificial intelligence and machine learning has numerous applications in ecommerce, business management, and finance covered within this chapter. Portfolio leadership, identifying fraudulent activity, managing inventory, forecasting of sales, revenue optimization, and increased revenue are just a few of the primary applications.

Introduction

The term artificial intelligence (AI) has been described as a field in computer science that replicates human thought processes, learning capacity, as well as knowledge storage (1, 2). Artificial intelligence–integrated systems or self-contained systems are widely used in almost every aspect of technology. It allows the countries across the globe to optimize the issues efficiently, the food sector should be computerized, and food products should change (3). The business sector could evaluate and make certain best conditions, such as selection of seed, crop monitoring, watering, and temperature surveillance, may have been improved through utilizing a technological arrangement, as a consequence into the food's culinary excellence sector goods (4, 5, 6). These are not the only applications of AI. Strong and weak AI are two categories into which AI can be divided (7). AI with strong principles claims that computers can reflect the human mind, whereas according to the weak AI concept, the machine ought to be constructed to operate as a self-contained programmable entity that mirrors human judgments (8). Strong AI does not yet exist; research about it is still ongoing. Among the domains that have utilized AI methods are the gaming sector, weather forecasting, heavy sector industry, process industry, food sector, medical sector, data mining, stem cells, as well as representation of knowledge (7, 9–16). It may also be used for processing, storage, and transportation of food. Automation and intelligence drones are two instances of technological innovations that could have a large and vital contribution to reducing packaging costs. In the food industry, concerns for food safety resulted in the creation of an innovative wrapping system that ensures a hygienic and contamination-free food supply chain (7, 36).

With the help of AI, it will be easier to monitor the quality and condition of food products in storage and during transportation (7, 37). Along with the use of 45 advanced optical systems, freshness monitoring through the use of AI, packaging with intelligence reduces the wastage of food (7), and the most important fields of application cover meat, fruits, vegetables, and fish products (37). Food factories using intelligent packaging is an important factor as they are in the food system capable of keeping track of the quality of crops and products (35, 36–42). Additionally, AI helps in delivering various products, completing tasks in dangerous situations, and providing high-quality products (17, 18). Food quality and security management are the two classifications of AI's important tasks across food industry sectors (Figure 15-1) (6).

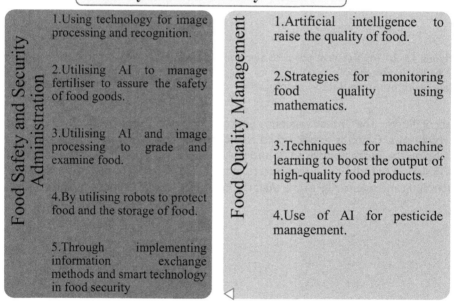

Artificial intelligence in the food industry
industrybusinessindustry

Food Safety and Security Administration

1. Using technology for image processing and recognition.

2. Utilising AI to manage fertiliser to assure the safety of food goods.

3. Utilising AI and image processing to grade and examine food.

4. By utilising robots to protect food and the storage of food.

5. Through implementing information exchange methods and smart technology in food security

Food Quality Management

1. Artificial intelligence to raise the quality of food.

2. Strategies for monitoring food quality using mathematics.

3. Techniques for machine learning to boost the output of high-quality food products.

4. Use of AI for pesticide management.

Figure 15-1. AI in the food industry

To feed 9–10 billion people by 2050, the estimated global food production must increase by 60–110% (19, 21) (Figure 15-2). One in every nine people worldwide, or 793 million people, lacks sufficient food to sustain their everyday lives. The Food and Agriculture Organization (FAO) data indicates how few Asian nations still experience undernourishment. According to intuition, due to their expanding populations and economic advancements, India and China share the first and second spots, subsequently (22).

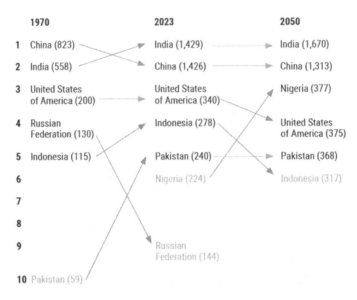

Figure 15-2. Top five most populous countries, estimated for 1970 and projected for 2023 and 2050. Projected
Source: https://population.un.org/wpp/

Accordingly, the most recent United Nations population figures and projections, China is expected to relinquish its belief with long-held position as being the most populated country. As shown in Figure 15-3, the estimated population of India is supposed to turn up 1,425,775,850 people in April 2023, matching and eventually more than the populace of the Chinese mainland (21).

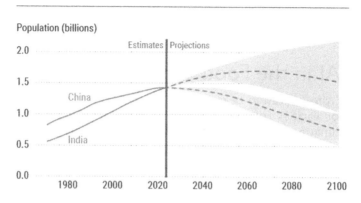

Population (billions)

Data source: United Nations, *World Population Prospects 2022*, https://population.un.org/wpp/.

Figure 15-3. Total population growth in China and India, calculated for 1970–2023 and projected for 2023-2100

According to statistics, unbiased global estimates could result from the unreliability of track records calculated by several causes, such as increasing substantial wealth levels in nations that are developing and rising levels in economic inequality, etc. (24). Ultimately, food supply will continue to be a contentious issue as a crucial link in the demand-supply cycle. The technique of selecting an appropriate strategy among modern, sustainable practices can produce better outcomes, sustaining production with corresponding demand as well. Conceptually, compared to other business sectors, the food service sector has remained reasonably stable, developed, and slow-growing, with low-level R&D investments (19, 25).

Artificial intelligence has therefore been implemented to feed food demand, such as managing the supply chain, sorting the food, developing production techniques, improving the quality of food, and ensuring proper safety in the workplace (26–28). Sharma claims that the culinary preparation and handling sectors will grow at least 5% until 2021 (27). As Funes and coworkers (29) report, artificial neural networks (ANNs) might be employed to resolve complex issues in the food business, while according to Correa (30), parameter classification and prediction are more straightforward when ANN is used, leading to an increase in ANN usage during the last couple years. Furthermore, fuzzy logic (FL) and artificial neural networks (ANNs) have additionally been utilized for integrators to ensure the safety of food, control of quality, yield increase, as well as expense reduction (31, 32). In addition to food drying technology, artificial intelligence using an expert system, FL, and ANN implemented into a process control tool for drying of fresh fruits (33–35). In previous studies, AI has been found to be used in a variety of food industries, focusing on specific targets. There has been an analysis of the various applications of AI in food process modeling using an ANN (36).

Use of AI in the Food Sector

For decades, the utilization of computer vision in the food sector has been developing for various reasons, including food separation, classification and attribute estimation, quality assurance, and food security. Expert systems, fuzzy logic, artificial neural networks, ANFIS (adaptive neuro-fuzzy inference system), and the use of machine learning are among the popular approaches used in the food industry. Previously adopting AI, for several decades, associated with food research had been carried out to notify the general people regarding food-related topics and enhance visual ultimate results related to cuisine characteristics and the cultivation of food (43–47). The AI technique has various advantages, and its adoption for many years, people have been working in the food industry and continues to grow (43–44, 48–50). Nonetheless, this study will concentrate on the use of AI in the food industry since 2015 onward due to the great boost and begin to implement innovation shown up to date. It is important to note that a number of techniques, such as limited minimal squares, gastrointestinal cohesive theory framework, in silico designs, models based on empirical data, scant regression analysis, and sequential projector methods, are used, and profitable reweighting of samples that is employed for predictions, food improvement, and beverage sectors is not addressed here; rather, the emphasis is on the widespread application of artificial intelligence (AI) in the food industry.

Expert System Based on Knowledge in the Food Industry

A system that relies on knowledge is a piece of software for computers that employs information to tackle complex problems gathered using a variety of resources, data, and expertise. It is classified into three types: systems of experts, knowledge-based artificial intelligence, and knowledge-based engineering. Figure 15-4 displays the knowledge-based system's breakdown. The commonly utilized expert knowledge–based system is a decisive and collective capable computer system of imitating the procedure for making decisions expert (51). It is a structure of an information-based system widely regarded as one of the very first efficient models for artificial intelligence.

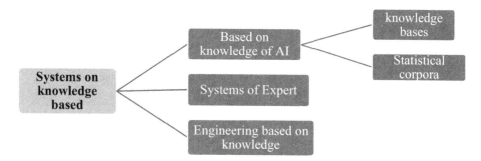

Figure 15-4. Knowledge-based system

An expert system relies on specialists to solve complex problems in a specific domain. It has two subsystems: the knowledge base and the inference machine. The Knowledge base stores information about the globe, while the inference engine represents the rules and facts about the world, which are typically expressed using IF-THEN rules (52). Normally, it is capable of resolving complex challenges with the assistance of a human specialist. This system is built on the expertise of specialists. The key elements of an expert system (ES) are the human specialist, information technician, material base, prediction vehicle's engine, graphical user interface, and client. The professional mechanism's fowl is displayed. The ES has already been employed within the food industry to serve various purposes because it has proven to be efficient, particularly during the decision-making process. A knowledge-driven system of experts was implemented through the white wine fermenting process for data recovery, intelligence management, and surveillance (53). Apart from the fact that by adopting the ES, a web-based program has been created to determine the nutritional content of food products for consumers, while the creation of ES was able to aid the Strategic management instruments (SMIs) in acquiring the information needed to demonstrate accreditation for food manufacturing licenses (54).

Food security is extremely important within the foodstuff business; hence, ES service which is connected closely modifications have been made to safeguard food widely employed, spanning beyond designing processes to danger evaluations, nutritional value, and security monitoring (55) shown in Figure 15-5. Furthermore, for the food sector, an early-stage technology-based platform and correction recommendations measures the addressed specifications of the model ES were built, and some important factors consist of the safety of food, dietary habits, excellence, and price were evaluated (56). MESTRAL, an online educational tool, has been established which aid persons employed in the processing of food utilizing items produced of studies in technology of food science as well as in training purpose. Entire technology built on engineering knowledge and its utilization in the real world which transferred to scales in system and foundations for information. Leo Kumar thorough examination of the applicability within the expertise system based on experience industrial outline (55, 56). Article explore the use employing

ES across three scenarios for decisions broad areas: actions for process scheduling, various utilization, and production approach.

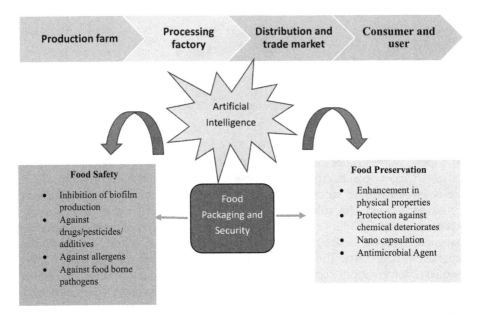

Figure 15-5. Use of AI in food safety and preservation

The Use of Fuzzy Logic in the Food Industry

Zadeh pioneered fuzzy logic (FL) in the year 1965, according to the superior human potential mind. When resolving issues, you must make decisions or decipher unclear, unreliable, and contradictory facts (57, 58). The concept of fuzzy sets is recognized in a way that a component is a member of a set that's fuzzy that specified status of membership and a real integer between (57). FL models are made up of multiple phases, including fuzzification, inference, and defuzzification (59, 60). Fuzzification is a procedure that converts the sharp price into a level of service as well as produces the sets of uncertain inputs.

In most affiliation duties, the associated degree is 0 and 1 (61). There are various aspects of membership to pick from, with the most frequent being Z-shaped, triangular, trapezoidal, S-shaped, and Gaussian-shaped (62). The imprecise signal processed by a deductive algorithm is transformed into output utilizing fuzzy rules. The rules that are uncertain are referred to as IF-THEN logic because they are expressed as IF premise, THEN consequence, with the IF containing input parameters and the THEN containing output parameters (63). The inference system is made up of two styles: Mamdani and Takagi-Sugeno-Kang (TSK). Defuzzification is the final stage of the fuzzy logic model in which crisp values are achieved (64). Defuzzification approaches include the center of gravity, maximal mean, shortest high, greatest maximum, maximal center, and the center of mass (65). FL has long been used due to its straightforwardness and capacity to solve difficulties in the business quickly and accurately. FL used in the business for food modeling, its control, and classification, as well as for problem solving in the food industry by regulating human reasoning in language terms (66). The use of fuzzy logic enhanced the food manufacturing system by reducing electricity losses by roughly 7% when compared to the traditional regulating approach (67). The sensory assessment of food is another prominent area in which FL plays a major role. In addition, a system based on fuzzy rules can provide a faster solution to problems (68). According to a prior study, FL effectively maintains food quality and serves as a forecasting tool as well as monitoring system for food manufacturing processes.

Methods of Learning Through Machine Learning (ML)

Machine learning is recognized as an AI subset (69, 70). It is a computer algorithm that understands from knowledge and flourishes on its own. There are three broad kinds of ML: supervised learning, unsupervised learning, and reinforcement learning (71). The goal of guided training is to forecast an expected target or outcome, using the provided set of inputs (72). Unsupervised training, on the contrary, lacks any outputs for forecasting and is used to categorize data and spontaneously find patterns of its occurrence (73). When there is an interaction between the program and the natural world for the purpose of attaining specific goals, this is known as reinforcement learning (74). ANN, decision trees (DT), support vector machines (SVM), regression analysis, Bayesian networks, genetic algorithms, kernel machines, and federated learning are examples of well-known machine learning models. ML has been widely utilized to handle complicated jobs, large amounts of data, and a wide range of variables when no preformulate or existing formula exists for the problem. Aside from that, ML models have the potential to learn from instances rather than being coded with rules (71, 74). Ordinary least square regression (OLS-R), stepwise linear regression (SL-R), principal component regression (PC-R), partial least square regression (PLS-R), support vector regression (SVM-R), boosted logistic regression (BLR), random forest regression (RF-R), and k-nearest neighbors' regression (kNN-R) are among the ML methods used in the food industry (75). According to studies, the application of ML has aided in lowering the cost of sensory evaluation, decision making, and improving business strategies to meet the needs of users (76). Long short-term memory (LSTM), a synthetic recurrent neural network, has been used in the food industry to detect pH during the cheese fermentation process (77). Genetic Algorithm (GA), on the other hand, has been used to find the best food parameters, whereas Neural Network (NN) has been used in the processing of food, to forecast the ultimate clogging rate (78). ML has been demonstrated to be useful in forecasting food insecurity in the United Kingdom (79). Aside from that, ML has been shown to predict sales of food patterns market (80). ML is also capable of predicting the quantity of wasted food consumed and offers knowledge about the system of production (81, 82).

Food Manufacturing: ANN Technique

An AI component that is often used in the food sector is ANN. ANN intended replication development as well as the human being's brain information via education and interaction-neuronal synapses mass are connections between neurons (83, 84). Gandhi along with his collaborators has claimed that the ANN setup is created to handle certain applications, for instance, data sorting or detection of patterns (85). ANN, according to Gonzalez-Fernandez, is flexible and applicable to a variety of challenges and scenarios. Furthermore, Gonzalez et al. (2019) said that ANN is suitable for modeling most chaotic systems and thus is adaptable to new situations or scenarios, even if adjustments are required. One of the most notable characteristics of ANN is its nonlinear regression (86). A feedforward neural network, radial basis function neural network (RBFNN), Kohonen self-organizing neural network, recurrent neural network, convolutional neural network, and modular neural network are some of the neural networks that can be used (87). When it comes to tackling real-world problems, the most effective varieties of NN include MLP, RBFNN, and Kohonen self-organizing algorithms, which are examples of the multilayer perceptron (88). The multilayer perceptron is the most commonly used network for prediction and pattern recognition (89).

Furthermore, depending on the learning techniques, learning on ANN can be classified as supervised or unsupervised (90). In general, ANN structures consisted of an input layer, a hidden layer, and an output layer, which might be single or several layers (91, 92). The architecture includes activation functions, such as feedforward or feedback (93). Backpropagation learning is commonly employed because it may minimize prediction error by feeding it back as an input until the minimal acceptable error is attained (94). An extra input known as bias is provided to neurons, allowing for the depiction of events with thresholds (95, 96).

AI-Based Compensation Within the Food Manufacturing Sector

The following are some of the benefits of artificial intelligence in the food industry: (i) In recent years, practically any kind of food processing sectors have unquestionably embraced AI to develop demanding management for supply chains, careful logistics, and predictive analysis, as well as to increase system accuracy. (ii) The computerization of demand-supply network systems for management ultimately requires and gives incentives for better understanding of the situation. AI can analyze large volumes of data in ways that humans cannot. (iii) AI assists the industry in reducing time to market and improving agreement with suspicions. (iv) Automated ordering will favorably reduce labor costs, increase manufacturing speed, and improve product quality.

Emerging AI Implementation Ideas in the Food Manufacturing Sector

According to research conducted in recent years, the use of AI approaches increased from 2015 to 2020 and is expected to continue over ten years according to current developments. The introduction of Industrial Revolution 4.0 (IR 4.0) has among rising factors for the application of intelligent systems in the food sector. Incorporation new or intelligent technologies onto traditional IR 4.0 refers to the manufacturing sector, sometimes known as smart factory (98, 99). AI, which is classified as an IR 4.0 technology, is concerned with creating a generation of intelligent machines that function similarly to humans (99). The effect of IR 4.0 on recalls of goods is enormous caused by food inspectors or claims industry. The implementation of artificial intelligence (AI) in sensors allows detecting and correcting faults throughout the manufacturing process. Aside from that, IR 4.0 has a significant influence in human behavior, as consumers in the twenty-first century frequently get information on meals on the Internet. The growing concern about food quality allows for further use of AI because it can improve food quality and aid in the manufacturing process. The greatest as more academics conduct investigations, the quantity of AI application in the food industry is predicted to grow by 2020, employing the AI technology, and is projected to rise further in the future years as food consumption rises as worries regarding the hygiene of foods produced grow. In the food industry, integration with external sensors has a larger rate than those without sensor integration. External sensors were used to collect data from samples, which were then used by AI algorithms to do various tasks, such as classification, prediction, quality control, and others, as previously indicated. However, data collected in 2017 revealed that the percentage of AI without external sensors is higher than that of integration with sensors. This is owing to the extensive investigation that was completed without the use of the external sensors specified in this publication. In summary, as the world of AI evolves 2.0 (100), it is possible to forecast that the use of AI in the food industry will increase indefinitely due to the benefits that it can provide, such as money, time, and energy savings, in addition to precision in anticipating the major elements influencing the food sectors. Aside from the recent crisis caused by the COVID-19 pandemic, it is expected that more organizations will use AI in their sectors to save costs and improve performance.

Table 15-1. Utilization of Artificial Intelligence in the Food Sector Network of Experts (101, 102)

Objective	Use	Industry Category	Outcomes
To evaluate the taro's quality in relation to market requirement	Taro	Raw material/ agriculture	The newly created ANFIS model, in conjunction with responsive surface approaches, can be utilized to optimize antioxidant extraction efficiency from taro four. The predicted values of the generated model were validated using when compared to experiment data, and the results were nearly compatible with the projected values of the generated model
To determine a fresh orange's maturation	Orange	Raw material/ agriculture	The developed ANFIS model fared better than the multiple regression model in predicting the orange flavor
To determine the food additives' halal compatibility score	Food additives	Food safety	Customers are provided with an assessment of the safety criteria based on their prior consumption record experience by the newly developed Halal Food Additive with ES
To strengthen the distribution systems for fresh food	Fresh food	Sustainability	The best possible distribution method was generated by the suggested expert system, Food Distribution Planner, which reduces carbon dioxide emissions by 9.6% and increases operating expenses by 2.7% and during the delivery term generates no waste, because of the shipping method's preservation measures
To identify diseases in oil	Fish oil	Sustainability and processing	ANFIS, multilinear recurrent neural networks, and multiple regression were used to estimate the oxidation parameters. The proposed strategy has been demonstrated to have the greatest accuracy for forecasting the variables
To understand the banana disease and how to get over it	Banana	Raw material/ agriculture	In order to prevent the disease, the approach was able to evaluate issues in plant samples on the stems, leaves, and roots
To recognize corn pests and illnesses	Corn	Agriculture/ raw material	The system's efficiency in identifying pests and diseases was 76.6%, and it also offered solutions for eradicating them. The suggested approach could give medical facilities explanations of the findings of the diagnosis

Conclusion

AI serves a crucial part in the food sector through various factors, such as training, forecasting, and recommendation. The food drying process, sensory assessment, quality supervision, and various other services solving complex food processing challenges are all examples of control tools. Aside from that, AI is capable of enhancing commercial approaches as a result of their capacity to conduct vending forecast which allows an increase in production. In the food sector, AI is generally recognized for its simplicity, precision, and cost-saving strategy. AI applications include their benefits, drawbacks, in addition to the incorporation into technologies various eating detectors that include e-nose and e-tongue business summarized. Furthermore, a comprehensive process to designing the right algorithm beforehand before employing an artificial intelligence algorithm within any food industry-related farm is being suggested the entirety of which are intended to help motivate scientists and business entities to branch out into modern technology it can be demonstrated to offer more effective outcomes.

Unlocking Emotional Intelligence with AI Marketing: Connecting Brands to Hearts

Prof. Anushka Lydia Issac*, ORCID: https://orcid.org/0000-0002-1493-1047 Faculty and Course Leader – L3 Pearson Foundation Program Westford University College, Sharjah, United Arab Emirates, Email: anulydia@gmail.com

Emotional intelligence (EI) has emerged as a key concept in various domains, including psychology, leadership, and education (Gladson Nwokah & Ahiauzu, 2009). In recent years, it has found its way into the realm of marketing as an essential factor in building strong and lasting connections with consumers. At its core, emotional intelligence refers to the ability to perceive, understand, manage, and influence emotions, both in oneself and others. In the context of marketing, EI is the capacity of brands and marketers to recognize and respond to consumers' emotional states to create impactful and authentic experiences. However, while EI has gained popularity as a marketing buzzword, it warrants a critical examination to understand its true implications and potential pitfalls.

Defining Emotional Intelligence in the Context of Marketing

Emotional intelligence in marketing refers to the strategic understanding and application of emotions to build deeper connections with consumers. It involves perceiving, interpreting, and responding to consumer emotions in a way that enhances brand-consumer relationships. This section will delve into two critical aspects.

Emotional Intelligence and Consumer Behavior

Proponents of emotional intelligence in marketing argue that understanding consumer emotions can lead to more effective advertising, personalized messaging, and increased brand loyalty. Emotional responses can significantly influence purchase decisions, and tailoring marketing strategies to evoke specific emotions seems promising. However, critics argue that relying solely on EI to drive marketing decisions may oversimplify consumer behavior. Emotions are multifaceted and can vary significantly between individuals and cultures, making it challenging to create a one-size-fits-all approach.

One of the most contentious issues surrounding emotional intelligence in marketing is the fine line between establishing authentic emotional connections and emotional manipulation. While connecting with consumers on an emotional level can lead to genuine relationships, some marketers might exploit emotions to push products or services aggressively (Gladson Nwokah & Ahiauzu, 2009). Ethical concerns arise when emotional triggers are used to sway consumers without considering their best interests. Marketers must be mindful of the ethical implications of leveraging emotions for commercial gain.

Quantifying emotional responses presents a significant challenge for marketers. Emotional experiences are often intangible and challenging to quantify accurately. Traditional marketing metrics like click-through rates and conversion rates might not fully capture the emotional impact of a campaign. Developing reliable methods for measuring emotional engagement remains a pressing issue in the integration of emotional intelligence into marketing strategies.

The Impact of Technology and AI

Advancements in technology and artificial intelligence have enabled marketers to harness vast amounts of data, including emotional data from social media and other sources. While AI can help identify emotional patterns and sentiments, it is not a substitute for genuine human understanding. The danger lies in relying solely on AI-driven emotional analytics, potentially overlooking the nuances that only human empathy and intuition can grasp. Emotional intelligence is not universally understood or expressed in the same way across cultures and regions (Gladson Nwokah & Ahiauzu, 2009). Emotional cues that resonate with one demographic might fall flat with another. Marketers must be sensitive to cultural differences and adapt their emotional appeals accordingly. A lack of cultural awareness could lead to unintended consequences, damaging brand reputation and relationships with consumers.

The Significance of Emotional Connections Between Brands and Consumers

In the competitive landscape of modern marketing, emotional connections between brands and consumers have gained increasing attention as a potent tool for fostering loyalty, advocacy, and lasting relationships. By tapping into consumers' emotions, brands aim to create memorable experiences that transcend transactional interactions. While emotional connections can undoubtedly yield substantial benefits, a critical examination is necessary to understand the genuine significance and potential drawbacks of relying on emotions in brand-consumer relationships.

Emotional connections have the power to transform passive consumers into loyal brand advocates. When consumers feel a strong emotional attachment to a brand, they are more likely to remain loyal over time, even in the face of competing offers. This loyalty can extend beyond individual transactions, leading to increased customer lifetime value (Kidwell et al., 2011). Loyal customers are also more inclined to recommend the brand to friends and family, acting as organic brand ambassadors. However, critics argue that loyalty built solely on emotions might be fickle, susceptible to shifting sentiments or the appeal of competitors.

In markets flooded with similar products and services, forging emotional connections can be a way for brands to differentiate themselves. Emotional experiences that resonate with consumers can create a unique brand identity, setting the brand apart from competitors solely focused on functional attributes. Emotional connections become part of the brand's narrative and are often more memorable than features or benefits. However, relying heavily on emotional appeals might overshadow the actual value proposition and may not be sufficient to sustain long-term success. During times of crisis or economic turbulence, brands with strong emotional connections are often better equipped to weather the storm. Consumers who feel emotionally connected are more forgiving of occasional missteps, giving the brand the benefit of the doubt (Gladson Nwokah & Ahiauzu, 2009; Peter, 2010). These connections can serve as a buffer against negative publicity and public relations challenges. Nevertheless, critics caution against overestimating emotional connections as a panacea for all adversities, as the effectiveness of emotional appeals may vary depending on the nature and severity of the crisis.

Impact on Consumer Decision-Making

Emotional connections can significantly influence consumer decision-making processes. Emotions can lead to impulse purchases, particularly when aligned with the consumer's self-identity or aspirations. Marketers' adept at tapping into emotions can create a sense of urgency or exclusivity, triggering quick decisions. However, critics argue that emotional appeals may not be sufficient when complex rational considerations are involved, such as major financial decisions, where logic and practicality play a more significant role.

While emotional connections can captivate consumers, it is essential not to overshadow product or service quality. A strong emotional bond may initially attract consumers, but the product's performance and value will determine long-term satisfaction. Some brands may focus excessively on emotional marketing without investing in the underlying quality, leading to disillusioned customers and eroding brand trust over time (Willman-livarinen, 2017).

Emotional intelligence (EI) has become a focal point in the study of consumer behavior, as marketers seek to understand and influence consumers' emotional responses to their brand messages and products. EI's influence on consumer decision-making has been touted as a key driver of successful marketing strategies. However, a critical examination of this relationship reveals both its potential benefits and inherent complexities. Emotional intelligence in marketing involves identifying emotional triggers that resonate with consumers, evoking positive feelings such as joy, nostalgia, or a sense of belonging. Marketers use emotional cues to craft compelling stories and experiences that connect with consumers on a deeper level. While emotional triggers can be effective in capturing attention and generating initial interest, critics argue that solely relying on emotions may distract consumers from assessing the product's functional attributes and long-term benefits. Emotional intelligence plays a pivotal role in shaping consumers' perceptions of brands. Brands that display high emotional intelligence can foster a sense of trust, authenticity, and empathy, leading to increased brand loyalty (Mowen, 1988; Willman-livarinen, 2017). Consumers may perceive such brands as being genuinely invested in their well-being, resulting in a stronger emotional attachment. However, some marketers may exploit emotional intelligence to create artificial emotional associations, leading to a shallow and fleeting connection that ultimately fails to build lasting loyalty. EI's impact on consumer behavior often manifests in emotional decision-making. Consumers make many purchase decisions based on emotions rather than rational evaluations of product features or price points. Emotional appeals can sway consumers' choices, leading to impulse purchases or preference for familiar brands associated with positive emotions. However, critics argue that heavy reliance on emotional decision-making might lead to buyers' remorse or dissatisfaction when emotions subside, potentially affecting brand credibility in the long run.

Emotional intelligence continues to play a role in post-purchase behavior and customer retention. Brands that maintain emotional connections beyond the initial purchase are more likely to encourage repeat purchases and foster brand advocates (Mowen, 1988; Willman-livarinen, 2017). Emotional intelligence facilitates personalized customer interactions, such as personalized thank-you messages or tailored offers, which can enhance customer satisfaction and loyalty. However, striking the right balance between emotional engagement and privacy concerns remains a challenge. As emotional engagement emerges as a central focus in modern marketing, the integration of artificial intelligence (AI) has become a game-changer in cultivating deeper and more meaningful connections with consumers. AI's ability to process vast amounts of data, analyze emotions, and deliver personalized experiences has transformed the way brands approach emotional engagement. However, a critical examination of AI's role in this domain is essential to understand its true potential, ethical implications, and limitations.

AI's most significant contribution to emotional engagement lies in its capacity to analyze vast datasets containing emotional cues from various sources such as social media, customer reviews, and consumer interactions. By applying advanced natural language processing (NLP) and sentiment analysis algorithms, AI can extract valuable insights into consumers' emotional responses to brands and products. This enables marketers to gauge sentiment trends, identify emotional triggers, and adapt their strategies accordingly. However, critics caution against overreliance on data-driven insights, as AI might not fully capture the context and nuances of human emotions. AI-powered personalization has redefined emotional engagement by enabling brands to deliver tailored content, products, and experiences to individual consumers (Peter, 2010). By analyzing consumer preferences and behavior, AI can craft emotionally resonant messages that cater to each person's unique emotional triggers. Personalization fosters a sense of intimacy and connection, elevating emotional engagement to new heights. Nonetheless, there are concerns about privacy and data security, as personalization requires access to substantial amounts of consumer data. The emergence of AI-driven chatbots has revolutionized customer interactions, especially in customer support and service. By employing AI and natural language understanding, chatbots can simulate empathetic conversations and respond to emotional cues from consumers. Emotional chatbots aim to create a more human-like experience, showing understanding and empathy during interactions. However, critics highlight that while AI chatbots can handle basic emotional interactions, they lack true emotional intelligence and may fall short in addressing complex emotional needs.

AI-generated content, such as emotionally driven advertisements, social media posts, and product descriptions, has become increasingly prevalent. AI algorithms can analyze successful emotional content and create new, emotionally appealing material. This approach saves time and resources while allowing brands to engage with consumers on an emotional level (Peter, 2010). Nevertheless, critics argue that AI-generated content may lack genuine emotional authenticity, potentially leading to consumer skepticism or even backlash if it appears insincere or manipulative.

AI's involvement in emotional engagement raises ethical concerns, particularly regarding data privacy, emotional manipulation, and transparency. Collecting and analyzing emotional data requires careful consideration of consumers' consent and their right to data protection. Ensuring that emotional engagement is used ethically and responsibly is essential to avoid crossing ethical boundaries or exploiting consumers' vulnerabilities.

Understanding Consumer Emotions with AI

As consumer behavior increasingly becomes driven by emotions, understanding and deciphering these complex human responses have become crucial for marketers seeking to forge meaningful connections with their target audience. The advent of artificial intelligence (AI) has provided a novel approach to unraveling the intricacies of consumer emotions. However, a critical examination of the role of AI in this domain is essential to grasp both its potential and limitations (Turner, 2020). AI has revolutionized emotional analysis by allowing marketers to process massive amounts of unstructured data, including text, images, and videos, to gain insights into consumers' emotional states. Through sentiment analysis and natural language processing, AI algorithms can identify emotional triggers and patterns in customer feedback, social media interactions, and product reviews. This data-driven approach offers marketers a wealth of information to craft emotionally resonant campaigns. Nonetheless, critics caution against relying solely on data-driven insights, as AI might overlook the complexities and subtleties of human emotions.

While AI can detect and categorize basic emotions like happiness, sadness, or anger, understanding the deeper context and nuances of these emotions remains a challenge. Human emotions are often multilayered and influenced by a myriad of factors, including cultural background, personal experiences, and social context (Jorfi et al., 2012). AI's reliance on data may not fully capture the depth and intricacy of emotional responses, leading to potential misinterpretations and oversimplifications. Brands must strike a balance between leveraging AI insights and incorporating human empathy to comprehend complex emotional experiences. Emotionally intelligent AI chatbots are designed to respond empathetically to consumers, providing a more personalized and human-like interaction. These chatbots are programmed to recognize and address emotions, such as frustration or satisfaction, to enhance the customer experience. However, critics argue that AI's understanding of emotions might be superficial, lacking true empathy and genuine emotional connection. AI's responses, no matter how sophisticated, may feel artificial and insincere, potentially leaving consumers dissatisfied.

To harness the true potential of AI in understanding consumer emotions, marketers must complement data-driven insights with genuine human empathy (Jorfi et al., 2012; Turner, 2020). AI can provide valuable data points, but it is human understanding and emotional intelligence that can bridge the gap between data and authentic emotional connections. Combining the strengths of AI with the emotional intelligence of marketers can lead to more impactful emotional engagement strategies.

Utilizing AI to Gather and Analyze Emotional Data from Various Sources

In the quest to unlock deeper insights into consumer emotions, the integration of artificial intelligence (AI) has emerged as a powerful tool for gathering and analyzing emotional data from a myriad of sources. AI's ability to process vast amounts of unstructured data, coupled with sophisticated sentiment analysis algorithms, has promised to revolutionize emotional engagement in marketing (Jorfi et al., 2012). Social media platforms, customer feedback, online reviews, and chat interactions serve as troves of emotional data that can provide a comprehensive view of consumer sentiments and preferences. This data-rich approach empowers marketers to create emotionally resonant campaigns tailored to specific audiences. However, the deluge of data raises concerns about data quality, accuracy, and the risk of misinterpretation.

AI can simulate emotionally intelligent responses, providing consumers with empathetic interactions. While emotionally intelligent AI chatbots may impress consumers with their understanding of emotions, they lack genuine emotional comprehension. Human emotional intelligence and empathy cannot be replicated entirely by AI, and the risk of consumers feeling emotionally manipulated by AI-driven interactions remains a concern.

Sentiment Analysis and Its Applications in Understanding Consumer Sentiment

Sentiment analysis, also known as opinion mining, has become a prominent tool in understanding consumer sentiment, attitudes, and emotions. This AI-powered technique involves analyzing textual data, such as customer reviews, social media posts, and online discussions, to determine whether the expressed sentiments are positive, negative, or neutral (Zhang et al., 2018). Sentiment analysis offers marketers an automated and scalable approach to process large volumes of textual data, providing insights into consumers' feelings and opinions (Feldman, 2013). This speed and efficiency allow marketers to respond swiftly to customer feedback, track brand sentiment, and assess the impact of marketing campaigns (Feldman, 2013). However, an overreliance on automated insights may risk overlooking the nuances and context that influence consumer sentiment, leading to incomplete or inaccurate interpretations (Lin et al., 2020).

Natural Language Processing (NLP) for Deciphering Emotions from Customer Interactions

Natural language processing (NLP) has emerged as a pivotal technology for understanding and interpreting human language, including emotions, in customer interactions. By enabling machines to comprehend and respond to written or spoken language, NLP has revolutionized customer service, sentiment analysis, and chatbot interactions. While NLP's applications in deciphering emotions appear promising, a critical examination is necessary to assess its accuracy, limitations, and potential ethical concerns.

NLP has made significant strides in emotion detection, allowing algorithms to identify and categorize emotions in textual customer interactions. Through sentiment analysis and emotion recognition, NLP can classify expressions as positive, negative, or neutral, providing valuable insights into consumer sentiments (Shankar & Parsana, 2022). However, the accuracy of emotion detection remains a challenge, as NLP models may struggle to interpret nuances, context, and cultural variations in emotional expression. Emotional expression is highly subjective and context dependent, making it challenging for NLP algorithms to capture the depth and intricacies of human emotions accurately. The lack of contextual understanding can lead to misinterpretations or inaccurate emotion labels, potentially impacting customer interactions and decision-making processes. Human intervention is often required to provide a more nuanced interpretation of emotions in complex customer interactions.

As businesses operate in increasingly global markets, multilingual emotion analysis becomes essential. However, NLP models may not be equally effective across various languages due to linguistic variations and cultural nuances in emotional expression (Shankar & Parsana, 2022). This limitation raises concerns about the reliability of emotion detection in multicultural settings and highlights the need for language-specific adaptations of NLP models. NLP's ability to decipher emotions from customer interactions raises privacy and ethical concerns. Extracting emotional insights from customer communications may intrude on individuals' personal experiences and preferences, leading to potential privacy violations. Companies must ensure transparency, obtain informed consent, and adhere to data protection regulations to safeguard customer data used in emotion analysis. NLP models for emotion detection are trained on vast datasets, which may introduce biases present in the training data. Biased emotion analysis can lead to skewed results, reflecting preexisting stereotypes or cultural prejudices. Ensuring fair and unbiased emotion detection requires continuous monitoring, fine-tuning, and diverse and representative training data (Liu et al., 2021; Shankar & Parsana, 2022).

While NLP can simulate emotionally intelligent responses, it lacks genuine emotional comprehension and empathy. Emotionally intelligent customer interactions can positively influence user experiences, but relying solely on NLP-driven responses may lead to artificial or insincere interactions (Liu et al., 2021). Combining NLP's capabilities with human empathy and emotional intelligence can bridge this gap, offering more authentic and empathetic customer interactions.

Case Studies and Examples of Successful Emotional Data Analysis

Case Study 1: Coca-Cola's "Share a Coke" Campaign

Challenge: Coca-Cola, a global beverage giant, faced the challenge of declining sales and a perception of being disconnected from younger generations. They needed to reignite emotional connections with their audience and increase brand engagement (Chen, 2022).

Solution: Coca-Cola launched the "Share a Coke" campaign, which involved printing individual names on their bottles and cans. To ensure the campaign's success, the company conducted emotional data analysis through sentiment analysis of social media posts and customer feedback.

Insights: Emotional data analysis revealed that consumers had a strong emotional attachment to their names and found personalized products highly appealing. Additionally, the sentiment analysis indicated that sharing a Coca-Cola with someone evoked positive emotions of happiness, friendship, and nostalgia (Tien et al., 2019).

Outcome: The "Share a Coke" campaign leveraged emotional data analysis to create personalized and emotional connections with consumers. By associating the brand with personalization and fostering emotional experiences around sharing, Coca-Cola successfully rekindled its emotional bond with customers. The campaign generated widespread social media engagement, with users sharing images of personalized Coca-Cola bottles, and resulted in a significant increase in sales and brand loyalty.

Case Study 2: Spotify's "Wrapped" Campaign

Challenge: Spotify, a music streaming service, aimed to strengthen its emotional connection with users and improve brand engagement by celebrating their individual music experiences (Yoga et al., 2022).

Solution: Spotify launched its annual "Wrapped" campaign, which uses emotional data analysis to curate personalized music statistics for each user. The campaign showcases users' most-played songs, artists, and genres, reflecting their unique music preferences and emotions.

Insights: Emotional data analysis allowed Spotify to understand users' emotional responses to music, revealing their favorite songs, moods, and sentimental attachments to specific tracks and artists.

Outcome: By providing users with personalized insights into their music habits and emotional connections with songs, Spotify deepened its emotional engagement with its audience. Users embraced the campaign, sharing their "Wrapped" results on social media, creating a sense of community and emotional connection around the shared experience. The campaign's success led to increased brand loyalty and user retention as users eagerly awaited each year's "Wrapped" report (Yoga et al., 2022).

Case Study 3: Nike's "Dream Crazy" Ad

Challenge: Nike, a leading sports brand, wanted to create an emotionally compelling ad campaign to resonate with consumers and reinforce its brand values (Eyada, 2020).

Solution: Nike launched the "Dream Crazy" ad featuring Colin Kaepernick, a former NFL player known for his activism. The ad aimed to inspire audiences to pursue their dreams fearlessly while tackling societal issues.

Insights: Emotional data analysis conducted on social media discussions and reactions revealed that the campaign sparked intense emotional responses, with both positive and negative sentiments expressed.

Outcome: Despite some controversy, the "Dream Crazy" ad effectively captured consumers' attention and evoked powerful emotional reactions. The ad generated widespread discussions, with consumers expressing their support for or opposition to the campaign's message. Ultimately, the emotional resonance of the ad strengthened Nike's brand identity as a champion of empowerment and social activism, leading to increased brand loyalty and a surge in sales (Aniskova, 2020).

Case Study 4: Airbnb's "Belong Anywhere" Campaign

Challenge: Airbnb, an online marketplace for lodging, aimed to foster a sense of belonging and emotional connection among travelers and hosts (Medvedeva, 2021).

Solution: Airbnb launched the "Belong Anywhere" campaign, which utilized emotional data analysis to identify unique and emotional travel experiences shared by guests and hosts.

Insights: Emotional data analysis allowed Airbnb to understand the sentiments and emotions associated with travel experiences. The analysis highlighted the significance of feeling welcomed, accepted, and part of a community.

Outcome: By focusing on emotional connections and a sense of belonging, Airbnb successfully differentiated itself in the crowded travel industry. The "Belong Anywhere" campaign touched hearts, resonating with travelers who sought authentic and emotional experiences during their journeys. The emotional appeal strengthened Airbnb's brand identity and contributed to significant growth in bookings and customer loyalty (Medvedeva, 2021; Menapace, 2019).

Case Study 5: Always' "#LikeAGirl" Campaign

Challenge: Always, a feminine hygiene brand, sought to challenge societal stereotypes and empower young girls to embrace their strengths and capabilities (Feng & Chen, 2022).

Solution: Always launched the "#LikeAGirl" campaign, which utilized emotional data analysis to understand the emotions and sentiments surrounding the phrase "like a girl." The campaign aimed to redefine the phrase and empower girls to embrace it as a compliment.

Insights: Emotional data analysis revealed that the phrase "like a girl" was often used in a derogatory manner, implying weakness or incompetence. The analysis also showcased the positive emotions associated with empowering young girls and challenging gender stereotypes.

Outcome: The "#LikeAGirl" campaign went viral, sparking a global conversation about gender bias and empowering young girls to redefine what it means to be strong, capable, and confident. The emotional resonance of the campaign led to widespread support and engagement, with people sharing their own stories and experiences. The campaign significantly strengthened Always' brand perception and resulted in increased brand loyalty among both existing and new customers.

Case Study 6: Google's "Year in Search" Videos

Challenge: Google aimed to create an emotional connection with its users by reflecting on the most significant events and moments of each year.

Solution: Google released annual "Year in Search" videos, which utilized emotional data analysis to identify the most searched topics and events that evoked strong emotional responses from users.

Insights: Emotional data analysis allowed Google to understand the emotional impact of various events, such as natural disasters, social movements, and cultural milestones, on users worldwide.

Outcome: The "Year in Search" videos struck an emotional chord with users, reflecting on both triumphs and challenges of the year. The emotional resonance of the videos reinforced Google's role as a platform that reflects and connects users to significant global events. The videos garnered millions of views and widespread social media sharing, contributing to increased brand engagement and positive user sentiment toward Google.

Case Study 7: Dove's "Real Beauty" Campaign

Challenge: Dove, a personal care brand, aimed to challenge societal beauty standards and celebrate real beauty in all its forms (Millard, 2009).

Solution: Dove launched the "Real Beauty" campaign, which utilized emotional data analysis to understand women's perspectives on beauty and self-esteem.

Insights: Emotional data analysis revealed that many women struggled with low self-esteem and felt pressured by unrealistic beauty standards portrayed in media.

Outcome: The "Real Beauty" campaign celebrated diversity and challenged conventional beauty norms, striking a deep emotional chord with women worldwide. The campaign encouraged women to embrace their unique beauty and reject harmful beauty stereotypes. The emotional resonance of the campaign resonated with consumers, leading to increased brand loyalty and a surge in sales for Dove's products (Millard, 2009).

AI-Driven Personalization for Emotional Resonance

In the era of data-driven marketing, AI-powered personalization has emerged as a key strategy for enhancing emotional resonance with consumers. By analyzing vast amounts of customer data, AI algorithms can create tailored experiences that cater to individual preferences and emotional triggers. AI-driven personalization offers marketers the ability to deliver highly relevant and emotionally resonant experiences to each individual customer (Alvarez & Fournier, 2016; Hwang & Kandampully, 2012). By processing data on past behaviors, preferences, and emotions, AI algorithms can predict and anticipate customer needs, serving content and recommendations that are likely to evoke positive emotions. Personalization creates a sense of exclusivity and care, fostering emotional connections between consumers and brands. While AI-driven personalization can enhance emotional resonance, it must be balanced with data privacy concerns (Alvarez & Fournier, 2016; Hwang & Kandampully, 2012; Vredeveld, 2018). Gathering and analyzing vast amounts of customer data raises ethical questions about data security and consumer consent. Marketers must ensure transparency in data collection practices, allowing customers to opt in for personalized experiences while respecting their right to privacy.

Leveraging AI Algorithms to Match Emotional Triggers with Individual Consumers

The utilization of AI algorithms to match emotional triggers with individual consumers has emerged as a powerful strategy in modern marketing. By analyzing vast datasets and using sophisticated algorithms, AI can identify emotional cues and preferences to deliver personalized content that resonates deeply with each consumer. While this approach shows great potential, a critical examination is essential to address ethical concerns, data privacy, and the potential risks associated with AI-driven emotional personalization (Vredeveld, 2018).

The Potential of AI in Emotional Personalization

AI algorithms have the capacity to analyze large amounts of customer data, including browsing behavior, purchase history, social media interactions, and feedback, to discern emotional triggers. Armed with this information, AI can craft tailored marketing messages that align with individual preferences, aspirations, and emotions. Personalized emotional experiences can strengthen brand-consumer relationships and drive consumer engagement (Banerjee & Shaikh, 2022; Patterson & O'malley, 2006).

AI algorithms are only as good as the data on which they are trained. Biases present in the training data can lead to biased emotional personalization, inadvertently reinforcing stereotypes or excluding certain consumer segments. Marketers must diligently address biases, regularly assess AI models, and strive for inclusivity to ensure fair and equitable emotional matching. AI algorithms excel in identifying emotional triggers, but marketers must strike a delicate balance between personalization and privacy. While consumers may appreciate emotionally resonant content, they may also feel uncomfortable or intruded upon when their emotions are excessively targeted. Brands must find the right level of personalization that enhances the consumer experience without compromising individual privacy (Patterson & O'malley, 2006). While AI algorithms can analyze data to predict emotional triggers, they may lack genuine emotional intelligence and empathy. Emotional personalization requires a deeper understanding of human emotions and context, aspects that AI may not fully grasp. Human creativity, emotional intelligence, and empathy remain essential in crafting emotionally authentic content. AI-driven emotional personalization carries the risk of unintentional emotional manipulation (Patterson & O'malley, 2006). Crafting content solely to trigger specific emotions for marketing gains can lead to negative consumer perceptions and harm brand trust. Brands must prioritize ethical marketing practices, ensuring that emotional personalization aims for authentic connections rather than manipulative tactics.

Balancing Personalization and Privacy Concerns

The pursuit of personalization in marketing has revolutionized the way brands engage with consumers, offering tailored experiences that resonate on an individual level. However, this trend raises significant privacy concerns as brands collect and analyze vast amounts of consumer data to deliver personalized content. Striking the right balance between personalization and privacy is paramount to ensure ethical practices, consumer trust, and sustained business success. A critical examination of this balance is essential to navigate the challenges and complexities surrounding data privacy in the age of personalization. Personalization holds the promise of delivering relevant and engaging content that caters to consumers' specific needs, preferences, and emotional triggers. By leveraging AI algorithms and data analysis, brands can create tailored marketing messages, product recommendations, and user experiences that increase customer satisfaction and foster brand loyalty. To achieve personalization, brands often collect extensive consumer data, including browsing history, location information, purchase behavior, and demographic details. Respecting consumer privacy and obtaining informed consent are essential ethical considerations. Brands must prioritize transparency, ensuring consumers understand how their data is used and providing options for data control and opt-out. Balancing personalization and privacy becomes particularly crucial when dealing with sensitive consumer information, such as health data, financial records, or personal beliefs. Brands must implement robust security measures to protect such data from breaches or misuse, earning consumers' trust and confidence. While personalization enhances customer experiences, overpersonalization can be detrimental. Brands must be cautious not to inundate consumers with overly customized content, leading to a sense of intrusiveness or manipulation. Balancing personalization with serendipity and discovery ensures a well-rounded and engaging customer journey. As data privacy regulations continue to evolve globally, brands must comply with legal requirements to safeguard consumer data and maintain trust. The General Data Protection Regulation (GDPR) in Europe and other similar laws place a significant emphasis on consumer data protection and impose strict penalties for noncompliance. Data breaches and mishandling of personal information have led to a trust deficit among consumers. Brands must work diligently to rebuild trust by being transparent about data collection and usage practices, actively addressing privacy concerns, and prioritizing data security.

The Risk of Emotional Manipulation

Empathetic AI-driven chatbots may inadvertently manipulate emotions to keep users engaged or achieve specific business outcomes. While providing empathetic responses can enhance user experiences, using emotional responses solely to influence consumer behavior raises ethical concerns about emotional manipulation.

AI models are trained on vast datasets that may contain biases, leading to biased empathetic responses. Bias in chatbot interactions can reinforce stereotypes, alienate certain user groups, or unintentionally discriminate. Brands must diligently address biases in chatbot training data to ensure fair and unbiased responses (Mowen, 1988; Willman-Iivarinen, 2017).

While empathy is essential for customer interactions, chatbots must also prioritize accuracy and effectiveness in addressing user queries. Striking the right balance between empathetic responses and providing accurate information is critical to maintain trust and credibility with consumers.

To avoid potential backlash, brands must be transparent about chatbots' AI nature and limitations. Users should be informed that they are interacting with an AI-driven chatbot and understand its capabilities. Setting appropriate user expectations ensures that consumers do not feel deceived or disappointed by the chatbot's responses (Mowen, 1988).

Emotional Storytelling Through AI-Generated Content

Emotional storytelling has long been a powerful tool for brands to connect with audiences, evoke emotions, and foster meaningful relationships. AI-generated content holds the promise of creating emotionally resonant narratives at scale. By analyzing vast amounts of data, AI algorithms can identify patterns in emotional responses and storytelling structures, potentially delivering content that aligns with audience preferences and emotional triggers. Emotional storytelling relies on authentic human experiences and perspectives (Gladson Nwokah & Ahiauzu, 2009). AI-generated content may struggle to capture the subtleties and complexities of human emotions and experiences, leading to narratives that feel generic or manufactured. AI-generated emotional storytelling raises concerns about potential emotional manipulation. Crafting content solely to evoke specific emotions for marketing or persuasive purposes may be perceived as disingenuous and undermines consumer trust. While AI can generate content based on patterns and data, human creativity remains essential for crafting emotionally authentic and unique narratives. Emotional storytelling often involves vulnerability, empathy, and an understanding of human psychology, aspects that AI may lack.

AI-generated emotional storytelling often relies on personal data to tailor content to individual preferences and emotions. Striking the right balance between personalization and data privacy is critical to ensure ethical data handling and consumer trust. Brands must consider the ethical implications of using AI-generated emotional content (Heffernan et al., 2008). Transparency, informed consent, and adherence to data protection regulations are essential to safeguard consumer privacy and ensure responsible use of emotional data. Brands must be cautious about outsourcing their emotional storytelling entirely to AI. Maintaining brand authenticity and human connection is crucial in building genuine relationships with consumers.

The Fusion of AI Visual Recognition and Emotional Branding: A Critical Examination

The convergence of AI visual recognition and emotional branding marks a significant advancement in marketing and brand engagement. By harnessing the power of AI to analyze visual content and detect emotional cues, brands can create emotionally resonant experiences that connect with consumers on a deeper level. However, a critical examination is necessary to explore the potential benefits, challenges, and ethical considerations of this fusion in shaping emotional connections between brands and their audiences (Thomson et al., 2005).

Case Studies of Emotionally Driven Brand Visuals and Their Effectiveness: A Critical Examination

Case Study 1: Apple's "Shot on iPhone" Campaign

Apple's "Shot on iPhone" campaign showcased emotionally compelling user-generated photographs captured with iPhones. The campaign's visuals depicted a range of emotions – from joy and wonder to nostalgia and inspiration – captured through everyday moments (Niessen, 2021).

Effectiveness: The campaign's emotionally evocative visuals humanized the brand and resonated with consumers. By showcasing authentic, relatable moments, Apple established an emotional connection that extended beyond product features, fostering a sense of community and creativity among users.

Challenges: While the campaign successfully conveyed emotions, it required careful curation to ensure that visuals aligned with Apple's brand identity and values. Balancing the emotional appeal with the representation of the brand's technological prowess was a critical challenge.

Critique: Apple's campaign effectively harnessed emotions to drive brand engagement. However, the emphasis on user-generated content may have introduced some variability in the quality and consistency of the visuals, potentially impacting the overall emotional impact of the campaign (Goik & Tanazefti, 2016; Niessen, 2021).

Case Study 2: Dove's "Real Beauty" Campaign

Dove's "Real Beauty" campaign challenged conventional beauty standards and celebrated diverse body images through emotionally charged visuals. The campaign's images featured women of different shapes, sizes, and ethnicities, aiming to promote self-acceptance and positive self-esteem (Murray, 2013).

Effectiveness: The emotionally driven visuals resonated with consumers seeking authenticity and inclusivity. By addressing societal pressures and fostering self-confidence, Dove's campaign established an emotional connection that aligned with its commitment to empowering women.

Challenges: While the campaign aimed to promote positive emotions, navigating the complex landscape of body image and self-esteem required careful execution. Ensuring that visuals portrayed diversity and authenticity without exploiting emotions was a critical challenge.

Critique: Dove's campaign successfully harnessed emotional storytelling to promote a socially relevant message. However, some critics argue that the campaign could inadvertently reinforce the notion that appearance remains central to women's self-worth, which may counter the intended message of empowerment (Millard, 2009).

Case Study 3: Nike's "Just Do It" Campaign with Colin Kaepernick

Nike's "Just Do It" campaign featuring Colin Kaepernick used emotionally driven visuals to address societal issues and championed social justice. The campaign's visuals depicted Kaepernick's resilience and commitment to activism, resonating with consumers who shared similar values (Aniskova, 2020).

Effectiveness: The emotionally powerful visuals sparked conversations and ignited a cultural movement. By aligning with Kaepernick's values, Nike's campaign connected with socially conscious consumers, establishing an emotional bond rooted in shared beliefs.

Challenges: The campaign's emotionally charged visuals ignited both praise and controversy. Balancing the emotional connection with potential backlash required a careful assessment of the brand's risk tolerance and readiness to navigate polarizing responses.

Critique: Nike's campaign effectively harnessed emotions to engage consumers in a larger societal conversation. However, the campaign's success was polarized, with some praising the brand's stance while others criticized it, emphasizing the delicate balance required when addressing emotionally charged social issues (Eyada, 2020).

Developing AI-Powered Metrics for Emotional Engagement: A Critical Examination

Emotional engagement has traditionally been challenging to measure, often relying on subjective indicators such as sentiment analysis or surveys. AI-powered metrics offer the potential to quantify emotional responses more objectively, providing brands with a data-driven approach to evaluating the success of their emotional branding strategies. AI can analyze vast datasets, including social media interactions, customer feedback, and behavioral data, to discern emotional patterns and trends. This analysis can uncover insights into which emotional triggers resonate most with audiences, allowing brands to refine their messaging and strategies accordingly (Mowen, 1988; Munoko et al., 2020). While AI can analyze data for emotional patterns, the complexity of human emotions poses challenges. AI-powered metrics may struggle to capture the full spectrum of emotions and their nuances, potentially leading to oversimplification or misinterpretation. Developing AI-powered metrics involves collecting and analyzing consumer data, raising ethical concerns about data privacy and consent. Brands must handle emotional data with care, ensuring that data usage aligns with ethical standards and complies with data protection regulations. The pursuit of AI-powered emotional metrics should prioritize genuine emotional connections over manipulative tactics. Brands must be cautious not to use emotional engagement metrics as a means to manipulate consumer emotions for short-term gains, risking long-term trust and loyalty (Hwang & Kandampully, 2012). The adoption of AI-powered metrics requires transparency in how emotional data is collected, analyzed, and used. Brands must communicate openly with consumers about the data they collect and how it contributes to enhancing their experiences, thereby building and maintaining trust. While AI-powered metrics provide valuable insights, human judgment remains essential in interpreting emotional nuances and context. Integrating human insights with AI-powered analysis ensures a more comprehensive understanding of emotional engagement.

Assessing the ROI of Emotionally Driven Marketing Campaigns: A Critical Examination

Measuring the return on investment (ROI) of emotionally driven marketing campaigns presents a multifaceted challenge. While emotions play a vital role in driving brand engagement and loyalty, quantifying their impact in monetary terms requires a critical examination of methodologies, metrics, and the dynamic nature of emotional connections. This section delves into the complexities of assessing the ROI of emotionally driven marketing campaigns and explores key considerations, challenges, and ethical implications.

Emotions influence consumer behavior, but their effects are often intangible and may not translate directly into immediate sales (Alvarez & Fournier, 2016). Quantifying emotional ROI demands a shift from conventional metrics to capturing changes in brand perception, customer loyalty, and long-term value. Emotionally driven campaigns may focus on metrics such as sentiment analysis, social media engagement, and brand mentions. While these metrics provide insights into emotional responses, linking them directly to financial outcomes requires careful analysis and correlation. Attributing the impact of emotional campaigns to specific financial gains can be challenging. Emotional connections may lead to brand loyalty, repeat purchases, and word-of-mouth referrals, but isolating these effects from other marketing efforts requires advanced analytical techniques. Emotional branding often aims for long-term customer relationships, which may not yield immediate ROI. Balancing short-term sales goals with the potential for lasting brand equity requires aligning expectations and strategies (Vredeveld, 2018). Measuring the ROI of emotionally driven campaigns involves the responsible use of consumer data. Brands must prioritize data privacy, transparency, and informed consent, ensuring that emotional engagement does not come at the cost of ethical data handling. ROI assessment must consider customer-centric metrics, such as customer lifetime value and net promoter scores, which reflect the enduring impact of emotional connections on customer relationships and brand advocacy (Patterson & O'malley, 2006). The dynamic nature of emotions requires an adaptable approach to ROI assessment. Brands must be prepared to recalibrate metrics and strategies based on changing consumer sentiment and evolving emotional landscapes. Emotional campaigns that resonate with core brand values and establish authentic connections tend to yield higher emotional ROI. Striking a chord with consumers' emotions requires a deep understanding of their needs, desires, and emotional triggers. Assessing emotional ROI involves an integrated analysis of various data sources, including social media, surveys, customer feedback, and sales data (Patterson & O'malley, 2006). A holistic approach is necessary to capture the multifaceted impact of emotional engagement. Brands must strike a balance between financial objectives and emotional goals. An emotionally driven campaign may not always result in immediate revenue spikes, but its influence on long-term brand equity and customer loyalty can be substantial.

Integrating Emotional Metrics with Traditional Performance Indicators: A Critical Examination

The integration of emotional metrics with traditional performance indicators represents a transformative approach in assessing the holistic impact of marketing campaigns. By combining emotional insights with conventional measurements, brands can gain a comprehensive understanding of the emotional resonance of their strategies and their influence on tangible outcomes (Alvarez & Fournier, 2016; Vredeveld, 2018). This section critically examines the process of integrating emotional metrics with traditional performance indicators, highlighting its benefits, challenges, and ethical considerations.

Traditional performance indicators such as sales, conversion rates, and click-through rates provide quantitative insights into campaign effectiveness. Integrating emotional metrics, such as sentiment analysis, emotional engagement scores, and brand affinity measures, enriches the evaluation process by revealing the emotional impact on consumer behavior. Linking emotional metrics with traditional indicators bridges the gap between emotional engagement and tangible outcomes. Brands can uncover how emotional resonance directly influences consumer actions, shedding light on the underlying drivers of conversions and loyalty. The integration allows brands to pivot from transactional approaches to consumer-centric strategies. By understanding how emotions shape consumer decisions, brands can tailor their messaging and experiences to create deeper emotional connections. One critical challenge lies in attributing emotional impact to specific outcomes. Identifying whether emotional engagement directly leads to conversions or complements other influencing factors requires robust data analysis and modeling. Emotional metrics are often tied to long-term brand equity and loyalty, which may not translate immediately into short-term financial gains. Brands must strike a balance between short-term ROI objectives and the enduring impact of emotional engagement. The integration involves the responsible use of consumer data for emotional analysis (Vredeveld, 2018). Brands must ensure that data privacy, transparency, and informed consent are upheld throughout the process to ethically measure emotional metrics. Brands need a unified framework that combines emotional and traditional metrics seamlessly. This framework should facilitate data collection, analysis, and interpretation, providing a comprehensive view of campaign performance. The integration empowers brands to make informed decisions. By understanding how emotional resonance contributes to overall performance, brands can allocate resources more effectively, optimize strategies, and enhance customer experiences. Emotional metrics can be complex, encompassing a wide range of emotions and nuances. Brands must invest in advanced analytics and AI tools to accurately capture, analyze, and interpret emotional data alongside traditional performance indicators (Alvarez &

Fournier, 2016). For successful integration, emotional metrics must align with the brand's core values and objectives. A critical assessment of emotional metrics ensures that they authentically reflect the brand's essence and resonate with its target audience.

The Ethical Implications of Using AI for Emotional Engagement: A Critical Examination

The use of artificial intelligence (AI) for emotional engagement in marketing introduces a range of ethical considerations that demand careful examination. While AI offers exciting opportunities to enhance emotional connections between brands and consumers, it also raises concerns about privacy, manipulation, consent, and the potential impact on human relationships. This section critically explores the ethical implications of employing AI for emotional engagement, shedding light on the complexities that marketers and brands must navigate (Munoko et al., 2020). The ethical implications of using AI for emotional engagement underscore the need for a critical and responsible approach to leveraging technology for emotional connections. While AI offers the potential to enhance brand-consumer relationships, the considerations of informed consent, emotional manipulation, cultural sensitivity, and algorithmic biases demand vigilant ethical oversight. Brands must prioritize authenticity, consumer well-being, and ethical AI development to navigate the complexities of emotional engagement in an ethically sound manner (Munoko et al., 2020). By critically examining the ethical dimensions and ensuring responsible practices, brands can harness the transformative potential of AI while upholding ethical standards and fostering meaningful, genuine, and ethical emotional connections with their consumers.

Conclusion

Emphasizing the Transformative Potential of AI in Connecting Brands to Hearts: A Critical Examination

The transformative potential of artificial intelligence (AI) in connecting brands to the hearts of consumers is a pivotal evolution in the realm of marketing. As AI-driven technologies continue to advance, the critical examination of how they enable brands to forge profound emotional connections becomes paramount. This section critically explores the multifaceted dimensions of AI's transformative potential, underscoring the benefits, challenges, and ethical considerations that underpin the process of connecting brands to the hearts of consumers (Mowen, 1988). The transformative potential of AI in connecting brands to the hearts of consumers is a revolutionary force in the marketing landscape. Critical examination reveals how AI unlocks deeper emotional insights, fosters personalized experiences, and amplifies authenticity. By navigating ethical considerations and redefining emotional intelligence, brands can leverage AI to create emotionally resonant connections that transcend boundaries and cultivate enduring brand-consumer relationships. This critical examination underscores AI's role as a catalyst for transformative emotional marketing, shaping the future of brand-consumer interactions and driving unprecedented levels of emotional engagement (Willman-Iivarinen, 2017).

Striking the Balance Between Technology and Human Emotions: A Critical Conclusion

The journey through this book chapter has led us on a critical exploration of the dynamic interplay between technology and human emotions in the realm of marketing. As we conclude our examination, it becomes evident that the convergence of technology and emotions is not merely a trend, but a transformative shift that demands careful consideration, ethical scrutiny, and strategic alignment. Striking the delicate balance between these two forces emerges as a central theme, one that shapes the future of emotionally driven marketing strategies (Mowen, 1988).

The critical examination of integrating AI into emotional marketing strategies has revealed both the immense potential and the complex challenges that this synergy presents. The transformative power of AI in connecting brands to the hearts of consumers is undeniably remarkable. AI-driven emotional engagement offers the ability to decode emotional nuances, deliver personalized experiences, and craft compelling narratives that resonate deeply. It ushers in a new era where emotional connections can be fostered at an unprecedented scale, impacting consumer behavior, brand loyalty, and overall business success (Willman-Iivarinen, 2017).

However, this transformation is not without its critical considerations. Ethical dimensions cast a significant shadow over the use of technology to elicit emotions. The responsible use of AI in emotional engagement demands transparency, consent, and a vigilant commitment to authenticity. As technology becomes intertwined with human emotions, there is an imperative to ensure that emotional connections are genuine and that brands prioritize ethical practices over manipulative tactics.

Our critical exploration also underscores the need to preserve the irreplaceable value of human emotions and interactions. While AI augments emotional engagement, the essence of human connection must not be overshadowed. The fine balance lies in leveraging technology to enhance, not replace, human emotions. AI can guide strategies, analyze data, and deliver content, but the core of emotional engagement remains grounded in authentic human experiences and connections.

Conclusion

In the pursuit of deeper, more resonant connections between brands and consumers, the integration of emotional intelligence (EI) and artificial intelligence (AI) stands as a transformative force. This chapter has unraveled the profound impact of AI-driven emotional marketing, shedding light on its potential to forge authentic, enduring relationships with consumers. Critical exploration began with the foundational understanding of emotional intelligence in the context of marketing. We dissected how perceiving, interpreting, and responding to consumer emotions form the bedrock of effective emotional marketing strategies. This understanding served as the springboard for delving into two pivotal dimensions. The first dimension, "Emotional Intelligence and Consumer Behavior," underscored the significance of discerning and leveraging emotional triggers in shaping consumer decisions. It illuminated how emotional intelligence empowers brands to tailor their approaches, ensuring they resonate on a profound, emotional level. The second dimension, "The Impact of Technology and AI," propelled us into the future of emotional marketing. We witnessed how AI, with its data-driven insights and dynamic adaptability, amplifies emotional intelligence to an unprecedented scale. The integration of AI not only decodes complex emotional patterns but also delivers personalized experiences, redefining the way brands connect with hearts. Yet, amidst this technological revolution, a crucial thread emerged: the imperative to balance technology with genuine human connection. The fine art of emotionally resonant marketing lies not in replacing human interactions, but in enhancing them. AI serves as an invaluable tool, guiding strategies and optimizing experiences, but it is the authenticity of human emotions that remains the bedrock of enduring relationships. As we conclude this exploration, it is evident that the future of emotional marketing lies at the intersection of technology and human emotion. The brands that thrive will be those that master this delicate dance, leveraging the power of AI to augment, not replace, the profound connections that form the heart of human experiences. Through this critical examination, we have unearthed a path forward – one that marries innovation with ethics, and technology with empathy, to unlock emotional intelligence in ways that resonate, inspire, and endure.

Correction to: Building AI Driven Marketing Capabilities

Correction to:

**Tyagi, Pallavi; Grima, Simon; Maurya, Mohit; Zaidi, Neha (eds.,),
Building AI Driven Marketing Capabilities**
https://doi.org/10.1007/978-1-4842-9810-7

The updated version of this book can be found at https://doi.org/10.1007/
978-1-4842-9810-7

Owing to an unfortunate error on the part of the publisher the chapter authors were missing in the initially published online version of the book. This has now been corrected.

Editors: Neha Zaidi, Mohit Maurya, Simon Grima, Pallavi Tyagi

Chapter 1:

Dr. Harish Kumar*, Professor and Head, Department of Mass Communication, St. Xavier's University, Action Area III, B, Newtown, Kolkata, West Bengal 700160, Email: harish.kumar@sxuk.edu.in

Chapter 2:

Ambika Khurana*, Assistant Professor, School of Business Studies, Sharda University, Greater Noida, Uttar Pradesh, India, Email: ambika.khurana@sharda.ac.in

Shelly, MBAI (Pursuing), School of Business Studies, Sharda University, Greater Noida, Uttar Pradesh, India, Email: 2020518243. shelly@ug.sharda.ac.in

Tirthankar Dey, Integrated MBA (Pursuing), School of Business Studies, Sharda University, Greater Noida, Uttar Pradesh, India, Email: 2020435851. tirthankar@ug.sharda.ac.in

Chapter 3:

Reena Malik*, Chitkara Business School, Chitkara University, Punjab, India, Email: reenamalik2008@gmail.com

Ambuj Sharma, Ballabh Pant Social Science Institute, Jhusi, Allahabad, India

Chapter 4:

Dr. Rishab Manocha*, Associate Professor, School of Fashion Pearl Academy, Jaipur, Rajasthan, India, Email: rishab.manocha@pearlacademy.com www.linkedin.com/in/rishab-manocha-5935bbb8/ https://orcid.org/0000-00026754-4040 www.researchgate.net/profile/Rishab-Manocha

Chapter 5:

Pooja Chopra*, Assistant Professor, School of Computer Applications, Lovely Professional University, Phagwara, Punjab, India, pooja.27304@lpu.co.in, ORCID: 00000002-7624-9000

Munish Gupta, Associate Professor, Chandigarh University, Mohali, Punjab, India, gupta.munish2005@gmail.com ORCID: 0000-0002-1982-4136

Chapter 6:

Anshul Saxena*, Christ University, Bengaluru, Karnataka, India, Email: anshul.saxena@christuniversity.in

Rehan Mathew Kuruvilla, Christ University, Bengaluru, Karnataka, India

Jayant Mahajan, Christ University, Bengaluru, Karnataka, India

Sunil Vakayil, LIBA, Chennai, Tamil Nadu, India

Chapter 7:

Ms. Divya Rai*, Research Scholar, Abhilashi University, Chail Chowk, Distt. Mandi (H.P.), India, Email: divyaraa11@gmail.com

Dr. Jyoti Sondhi, Associate Professor, Abhilashi University, Chail Chowk, Distt. Mandi (H.P.), India, jyotisonisondhi@gmail.com

Chapter 8:

Himanshi Puri*, Assistant Professor, Sharda School of Business Studies, Sharda University, Greater Noida, Uttar Pradesh, India, Email: himanshi.puri@sharda.ac.in

Richa Pandey, Assistant Professor, Sharda School of Business Studies, Sharda University, Greater Noida, Uttar Pradesh, India

Apeksha Singh, Student, Sharda School of Business Studies, Sharda University, Greater Noida, Uttar Pradesh, India

Chapter 9:

Aderinola Ololade Dunmade, PhD, Centre for Open and Distance Learning, University of Ilorin/Computer Services and Information Technology (COMSIT), Ilorin, Kwara State, Nigeria, Directorate, University of Ilorin, Ilorin, Kwara State, Nigeria Email: derin_d@unilorin.edu.ng https://orcid.org/0000-0002-7745-0494

Timilehin Olasoji Olubiyi*, PhD, Department of Business Administration and Marketing, School of Management Sciences, Babcock University, Ilishan-Remo, Ogun State, Nigeria, Email: drtimiolubiyi@gmail.com https://orcid.org/0000-0003-0690-7722

Olorundamisi Daniel Dunmade, Faculty of Basic Medical Sciences, University of Ibadan, Ibadan, Oyo State, Nigeria, Email: olorundamisi1@gmail.com https://orcid.org/0009-00056368-6673

Chapter 10:

Madhu Rani*, Research Scholar, Sharda University, Greater Noida, Uttar Pradesh, India, rani.madhu01@gmail.com, ORCID ID: https://orcid.org/0000-0002-1712-2042

Dr. Satendar Singh, Associate Professor, School of Business Studies, Sharda University, Greater Noida, Uttar Pradesh, India, Email: satendar.singh@sharda.ac.in

Shagun Tomar, Research Scholar, Sharda University, Greater Noida, Uttar Pradesh, India, shaguntomar22@gmail.com, ORCID ID: https://orcid.org/0000-0001-5939-0371

Dr. Manisha Gupta, Associate Professor, Sharda University, Greater Noida, Uttar Pradesh, India, guptaamanisha@gmail.com, ORCID ID: https://orcid.org/0000-0001-6494-1094

Dr. Hari Shankar Shyam, Professor, Sharda University, Greater Noida, Uttar Pradesh, India, harishankar.shyam@sharda.ac.in

Chapter 11:

Dr. Vijay Prakash Gupta*, Associate Professor, Institute of Business Management, GLA University, Mathura, UP India, Email: vijayguptacmd@gmail.com

Chapter 12:

Dr. Madhavi Sripathi*, Associate Professor, Department of Business and Management Studies, SRGEC, Gudlavalleru, Andhra Pradesh, India, Email: sripathi.madhavi235@gmail.com

Dr. T. S. Leelavati, Assistant Professor, Department of Business and Management Studies, SRGEC, Gudlavalleru, Andhra Pradesh, India

Mr. T. Hemanth Kumar, Assistant Professor, Department of Business and Management Studies, SRGEC, Gudlavalleru, Andhra Pradesh, India

Chapter 13:

Shagun Sharma*, Research Scholar, Sharda School of Business Studies, Sharda University, Greater Noida, Uttar Pradesh, India, Email: 2021382123.shagun@dr.sharda.ac.in

Dr. K.R. Gola, Assistant Professor, Sharda School of Business Studies, Sharda University, Greater Noida, Uttar Pradesh, India, Email: kr.gola@sharda.ac.in

Nishtha Ujjawal, Research Scholar, Sharda School of Business Studies, Sharda University, Greater Noida, Uttar Pradesh, India, Email: 2021381091.nishtha@dr.sharda.ac.in

Chapter 14:

Disha Gupta, Research Scholar, Sharda School of Business Studies Sharda University, Greater Noida, India, Email: 2022300531.disha@dr.sharda.ac.in

Vidushi Nain*, Research Scholar, Sharda School of Business Studies Sharda University, Greater Noida, India, Email: 2017008152.vidushi@dr.sharda.ac.in; vidushinain1@gmail.com

Dr. Satendar Singh, Associate Professor, Sharda School of Business Studies Sharda University, Greater Noida, India, Email: satendar.singh@sharda.ac.in

Dr. Hari Shankar Shyam, Professor Sharda, School of Business Studies Sharda University, Greater Noida, India, Email: harishankar.shyam@sharda.ac.in

Chapter 15:

Neha Bisht* and **Amar P. Garg**, School of Biological Engineering & Life Sciences, Shobhit Institute of Engineering & Technology (NAAC "A" Grade Accredited, Deemed to-be-University), NH-58, Modipuram, Meerut -250110, Uttar Pradesh, India, bishtneha1993a@gmail.com; amarprakashgarg@yahoo.com https://orcid.org/0000-00026568-3469; https://orcid.org/0000-0003-0613-9495

Chapter 16:

Prof. Anushka Lydia Issac*, ORCID: https://orcid.org/0000-0002-1493-1047 Faculty and Course Leader – L3 Pearson Foundation Program, Westford University College, Sharjah, United Arab Emirates, Email: anulydia@gmail.com

R

References

Chapter 1

Boyd, D. M., & Ellison, N. B. (2008). "Social network sites: Definition, history, and scholarship." *Journal of Computer-Mediated Communication*, 13(1), 210–230.

Kietzmann, J. H., Hermkens, K., McCarthy, I. P., & Silvestre, B. S. (2011). "Social media? Get serious! Understanding the functional building blocks of social media." *Business Horizons*, 54(3), 241–251.

Kotler, P. (2003). *Marketing management*, 11th ed. Upper Saddle River, NJ: Prentice Hall.

Peppers, D., & Rogers, M. (2016). *Managing customer experience and relationships: A strategic framework.* John Wiley & Sons.

Chen, Y., & Chen, Y. (2017). "The impact of social media marketing on brand loyalty." *Journal of Research in Interactive Marketing*, 11(2), 145–164.

Hajli, N. (2014). "A study of the impact of social media on consumers." *International Journal of Market Research*, 56(3), 387–404.

Kaplan, A. M., & Haenlein, M. (2010). "Users of the world, unite! The challenges and opportunities of social media." *Business Horizons*, 53(1), 59–68.

Leung, X. Y., Bai, B., & Stahura, K. A. (2013). "Social media use for customer relationship building: An empirical study." *Journal of Database Marketing & Customer Strategy Management*, 20(2), 109–125.

© Neha Zaidi, Mohit Maurya, Simon Grima, Pallavi Tyagi 2024
N. Zaidi et al. (eds.), *Building AI Driven Marketing Capabilities*,
https://doi.org/10.1007/978-1-4842-9810-7

Verhoef, P. C., Reinartz, W. J., & Krafft, M. (2010). "Customer engagement as a new perspective in customer management." *Journal of Service Research*, 13(3), 247–252.

Casaló, L. V., Flavián, C., & Guinalíu, M. (2018). "Understanding the impact of social media on customer engagement and loyalty in the hotel industry." *Tourism Management*, 65, 41–51.

Hamzaoui-Essoussi, L., & Ben Mimoun, M. S. (2015). "The impact of social media on customer engagement: Evidence from the fast food industry in Tunisia." *International Journal of Information Management*, 35(4), 443–446.

Hussain, S., Khattak, J., Raza, S. H., Ali, S., & Zaman, K. (2020). "The impact of social media on customer engagement and brand loyalty: Evidence from Pakistan's telecommunication sector." *Journal of Retailing and Consumer Services*, 53, 101966.

Kapoor, K. K., Tamilmani, K., Rana, N. P., Patil, P., & Dwivedi, Y. K. (2018). "Advances in social media research: Past, present and future." *Information Systems Frontiers*, 20(3), 531–558.

Mangold, W. G., & Faulds, D. J. (2009). "Social media: The new hybrid element of the promotion mix." *Business Horizons*, 52(4), 357–365.

Tsimonis, G., & Dimitriadis, S. (2014). "Brand strategies in social media." *Marketing Intelligence & Planning*, 32(3), 328–344.

Yoo, B., & Donthu, N. (2001). "Developing a scale to measure the perceived quality of an Internet shopping site (SITEQUAL)." *Quarterly Journal of Electronic Commerce*, 2(1), 31–46.

Sharma, A., & Joshi, S. (2018). "Social media as a tool for customer engagement: An empirical study of Indian brands." *Journal of Indian Business Research*, 10(3), 191–210.

Singh, S., & Srivastava, R. K. (2018). "Social media marketing for customer engagement: A study of Indian FMCG sector." *Journal of Business and Retail Management Research*, 12(1), 29–41.

Chauhan, A., Kumar, A., & Gautam, V. (2019). "Measuring customer engagement in social media platforms: An exploratory study of Indian consumers." *Journal of Indian Business Research*, 11(2), 175–190.

Singh, R., & Saini, G. (2017). "Measuring customer engagement through social media: A study of Indian fashion industry." *International Journal of Business and Management Invention*, 6(10), 41-46.

Singh, R., & Saini, G. (2018). "Impact of social media on customer engagement: An empirical study of Indian hospitality industry." *Journal of Contemporary Hospitality Management*, 30(2), 714–731.

Chapter 2

1. Stark J (2015) "Product lifecycle management." In *Product lifecycle management*, vol 1. Springer, Cham, pp 1–29

2. Strong A I (2016) "Applications of artificial intelligence & associated technologies." In *2016 International conference on emerging technologies in engineering, biomedical, management and science*, pp 64–67

3. Wuest T, Weimer D, Irgens C, Thoben KD (2016) "Machine learning in manufacturing: advantages, challenges, and applications." *Prod Manuf Res* 4(1):23–45

4. Jackson PC (2019) *Introduction to artificial intelligence.* Courier Dover Publications, Mineola

5. Le Duigou J, Bernard A, Perry N (2011) "Framework for product lifecycle management integration in small and medium enterprises networks." *Comput Aided Des Appl* 8(4):531–544

6. Merayo D, Rodriguez-Prieto A, Camacho AM (2019) "Comparative analysis of artificial intelligence techniques for material selection applied to manufacturing in Industry 4.0." *Procedia Manuf* 41:42–49

7. Webster C, Ivanov S (2020) "Robotics, artificial intelligence, and the evolving nature of work." In *Digital transformation in business and society*. Palgrave Macmillan, Cham, pp 127–143

8. Wang L, Liu Z (2021) "Data-driven product design evaluation method based on multi-stage artificial neural network." *Appl Soft Comput* 103:107117

9. Keskin GA, İlhan S, Özkan C (2010) "The Fuzzy ART algorithm: A categorization method for supplier evaluation and selection." *Expert Syst Appl* 37(2):1235–1240

10. Kulkarni CS, Bhavsar AU, Pingale SR, Kumbhar SS (2017) BANK CHAT BOT–An intelligent assistant system using NLP and machine learning. IRJET (International Research Journal of Engineering and Technology, 4(05)

11. Mourtzis D, Vlachou E, Milas N, Dimitrakopoulos G (2016) "Energy consumption estimation for machining processes based on real-time shop floor monitoring via wireless sensor networks." *Procedia CIRP* 57:637–642

12. Neto P, Simão M, Mendes N, Safeea M (2019) "Gesture-based human-robot interaction for human assistance in manufacturing." *Int J Adv Manuf Technol* 101(1–4):119–135

13. Liu Z, Guo S, Wang L (2019) "Integrated green scheduling optimization of flexible job shop and crane transportation considering comprehensive energy consumption." *J Clean Prod* 211:765–786

14. Dorri A, Kanhere SS, Jurdak R, Gauravaram P (2017) "Blockchain for IoT security and privacy: The case study of a smart home." In *2017 IEEE international conference on pervasive computing and communications workshops (PerCom workshops)*. IEEE, pp 618–623

15. Grau A, Indri M, Bello LL, Sauter T (2017) "Industrial robotics in factory automation: From the early stage to the Internet of Things." In *IECON 2017-43rd annual conference of the IEEE Industrial Electronics Society*. IEEE, pp 6159–6164

16. Davis J, Edgar T, Porter J, Bernaden J, Sarli M (2012) "Smart manufacturing, manufacturing intelligence and demand-dynamic performance." *Comput Chem Eng* 47: 145–156

Chapter 3

[1] André, Q., Carmon, Z., Wertenbroch, K. et al. (2018). "Consumer choice and autonomy in the age of artificial intelligence and big data." *Customer Needs and Solutions*, 5, 28–37. https://link.springer.com/article/10.1007/s40547-017-0085-8

[2] Bertacchini, F., Bilotta, E., Pantano, P. (2017). "Shopping with a robotic companion." *Computers in Human Behavior*, 77, No C 382– 395.

[3] Concured Homepage. www.concured.com/blog/5-brands-that-are-successfully-leveraging-ai-for-marketing, Last Accessed 2022/12/29.

[4] Dumitriu, D., Popescu, M. A. M. (2020). "Artificial intelligence solutions for digital marketing." *Procedia Manufacturing*, 46, 630–636.

[5] Zumstein, D., Hundertmark, S. (2017). "Chatbots – An interactive technology for personalized communication, transactions and services." *IADIS International Journal*, 15(1), 96–109.

[6] Dash, R., McMurtrey, M., Rebman, C., Kar, U. K. (2019). "Application of artificial intelligence in automation of supply chain management." *Journal of Strategic Innovation and Sustainability*, 14(3). https://doi.org/10.33423/jsis.v14i3.2105Rupa

[7] Deb, S. K., Deb, V., Jain, R. (2018). "Artificial intelligence – Creating automated insights for customer relationship management," 758–764.

[8] Hermann, E. (2021). "Leveraging artificial intelligence in marketing for social good – An ethical perspective." *Journal of Business Ethics*, 1–19.

[9] Makarius, E. E., Mukherjee, D., Fox, J. D., Fox, A. K. (2020). "Rising with the machines: A sociotechnical framework for bringing artificial intelligence into the organization." *Journal of Business Research*, 120, 262–273. Econsultancy Homepage, https://econsultancy.com/how-wowcher-used-ai-copywriting-tool-reduce-facebook-adcpl/?zd_source=mta&zd_campaign=13370&zd_term=chiradeepbasumallick, Last Accessed 2022/12/30.

[10] Ergen, F. D. (2021). "Artificial intelligence applications for event management and marketing," in: *Impact of ICTs on Event Management and Marketing*, IGI Global, 199–215.

[11] Görgens, M. (2019). "How can Artificial Intelligence use big data to form a better customer experience." *Computer Science*, 1(1), 1–12.

[12] Ivanov, S., Webster, C. (2017). "Adoption of robots, artificial intelligence and service automation by travel, tourism and hospitality companies – A cost-benefit analysis," in: *International Scientific Conference "Contemporary Tourism – Traditions and Innovations"*, 19–21 October 2017, Sofia University.

[13] Cannella, J. (2018). Artificial intelligence in marketing. Honors Thesis. Available www.jamescannella.com/wpcontent/uploads/2018/04/Cannella_J_Spring_2018.pdf

[14] Johnson, M., Jain, R., Brennan-Tonetta, P., Swartz, E., Silver, D., Paolini, J., Mamonov, S., Hill, C. (2021). "Impact of big data and artificial intelligence on industry: Developing a workforce roadmap for a data driven economy." *Global Journal of Flexible Systems Management*, 1–21.

[15] Kuo, C.-M., Chen, L.-C., Tseng, C.-Y. (2017). "Investigating an innovative service with hospitality robots." *International Journal of Contemporary Hospitality Management*, 29(5), 1305–1321.

[16] Khatri, M. (2021). "How digital marketing along with artificial intelligence is transforming consumer behaviour." *International Journal for Research in Applied Science and Engineering Technology*, 9(7), 523–527. doi:10.22214/ijraset.2021.36287.

[17] Wu, L., Dodoo, N. A., Wen, T. J., Ke L. (2021). "Understanding Twitter conversations about artificial intelligence in advertising based on natural language processing." *International Journal of Advertising*, 1–18.

[18] Liu, X., Shin, H., Burns, A. C. (2021). "Examining the impact of luxury brand's social media marketing on customer engagement: Using big data analytics and natural language processing." *Journal of Business Research*, 125, 815–826. doi:10.1016/j.jbusres.

[19] Ammar, M., Haleem, A., Javaid, M., Walia, R., Bahl, S. (2021). "Improving material quality management and manufacturing organizations system through Industry 4.0 technologies." *Materials Today: Proceedings*, 45, 5089–5096.

[20] Khatri, M. (2021). "Digital marketing and artificial intelligence for evaluating powerful customer experience." *International Journal of Innovative Science and Research Technology*, 6.

[21] Martech Advisor Homepage. www.martechadvisor.com/articles/machine-learning-ai/5-examples-of-ai-inmarketing-in-2019/, Last Accessed 2022/12/30.

[22] Adam, M, Wessel, M., Benlian, A. (2020). "AI-based chatbots in customer service and their effects on user compliance." *Electron Markets*. Available: https://link.springer.com/article/10.1007%2Fs12525-020-00414-7.

[23] Moriuchi, E. (2019). "Okay, Google!: An empirical study on voice assistants on consumer engagement and loyalty." *Psychology and Marketing*, 36(5), 489–501. doi:10.1002/mar.21192.

[24] Ameen, N., Tarhini, A., Reppel, A., Anand A. (2021). "Customer experiences in the age of artificial intelligence." *Computers in Human Behavior*, 114, 106548.

[25] Mikalef, P., Fjørtoft, S. O., Torvatn, H. Y. (2019). "Developing an artificial intelligence capability: A theoretical framework for business value," in: *International Conference on Business Information Systems*, Springer, Cham, 2019, June, pp. 409–416.

[26] Purwanto, P., Kuswandi, K., Fatmah F. (2020). "Interactive applications with artificial intelligence: The role of trust among digital assistant users," *Форсайт*, 14(2), 64–75 (eng)).

[27] Pegasus One Homepage. www.pegasusone.com/top-5-real-world-applications-artificial-intelligence/, Last Accessed 2022/12/29.

[28] Brooks, R., Nguyen, D., Bhatti, A., Allender, S., Johnstone, M., Lim, C. P., Backholer, K. (2022). "Public health nutrition," in: *Use of Artificial Intelligence to Enable Dark Nudges by Transnational Food and Beverage Companies: Analysis of Company Documents*, 1–9.

[29] Perez-Vega, R., Kaartemo, V., Lages, C. R., Razavi, N. B., Mannist J. (2021). "Reshaping the contexts of online customer engagement behavior via artificial intelligence: A conceptual framework." *Journal of Business Research*, 129, 902–910.

[30] Dharmaputra, R. T., Fernando, Y., Aryshandy, G., Ikhsan, R. B. (2021). "Artificial intelligence and electronic marketing outcomes: An empirical study," in: *2021 3rd International Conference on Cybernetics and Intelligent Systems (ICORIS)*, IEEE, 2021, October, pp. 1–6.

[31] Dimitrieska, S., Stankovska, A., Efremova, T. (2021). "Artificial intelligence and marketing." *Entrepreneurship*, 6(2), 298–304.

[32] Rodgers, S. (2021). "Themed issue introduction: Promises and perils of artificial intelligence and advertising." *Journal of Advertising*, 50(1), 1–10.

[33] Verma, S., Sharma, R., Deb, S., Maitra D. (2021). "Artificial intelligence in marketing: Systematic review and future research direction." *International Journal of Information Management Data Insights*, 1(1), 100002.

[34] Saragih, M. H., Girsang, A. S. (2017). "Sentiment analysis of customer engagement on social media in transport online," in: 2017 *International Conference on Sustainable Information Engineering and Technology (SIET)*, IEEE, pp. 24–29. doi:10.1109/SIET.2017.8304103.

[35] Social Media Strategies Summit. https://blog.socialmediastrategiessummit.com/10-examples-of-ai-in-marketing/, Last Accessed 2019/12/30.

[36] Wang, Y., Petrina, S. (2013). "Using learning analytics to understand the design of an intelligent language tutor." *International Journal of Advanced Computer Science & Applications*, (11), 124–131.

[37] Sangeeta, Tandon, U. (2021). "Factors influencing adoption of online teaching by school teachers: A study during COVID-19 pandemic." *Journal of Public Affairs*, 21(4).

[38] Aggarwal, A., Chand, P. K., Jhamb, D., Mittal, A. (2020). "Leader–member exchange, work engagement, and psychological withdrawal behavior: The mediating role of psychological empowerment," 11.

[39] Luo, X., Qin, M. S., Fang, Z., Qu Z. (2021). "Artificial intelligence coaches for sales agents: Caveats and solutions." *Journal of Marketing*, 85(2), 14–32.

Chapter 4

- Project Muze: Fashion inspired by you, designed by code. (2016, September 2). Google. Retrieved 1, 2023, from https://blog.google/around-the-globe/google-europe/project-muze-fashion-inspired-by-you/

- Artificial neural network – Wikipedia. (2017, April 1). Retrieved January 4, 2023, from https://en.wikipedia.org/wiki/Artificial_neural_network

- About | Yuima Nakazato. (n.d.). Retrieved January 4, 2023, from www.yuimanakazato.com/about.html#:~:text= Designer%20Profile%20YUIMA%20NAKAZATO,Fine%20 Arts%20Antwerp's%20Fashion%20Department.

- Far infrared – Wikipedia. (2012, October 1). Retrieved January 7, 2023, from https://en.wikipedia.org/ wiki/Far_infrared

- Roadmap to Zero. (n.d.). Retrieved January 11, 2023, from www.roadmaptozero.com/?locale=en

- Understanding REACH – ECHA. (n.d.). Retrieved January 11, 2023, from https://echa.europa.eu/regulations/ reach/understanding-reach

- Meet MyloTM. (n.d.). MyloTM | Unleather. Retrieved January 12, 2023, from www.mylo-unleather.com

- Adam Pruden | frog, part of Capgemini Invent. (2022, September 6). www.frog.co/authors/adam-pruden

- Amazon Lab126. (2004). Amazon.jobs. https:// amazon.jobs/en/teams/lab126/

- Athos. (2012). Wearables.com. https://wearables. com/collections/athos

- CuteCircuit. (2004). https://cutecircuit.com/

- Firstinsight. (2020), Gen Z shoppers demand sustainable retail. Retrieved from www.firstinsight.com/ white-papers-posts/gen-z-shoppers-demand- sustainability

- Golub, A. (2019). DeepVogue AI: The era of AI design – Farewell human Karl Lagerfeld? ELSE research by ELSE Corp. https://blog.else-corp.com/2019/05/ deepvogue-ai-the-era-of-ai-design-farewell- human-karl-lagerfeld/

- Jacquard by Google – Home. (2015). Jacquard by Google. https://atap.google.com/jacquard/

- JCTC. (2020). 胜蓝股份官网-连接创造价值. https:// jctc.com.cn/

- On. (2010). www.on-running.com/en-in/

- Project Muze. (2016). Stink Studios. `www.stinkstudios.com/work/zalando-project-muze`
- ReTiSense. (2014). Stridalyzer Sensor Insoles – Sensor Insoles for Gait Research, Physiotherapy, Runners and Rehab. (n.d.). `www.retisense.com/`

Chapter 5

[1] P. Hájek, "Metamathematics of Fuzzy Logic," vol. 4, 1998, doi: 10.1007/978-94-011-5300-3.

[2] L. A. Zadeh, "Fuzzy Logic," *Computer (Long Beach Calif)*, vol. 21, no. 4, pp. 83–93, 1988.

[3] M. Gupta, S. Taneja, V. Sharma, A. Singh, R. Rupeika-Apoga, and K. Jangir, "Does Previous Experience with the Unified Payments Interface (UPI) Affect the Usage of Central Bank Digital Currency (CBDC)?," *Journal of Risk and Financial Management*, vol. 16, no. 6, p. 286, 2023.

[4] V. Sharma, M. Gupta, K. Jangir, P. Chopra, and N. Pathak, "The Impact of Post-Use Consumer Satisfaction on Smart Wearables Repurchase Intention in the Context of AI-Based Healthcare Information," in *Enhancing Customer Engagement Through Location-Based Marketing*, IGI Global, 2023, pp. 77–101.

[5] W. Holmes *et al.*, "Ethics of AI in Education: Towards a Community-Wide Framework," *Int J Artif Intell Educ*, vol. 32, no. 3, pp. 504–526, Sep. 2022.

[6] M. Lotfollahi, M. Jafari Siavoshani, R. Shirali Hossein Zade, and M. Saberian, "Deep Packet: A Novel Approach for Encrypted Traffic Classification Using Deep Learning," *Soft Computing*, vol. 24, no. 3, pp. 1999–2012, Feb. 2020, doi: 10.1007/S00500-019-04030-2/TABLES/12.

[7] P. Chopra and M. Gupta, "Fuzzy Logic and ANN in an Artificial Intelligent Cloud: A Comparative Study," in *Intelligent Communication Technologies and Virtual Mobile Networks*, Springer Nature Singapore, Singapore, 2023, pp. 559–570.

[8] N. J. Nilsson, "Probabilistic Logic," *Artificial Intelligence*, vol. 28, no. 1, pp. 71–87, Feb. 1986, doi: 10.1016/0004-3702(86)90031-7.

[9] E. Eiben and J. Smith, "From Evolutionary Computation to the Evolution of Things," *Nature,* vol. 521, no. 7553, pp. 476–482, May 2015, doi: 10.1038/nature14544.

[10] G. V. Benito, A. Sobrino Cerdeiriña, and A. Bugarín-Diz, "An Empirically Supported Approach to the Treatment of Imprecision in Vague Reasoning," *International Journal of Approximate Reasoning,* p. 108995, Jul. 2023.

[11] S. P. Gayathri, S. K. Selvi, and P. Nagaraja, "AI and ML Toward Sustainable Solar Energy," *Power Systems,* pp. 19–34, 2023, doi: 10.1007/978-3-031-15044-9_2/COVER.

[12] P. Sunhare, R. R. Chowdhary, and M. K. Chattopadhyay, "Internet of Things and Data Mining: An Application Oriented Survey," *Journal of King Saud University – Computer and Information Sciences,* vol. 34, no. 6, pp. 3569–3590, Jun. 2022, doi: 10.1016/J.JKSUCI.2020.07.002.

[13] F. Freudenstejn, "An Application of Boolean Algebra to the Motion of Epicyclic Drives," *Journal of Engineering for Industry,* vol. 93, no. 1, pp. 176–182, Feb. 1971, doi: 10.1115/1.3427871.

[14] L. Parreaux and C. Y. Chau, "MLstruct: Principal Type Inference in a Boolean Algebra of Structural Types," *Proceedings of the ACM on Programming Languages,* vol. 6, no. OOPSLA2, pp. 449–478, Oct. 2022, doi: 10.1145/3563304.

[15] B. van Tiel, M. Franke, and U. Sauerland, "Probabilistic Pragmatics Explains Gradience and Focality in Natural Language Quantification," *Proceedings of the National Academy of Sciences of the United States of America,* vol. 118, no. 9, p. e2005453118, Mar. 2021, doi: 10.1073/PNAS.2005453118/SUPPL_FILE/PNAS.2005453118.SAPP.PDF.

[16] M. Ozawa and A. Khrennikov, "Nondistributivity of Human Logic and Violation of Response Replicability Effect in Cognitive Psychology," *Journal of Mathematical Psychology,* vol. 112, p. 102739, Feb. 2023, doi: 10.1016/J.JMP.2022.102739.

[17] V. Laxmi Mohanta, S. Singh, and B. Kumar Mishra, "Human Health Risk Assessment of Fluoride-Rich Groundwater Using Fuzzy-Analytical Process over the Conventional Technique," *Groundwater for Sustainable Development*, vol. 10, p. 100291, Apr. 2020, doi: 10.1016/J.GSD.2019.100291.

[18] L. A. Zadeh, "The Role of Fuzzy Logic in the Management of Uncertainty in Expert Systems," *Fuzzy Sets and Systems*, vol. 11, no. 1–3, pp. 199–227, Jan. 1983, doi: 10.1016/S0165-0114(83)80081-5.

[19] R. S. Almeida, F. Vasconcelos da Silva, and S. S. V. Vianna, "Combining the Bow-Tie Method and Fuzzy Logic Using Mamdani Inference Model," *Process Safety and Environmental Protection*, vol. 169, pp. 159–168, Jan. 2023, doi: 10.1016/J.PSEP.2022.11.005.

[20] J. M. Kościelny and M. Bartyś, "A New Method of Diagnostic Row Reasoning Based on Trivalent Residuals," *Expert Systems With Applications*, vol. 214, p. 119116, Mar. 2023, doi: 10.1016/J.ESWA.2022.119116.

[21] L. A. Zadeh, "Fuzzy Logic, Neural Networks, and Soft Computing," *Communications of the ACM*, vol. 37, no. 3, pp. 77–84, Mar. 1994, doi: 10.1145/175247.175255.

[22] Y. Liu and E. E. Kerre, "An Overview of Fuzzy Quantifiers. (I). Interpretations," *Fuzzy Sets and Systems*, vol. 95, no. 1, pp. 1–21, Apr. 1998, doi: 10.1016/S0165-0114(97)00254-6.

[23] Z. Şen, "Philosophical and Logical Principles in Science," *Shallow and Deep Learning Principles*, pp. 67–139, 2023, doi: 10.1007/978-3-031-29555-3_3.

[24] H. Thiele, "On Fuzzy Quantifiers," *Fuzzy Logic and Its Applications to Engineering, Information Sciences, and Intelligent Systems*, pp. 343–352, 1995, doi: 10.1007/978-94-009-0125-4_34.

[25] J. Williams, N. Steele, and H. Robinson, "Modelling Non-Numeric Linguistic Variables," *Developments in Soft Computing*, pp. 124–131, 2001, doi: 10.1007/978-3-7908-1829-1_15.

[26] Wray, "Formulaic Sequences in Second Language Teaching: Principle and Practice," *Applied Linguistics*, vol. 21, no. 4, pp. 463–489, Dec. 2000.

[27] J. M. Terricabras, "Language, Fuzzy Logic, Metalogic," *Studies in Fuzziness and Soft Computing*, vol. 325, pp. 21–29, 2015, doi: 10.1007/978-3-319-18750-1_2/COVER.

[28] J. L. Ackrill, "Aristotle: The Philosopher." 1981. Accessed: Jan. 20, 2023. [Online]. Available: https://philpapers.org/rec/LACATP-2

[29] "Plato – Google Books." www.google.co.in/books/edition/Plato/EPZDAAAAYAAJ?hl=en&gbpv=1&pg=PR2&printsec=frontcover (accessed Jan. 20, 2023).

[30] George. Boole, "An Investigation of the Laws of Thought : On Which Are Founded the Mathematical Theories of Logic and Probabilities," p. 440, 2009, Accessed: Jan. 20, 2023. [Online]. Available: https://tiengtrung.cn/wiki/en/Laws_of_Thought

[31] B. J. Copeland, "The Genesis of Possible Worlds Semantics," *Journal of Philosophical Logic*, vol. 31, no. 2, pp. 99–137, 2002, doi: 10.1023/A:1015273407895/METRICS.

[32] L. A. Zadeh, "Fuzzy Sets," *Information and Control*, vol. 8, no. 3, pp. 338–353, Jun. 1965.

[33] S. Zhang, W. Zhang, A. H. Osman, and H. M. Aljahdali, "Important Arguments Nomination Based on Fuzzy Labeling for Recognizing Plagiarized Semantic Text," *Mathematics*, vol. 10, no. 23, p. 4613, Dec. 2022, doi: 10.3390/MATH10234613.

[34] R. G. Pirbalouti, M. K. Dehkordi, J. Mohammadpour, E. Zarei, and M. Yazdi, "An Advanced Framework for Leakage Risk Assessment of Hydrogen Refueling Stations Using Interval-Valued Spherical Fuzzy Sets (IV-SFS)," *International Journal of Hydrogen Energy,*, vol. 48, no. 54, pp. 20827–20842, Jun. 2023.

[35] S. K. K, L. Verghese and K. K. Mahapatra, "Fuzzy Logic Based Integrated Control of Anti-lock Brake System and Collision Avoidance System Using CAN for Electric Vehicles," *Proceedings of the IEEE International Conference on Industrial Technology*, 2009, doi: 10.1109/ICIT.2009.4939720.

[36] M. M. van Paassen, "Heidegger Versus Carthesian Dualism or Where Is My Hammer?" *Conference: Proceedings of the IEEE International Conference on Systems, Man and Cybernetics*, pp. 1684–1688, 2010, doi: 10.1109/ICSMC.2010.5642318.

[37] Yong-Hua Song and A. T. Johns, "Applications of Fuzzy Logic in Power Systems. Part 2: Comparison and Integration with Expert Systems, Neural Networks and Genetic Algorithms," *Power Engineering Journal*, vol. 12, no. 4, pp. 185–190, Aug. 1998, doi: 10.1049/PE:19980403 10.1049/PE:19980403.

[38] D. K. Ranaweera, N. F. Hubele, and G. G. Karady, "Fuzzy Logic for Short Term Load Forecasting," *International Journal of Electrical Power & Energy Systems*, vol. 18, no. 4, pp. 215–222, May 1996, doi: 10.1016/0142-0615(95)00060-7.

[39] H. Atmaca, B. Cetişli, and H. S. Yavuz, "The Comparison of Fuzzy Inference Systems and Neural Network Approaches with ANFIS Method for Fuel Consumption Data."

[40] P. Singhala, D. Shah, and B. Patel, "Temperature Control using Fuzzy Logic," *International Journal of Instrumentation and Control Systems*, vol. 4, no. 1, pp. 1–10, Feb. 2014, doi: 10.48550/arxiv.1402.3654.

[41] M. R. H. Mohd Adnan, A. Sarkheyli, A. Mohd Zain, and H. Haron, "Fuzzy Logic for Modeling Machining Process: A Review," *Artificial Intelligence Review*, vol. 43, no. 3, pp. 345–379, Mar. 2015, doi: 10.1007/S10462-012-9381-8/METRICS.

[42] S. Thaker and V. Nagori, "Analysis of Fuzzification Process in Fuzzy Expert System," *Procedia Computer Science*, vol. 132, pp. 1308–1316, Jan. 2018, doi: 10.1016/J.PROCS.2018.05.047.

[43] J. Williams and N. Steele, "Difference, Distance and Similarity as a Basis for Fuzzy Decision Support Based on Prototypical Decision Classes," *Fuzzy Sets and Systems*, vol. 131, no. 1, pp. 35–46, Oct. 2002, doi: 10.1016/S0165-0114(01)00253-6.

[44] W. Pedrycz, "Why Triangular Membership Functions?," *Fuzzy Sets and Systems*, vol. 64, no. 1, pp. 21–30, May 1994, doi: 10.1016/0165-0114(94)90003-5.

[45] F. Cuevas, O. Castillo, and P. Cortes, "Optimal Setting of Membership Functions for Interval Type-2 Fuzzy Tracking Controllers Using a Shark Smell Metaheuristic Algorithm," *International Journal of Fuzzy Systems*, vol. 24, no. 2, pp. 799–822, Mar. 2022.

[46] M. Serda *et al.*, "Synteza i aktywność biologiczna nowych analogów tiosemikarbazonowych chelatorów żelaza," *Uniwersytet śląski*, vol. 7, no. 1, pp. 343–354, 2013, doi: 10.2/JQUERY.MIN.JS.

[47] P. Scarabaggio, R. Carli, and M. Dotoli, "Noncooperative Equilibrium-Seeking in Distributed Energy Systems Under AC Power Flow Nonlinear Constraints," *IEEE Transactions on Control of Network Systems*, vol. 9, no. 4, pp. 1731–1742, Dec. 2022, doi: 10.1109/TCNS.2022.3181527.

[48] V. Radhakrishna, S. A. Aljawarneh, P. Veereswara Kumar, and V. Janaki, "ASTRA – A Novel Interest Measure for Unearthing Latent Temporal Associations and Trends Through Extending Basic Gaussian Membership Function," *Multimedia Tools and Applications*, vol. 78, no. 4, pp. 4217–4265, Feb. 2019.

[49] F. J. Lin, C. I. Chen, G. D. Xiao, and P. R. Chen, "Voltage Stabilization Control for Microgrid with Asymmetric Membership Function-Based Wavelet Petri Fuzzy Neural Network," *IEEE Transactions on Smart Grid*, vol. 12, no. 5, pp. 3731–3741, Sep. 2021, doi: 10.1109/TSG.2021.3071357.

[50] S. Medasani, J. Kim, and R. Krishnapuram, "An Overview of Membership Function Generation Techniques for Pattern Recognition," *International Journal of Approximate Reasoning*, vol. 19, no. 3–4, pp. 391–417, Oct. 1998.

[51] R. A. Aliev, A. v. Alizadeh, and O. H. Huseynov, "An Introduction to the Arithmetic of Z-Numbers by Using Horizontal Membership Functions," *Procedia Computer Science*, vol. 120, pp. 349–356, Jan. 2017, doi: 10.1016/J.PROCS.2017.11.249.

[52] "Proceedings of the Third IEEE Conference on Fuzzy Systems," *1994 IEEE 3rd International Fuzzy Systems Conference*, 1994, Accessed: Jan. 20, 2023. [Online]. Available: http://purl.oclc.org/DLF/benchrepro0212 H1 - THULB Jena H2 - H1 - HSB Emden/Leer H2 - H1 - FH Kiel H2 - H1 - ZHSB Flensburg H2 - H1 - Ostfalia Wolfenbüttel H2 - H1 - HSU Hamburg H2 - H1 - TIB Hannover H2 - H1 - UB Rostock H2 - H1 - HSB HS

[53] T. Samavat *et al.*, "A Comparative Analysis of the Mamdani and Sugeno Fuzzy Inference Systems for MPPT of an Islanded PV System," *International Journal of Energy Research*, vol. 2023, pp. 1–14, Apr. 2023, doi: 10.1155/2023/7676113.

[54] Y. Bai and D. Wang, "Fundamentals of Fuzzy Logic Control – Fuzzy Sets, Fuzzy Rules and Defuzzifications," *Advances in Industrial Control*, no. 9781846284687, pp. 17–36, 2006.

[55] S. Maalej and A. Kruszewski, "Stability and Performances Synthesis of a Class of Takagi–Sugeno Systems with Unmeasured Premises: Restricted-Model-Based Approach," vol. 54, no. 2, pp. 443–461, 2022, doi: 10.1080/00207721.2022.2122900.

[56] R. Khosravanian, M. Sabah, D. A. Wood, and A. Shahryari, "Weight on Drill Bit Prediction Models: Sugeno-Type and Mamdani-Type Fuzzy Inference Systems Compared," *Journal of Natural Gas Science and Engineering*, vol. 36, pp. 280–297, Nov. 2016, doi: 10.1016/J.JNGSE.2016.10.046.

[57] M. Rezaei, S. Molani, N. Firoozeh, H. Abbasi, F. Vahedifard, and M. Orouskhani, "Evolving Tsukamoto Neuro Fuzzy Model for Multiclass Covid 19 Classification with Chest X Ray Images," May 2023, Accessed: Aug. 09, 2023. [Online]. Available: https://arxiv.org/abs/2305.10421v1

[58] G. Acampora, R. Schiattarella, and A. Vitiello, "On the Implementation of Fuzzy Inference Engines on Quantum Computers," *IEEE Transactions on Fuzzy Systems*, vol. 31, no. 5, pp. 1419–1433, May 2023.

[59] E. Van Broekhoven and B. De Baets, "Fast and Accurate Center of Gravity Defuzzification of Fuzzy System Outputs Defined on Trapezoidal Fuzzy Partitions," *Fuzzy Sets and Systems*, vol. 157, no. 7, pp. 904–918, Apr. 2006.

[60] W. L. Hung and J. W. Wu, "Correlation of Intuitionistic Fuzzy Sets by Centroid Method," *Information Sciences (N Y)*, vol. 144, no. 1–4, pp. 219–225, Jul. 2002, doi: 10.1016/S0020-0255(02)00181-0.

[61] T. J. Ross, "Membership Functions, Fuzzification and Defuzzification," pp. 48–77, 2000, doi: 10.1007/978-3-7908-1859-8_3.

[62] M. Zhang, Y. Wu, W. Li, and W. Li, "Learning Universal Sentence Representations with Mean-Max Attention Autoencoder," *Proceedings of the 2018 Conference on Empirical Methods in Natural Language Processing, EMNLP 2018*, pp. 4514–4523, Sep. 2018.

Chapter 6

[1] R. Annisa, I. Surjandari, and Zulkarnain, "Opinion Mining on Mandalika Hotel Reviews Using Latent Dirichlet Allocation," *Procedia Comput. Sci.* vol. 161, pp. 739–746, 2019, doi: 10.1016/j.procs.2019.11.178.

[2] N. Akhtar, N. Zubair, A. Kumar, and T. Ahmad, "Aspect Based Sentiment Oriented Summarization of Hotel Reviews," *Procedia Comput. Sci.* vol. 115, pp. 563–571, 2017, doi: 10.1016/j.procs.2017.09.115.

[3] P. F. Muhammad, R. Kusumaningrum, and A. Wibowo, "Sentiment Analysis Using Word2vec and Long Short-Term Memory (LSTM) for Indonesian Hotel Reviews," *Procedia Comput. Sci.* vol. 179, no. 2020, pp. 728–735, 2021, doi:10.1016/j.procs.2021.01.061.

[4] E. Bjørkelund, T. H. Burnett, and K. Nørvåg, "A Study of Opinion Mining and Visualization of Hotel Reviews," *ACM Int. Conf. Proceeding Ser.* pp. 229–238, 2012, doi: 10.1145/2428736.2428773.

[5] R. A. Priyantina and R. Sarno, "Sentiment analysis of Hotel Reviews Using Latent Dirichlet Allocation, Semantic Similarity and LSTM," *Int. J. Intell. Eng. Syst.* vol. 12, no. 4, pp. 142–155, 2019, doi: 10.22266/ijies2019.0831.14.

[6] A. Farisi, Y. Sibaroni, and S. Al Faraby, "Sentiment Analysis on Hotel Reviews Using Multinomial Naïve Bayes Classifier," *J. Phys. Conf. Ser.* vol. 1192, no. 1, 2019, doi: 10.1088/1742- 6596/1192/1/012024.

[7] H. Hyun Jeong, S. Mankad, N. Gavirneni, and V. Rohit, "What Guests Really Think of Your Hotel," *Cornell Hosp. Rep.* vol. 16, no. 2, pp. 1–19, 2016.

[8] M. Sodanil, "Multi-Language Sentiment Analysis for Hotel Reviews," *MATEC Web Conf.* vol. 75, pp. 5–8, 2016, doi: 10.1051/matecconf/20167503002.

[9] K. Berezina, A. Bilgihan, C. Cobanoglu, and F. Okumus, "Understanding Satisfied and Dissatisfied Hotel Customers: Text Mining of Online Hotel Reviews," *J. Hosp. Mark. Manag.* vol. 25, no. 1, pp. 1–24, 2016, doi: 10.1080/19368623.2015.983631.

[10] M. Ristova, "What Do Hotel Guests Really Want?: An Analysis of Online Reviews Using Text Mining," *Menadzment u Hotel. i Tur.* vol. 8, no. 1, pp. 37–48, 2020, doi: 10.5937/menhottur2001037r.

[11] P. Chanwisitkul, A. Shahgholian, and N. Mehandjiev, "The Reason Behind the Rating: Text Mining of Online Hotel Reviews," *Proceeding – 2018 20th IEEE Int. Conf. Bus. Informatics*, CBI 2018, vol. 1, pp. 149–157, 2018, doi: 10.1109/CBI.2018.00025.

Chapter 7

1. https://medium.com/swlh/the-growth-of-ecommerce-2220cf2851f3

2. García-Crespo, Á., Colomo-Palacios, R., Mencke, M., & Gómez-Berbís, J. M. (2009). "CUSENT: Social sentiment analysis using semantics for customer feedback." In *Social Web Evolution: Integrating semantic applications and web 2.0 technologies* (pp. 89–101). IGI Global.

3. Philander, K., & Zhong, Y. (2016). "Twitter sentiment analysis: Capturing sentiment from integrated resort tweets." *International Journal of Hospitality Management,* 55(2016), 16–24.

4. Ireland, R., & Liu, A. (2018). "Application of data analytics for product design: Sentiment analysis of online product reviews." *CIRP Journal of Manufacturing Science and Technology,* 23, 128–144.

5. Rambocas, M., & Pacheco, B. G. (2018). "Online sentiment analysis in marketing research: a review." *Journal of Research in Interactive Marketing.*

6. Thelwall, M. (2019). "Sentiment analysis for tourism." *Big Data and Innovation in Tourism, Travel, and Hospitality,* 87–104.

7. Jain, P. K., Pamula, R., & Srivastava, G. (2021). "A systematic literature review on machine learning applications for consumer sentiment analysis using online reviews." *Computer Science Review, 41,* 100413.

8. Dr. Sondhi, J. (2019). "E-Commerce growth in international market: Impact on supply chain management." *International Journal of Commerce and Management Research, 5*(4), 91–93.

9. Gujjar, J. P., & Kumar, H. P. (2021). "Sentiment analysis: Textblob for decision making." *International Journal of Scientific Research & Engineering Trends, 7*(2), 1097–1099.

10. Rashid, A., & Huang, C. Y. (2021). "Sentiment Analysis on Consumer Reviews of Amazon Products." *International Journal of Computer Theory and Engineering, 13*(2). https://shabdbooks.com/index.php/volume-10-issue-9-2021/

Chapter 8

Razmak, J., Bélanger, C. H., & Farhan, W. "Development of a techno-humanist model for e-health adoption of innovative technology," *International Journal of Medical Informatics* (excess research paper) https://doi.org/10.1016/j.ijmedinf.2018.09.022

Agarwal, R., Anderson, C., Zarate, J., & Ward, C. "If we offer it, will they accept? Factors affecting patient use intentions of personal health records and secure messaging," *Journal of Medical Internet Research,* 15(2), e43 (2013). www.jmir.org/2013/2/e43. DOI: 10.2196/jmir.2243

Kumar, P., Dwivedi, Y. K., & Anand. "Responsible artificial intelligence (AI) for value formation and market performance in healthcare: The mediating role of patient's cognitive engagement," *Information Systems Frontiers* (2021). https://doi.org/10.1007/s10796-021-10136-6

Rahman, M. S., Ko, M., Warren, J., & Carpenter, D. "Healthcare Technology Self-Efficacy (HTSE) and its influence on individual attitude: An empirical study," *Computers in Human Behavior.* https://doi.org/10.1016/j.chb.2015.12.016

Rhee, H.-S., Kim, C., & Ryu, Y. U. "Self-efficacy in information security: Its influence on end users' information security practice behaviour," *Computers & Security* (2009). `https://doi.org/10.1016/j.cose.2009.05.008`

Russell, S. J., & Norvig, P. *Artificial Intelligence: A Modern Approach* (Prentice Hall, New Jersey, 2010).

Krizhevsky, A., Sutskever, I., & Hinton, G. E. in *Advances in Neural Information Processing Systems* 1097–1105 (Curran Associates, Nevada, 2012).

Lewis-Kraus, G. The great A.I. awakening. *The New York Times Magazine* (14 December 2016).

Yu, K.-H., Beam, A. L., & Kohane, I. S. *Nature Biomedical Engineering*, October 2018, 719–731 (accessed on January 2023)

Coccia, M. "Deep learning technology for improving cancer care in society: New directions in cancer imaging driven by artificial intelligence," *Technology in Society*, 60, 101198 (2020).

Dutta, G., Gupta, N., Mandal, J., & Tiwari, M. K. "New decision support system for strategic planning in process industries: Computational results," *Computers & Industrial Engineering*, 124, 36–47 (2018).

Ghasemi, P., Goodarzian, F., Gunasekaren, A., & Abraham, A. "A bi-level mathematical model for logistic management considering the evolutionary game with environmental feedbacks," *The International Journal of Logistics Management* (2021).

Ghasemi, P., Khalili-Damghani, K., Hafezalkotob, A., & Raissi, S. "Stochastic optimization model for distribution and evacuation planning (A case study of Tehran earthquake)," *Socio-Economic Planning Sciences*, 71, 100745 (2020).

Ghasemi, P., Khalili-Damghani, K., Hafezalkotob, A., & Raissi, S. "Uncertain multi-objective multi-commodity multi-period multi-vehicle location-allocation model for earthquake evacuation planning," *Applied Mathematics and Computation*, 350, 105–132 (2019).

Goodarzian, F., Taleizadeh, A. A., Ghasemi, P., & Abraham, A. "An integrated sustainable medical supply chain network during COVID-19," *Engineering Applications of Artificial Intelligence*, 100, 104188 (2021a).

Goodarzian, F., Wamba, S. F., Mathiyazhagan, K., & Taghipour, A. "A new bi-objective green medicine supply chain network design under fuzzy environment: Hybrid metaheuristic algorithms," *Computers & Industrial Engineering*, 160, 107535 (2021c).

Simonite, T. Google's AI eye doctor gets ready to go to work in India. *WIRED* (6 August 2017).

Lee, R., Wong, T. Y., & Sabanayagam, C. "Epidemiology of diabetic retinopathy, diabetic macular edema and related vision loss," *Eye and Vision*, 2, 17 (2015).

Lin, D. Y., Blumenkranz, M. S., Brothers, R. J., & Grosvenor, D. M. "The sensitivity and specificity of single-field nonmydriatic monochromatic digital fundus photography with remote image interpretation for diabetic retinopathy screening: A comparison with ophthalmoscopy and standardized mydriatic color photography," *American Journal of Ophthalmology*, 134, 204–213 (2002).

Zheng, Y., He, M., & Congdon, N. "The worldwide epidemic of diabetic retinopathy," *Indian Journal of Ophthalmology*, 60, 428–431 (2012).

Gulshan, V. et al. "Development and validation of a deep learning algorithm for detection of diabetic retinopathy in retinal fundus photographs," *JAMA*, 316, 2402–2410 (2016).

Poplin, R. et al. "Prediction of cardiovascular risk factors from retinal fundus photographs via deep learning," *Nature Biomedical Engineering*, 2, 158–164 (2018).

Abràmof, M. D., Lavin, P. T., Birch, M., Shah, N., & Folk, J. C. "Pivotal trial of an autonomous AI-based diagnostic system for detection of diabetic retinopathy in primary care offices," *NPJ Digital Medicine*, 1, 39 (2018).

Chapter 9

Abdolmohammadi, M. J., & Baker, C. R. (2007). "The relationship between moral reasoning and plagiarism in accounting courses: A replication study." *Issues in Accounting Education*. 22 (1).

Adetayo, A. J. (2023). "ChatGPT and librarians for reference consultations." *Internet Reference Services Quarterly*, 1–17.

Baig, A. I. (2023). *Learning in the Metaverse: Challenges, Opportunities, and Threats* (Doctoral dissertation, National University of Sciences and Technology).

Chan, C. K. Y. (2023). A comprehensive AI policy education framework for university teaching and learning. *arXiv preprint arXiv:2305.00280*.

Chikkam, S. G. K. (2023). Plagiarism checker. https://opus.govst.edu/cgi/viewcontent.cgi?article=1615&context=capstones

Cotton, D. R., Cotton, P. A., & Shipway, J. R. (2023). "Chatting and cheating: Ensuring academic integrity in the era of ChatGPT." *Innovations in Education and Teaching International*, 1–12.

Dunmade, A. O. (2022). *Perception, Awareness and Attitude of Female Postgraduate Students Towards Cyber-Ethical Behaviour in North-Central Nigeria Universities* (Doctoral dissertation, Adeleke University).

Dunmade, A. O., & Tella, A. (2023). "Libraries and librarians' roles in ensuring cyber-ethical behaviour." *Library Hi Tech News*.

Djokovic, R., Janinovic, J., Pekovic, S., Vuckovic, D., & Blecic, M. (2022). "Relying on technology for countering academic dishonesty: the impact of online tutorial on students' perception of academic misconduct." *Sustainability*, *14*(3), 1756.

Fernández Fernández, J. L. (2022). Ethical considerations regarding biases in algorithms. https://repositorio.comillas.edu/xmlui/bitstream/handle/11531/66640/JLF._Ethical%20considerations%20regarding%20baises%20in%20algoritms%20GE_EE_10_isbn9782889314423.pdf?sequence=1

Fitria, T. N. (2023, March). "Artificial intelligence (AI) technology in OpenAI ChatGPT application: A review of ChatGPT in writing English essay." *ELT Forum: Journal of English Language Teaching*, *12*(1), 44–58.

Floridi, L., & Sanders, J. W. (2005). Internet ethics: The constructionist values of homo poieticus. https://philpapers.org/archive/FLOIET.pdf

Fox, A. (2022). "Educational research and AIED: Identifying ethical challenges." In *The Ethics of Artificial Intelligence in Education* (pp. 47–73). Routledge.

Gumede, L., & Badriparsad, N. (2022). "Online teaching and learning through the students' eyes–Uncertainty through the COVID-19 lockdown: A qualitative case study in Gauteng province, South Africa." *Radiography*, *28*(1), 193–198.

Himma, K. E., & Tavani, H. T. (Eds.). (2008). *The handbook of information and computer ethics* (pp. 135–156). Hoboken: Wiley.

Kasneci, E., Seßler, K., Küchemann, S., Bannert, M., Dementieva, D., Fischer, F., ... & Kasneci, G. (2023). "ChatGPT for good? On opportunities and challenges of large language models for education." *Learning and Individual Differences*, *103*, 102274.

Kooli, C. (2023). "Chatbots in education and research: a critical examination of ethical implications and solutions." *Sustainability*, *15*(7), 5614.

Masenya, T. M. (2023). "Awareness and knowledge of cyber ethical behaviour by students in higher education institutions in South Africa." In *Handbook of Research on Cybersecurity Risk in Contemporary Business Systems* (pp. 33–48). IGI Global.

Newman, J., Mintrom, M., & O'Neill, D. (2022). "Digital technologies, artificial intelligence, and bureaucratic transformation." *Futures*, *136*, 102886.

Ng, T. K., Reynolds, R., Chan, M. Y. H., LI, X., & Chu, S. K. W. (2020). "Business (teaching) as usual amid the COVID-19 pandemic: A case study of online teaching practice in Hong Kong." *Journal of Information Technology Education: Research*.

Noonan, N. (2023). "Creative mutation: A prescriptive approach to the use of ChatGPT and large language models in lawyering." *Available at SSRN 4406907.*

Okaphor, E. F., & Agbara, O. D. (2022). "Intentional and unintentional plagiarism by researchers in the Nigerian universities: The legal and social implications." *AJLHR, 6, 91.*

Olubiyi, T. O., Egwakhe, A. J., & Egwuonwu, T. K. (2019). "Managerial roles and competitive advantage: SMEs perspective from Lagos State, Nigeria." *International Journal of Small Business and Entrepreneurship Research, 7*(3), 1–14.

Olubiyi, O. T., Lawal, A, T., & Adeoye, O. O. (2022). "Succession planning and family business continuity: Perspectives from Lagos State, Nigeria." *Organization and Human Capital Development, 1*(1), 40–52. https://doi.org/10.31098/orcadev.v1i1.865

Olubiyi, T. O. (2022a). "Measuring technological capability and business performance post-COVID Era: Evidence from Small and Medium-Sized Enterprises (SMEs) in Nigeria." *Management & Marketing Journal, xx*(2), 234–248

Oyewole, O. (2017). "Awareness and perception of computer ethics by undergraduates of a Nigerian university." *Journal of Information Science Theory and Practice, 5*(4), 68–80

Ray, P. P. (2023). "ChatGPT: A comprehensive review on background, applications, key challenges, bias, ethics, limitations and future scope." *Internet of Things and Cyber-Physical Systems.*

Sullivan, M., Kelly, A., & McLaughlan, P. (2023). "ChatGPT in higher education: Considerations for academic integrity and student learning." *Journal of Applied Learning and Teaching, 6*(1).

Sweeney, S. (2023). "Who wrote this? Essay mills and assessment–Considerations regarding contract cheating and AI in higher education." *The International Journal of Management Education, 21*(2), 100818.

Tomar, A. K. (2022). "The abhorrent act of plagiarism in higher education." *Issue 4 Int'l JL Mgmt. & Human., 5,* 1045.

Torres, J. (2023). *Leadership Practices That Cultivate Responsible Online Behavior in Elementary and Middle Schools* (Doctoral dissertation, Widener University).

Ugbede, E. O., Ikani, V., Attah, A. H., & El-Kalash, K. I. (2021) Appraisal of availability and utilization of anti-plagiarism software by academic staff among the Public Colleges of Education in North-Central NIGERIA. www.globalacademicgroup.com/journals/the%20nigerian%20academic%20forum/V28N1P34_2021_NAF.pdf

Ukabi, O. B., Uba, U. J., Ewum, C. O., & Olubiyi, T. O. (2023). "Measuring entrepreneurial skills and sustainability in small business enterprises post-pandemic: Empirical study from Cross River State, Nigeria." *International Journal of Business, Management and Economics, 4*(2), 132–149.

Uwem, E. I., Oyedele, O. O., & Olubiyi, O. T. (2021). "Workplace green behavior for sustainable competitive advantage." In *Human resource management practices for promoting Sustainability* (pp. 248–263). IGI Global.

Wardat, Y., Tashtoush, M. A., AlAli, R., & Jarrah, A. M. (2023). "ChatGPT: A revolutionary tool for teaching and learning mathematics." *Eurasia Journal of Mathematics, Science and Technology Education, 19*(7), em2286.

Chapter 10

Joinson, A.N. 2008, April. "Looking at, looking up or keeping up with people? Motives and use of Facebook." In *Proceedings of the SIGCHI Conference on Human Factors in Computing Systems* (pp. 1027–1036).

Tonkin, E., Pfeiffer, H.D. and Tourte, G. 2012. "Twitter, information sharing and the London riots?" *Bulletin of the American Society for Information Science and Technology, 38*(2), pp. 49–57.

Mackenzie, G. 2018. "Twitter big data and infectious disease conferences." *The Lancet Infectious Diseases, 18*(2), p. 154.

Ahmed, W. and Lugovic, S. 2018. "Social media analytics: analysis and visualisation of news diffusion using NodeXL." *Online Information Review.*

PWC. 2016. "Videoquake 3.0: The evolution of TV's revolution," available at: www.pwc.com/us/en/ industry/entertainment-media/publications/consumer-intelligence-series/assets/pwc-videoconsumption-report-3.pdf (accessed 10 June 2016).

Rastogi, D., Parihar, T.S. and Kumar, H. 2023. "A parametric analysis of AVA to optimise Netflix performance." *International Journal of Information Technology,* pp. 1–8.

Song, M. 2013. "Global OTT landscape & strategic directions of CPND." *KT Economics & Management Research Lab.*

Netflix. 2022. "Netflix to announce second quarter 2022 financial results," available at: https://s22.q4cdn.com/959853165/files/doc_news/Netflix-to-Announce-Second-Quarter-2022-Financial-Results-2022.pdf

Moody, R. 2020. "Netflix subscribers and revenue by country." *Comparitech. com.*

Saha, S. and Prasad, S. 2021. "Consumption pattern of OTT platforms in India." *International Journal of Modern Agriculture, 10*(2), pp. 641–655.

Mishra, S. 2019, September 24. "Startup stories. The rise of OTT platforms in India," accessed from `www.startupstories.in/stories/the-rise-of-ott-platforms-in-india`

Humphreys, L. 2012. "Connecting, coordinating, cataloguing: Communicative practices on mobile social networks." *Journal of Broadcasting & Electronic Media*, *56*(4), pp. 494–510.

Wellman, B. 2004. "Connecting communities: On and offline." *Contexts*, *3*(4), pp. 22–28.

Delgado Reina, M., Lluis Gumiel, P., Paz, E., Navarro Bosch, C. and García Muñoz, N. 2018. TV news and social audience in Europe (EU5): on-screen and twitter strategies.

Pena, L.L. 2015. *Breaking Binge: Exploring the Effects of Binge Watching on Television Viewer Reception* (Doctoral dissertation, Syracuse University).

Wohn, D.Y. and Na, E.K. 2011. "Tweeting about TV: Sharing television viewing experiences via social media message streams." *First Monday*.

Fernández-Gómez, E. and Martín-Quevedo, J. 2018. The engagement strategy of Netflix Spain in Twitter.

Van Es, K. 2016. "Social TV and the participation dilemma in NBC's The Voice." *Television & new media*, *17*(2), pp. 108–123.

D'heer, E., Godin, F., Evens, T., De Neve, W., Verdegem, P. and Van de Walle, R. 2015. "How can Twitter data and viewing rates enrich one another? A conceptual and empirical comparison between viewing rates and Twitter data for TV audience research." In *ICA*.

Artt, S. and Schwan, A. 2016. "Screening women's imprisonment: Agency and exploitation in Orange Is the New Black." *Television & New Media*, *17*(6), pp. 467–472.

Schwan, A. 2016. "Postfeminism meets the women in prison genre: Privilege and Spectatorship in Orange Is the New Black." *Television & New Media*, *17*(6), pp. 473–490.

Belcher, C. 2016. "There is no such thing as a post-racial prison: Neoliberal multiculturalism and the white savior complex on orange is the new black." *Television & New Media*, *17*(6), pp. 491–503.

DeCarvalho, L.J. and Cox, N.B. 2016. "Extended "visiting hours" deconstructing identity in Netflix's promotional campaigns for Orange Is the New Black." *Television & New Media*, *17*(6), pp. 504–519.

Silverman, R.E. and Ryalls, E.D. 2016. ""Everything is different the second time around" The stigma of temporality on Orange Is the New Black." *Television & New Media, 17*(6), pp. 520–533.

De-Lara-González, A., Árias-Robles, F., Carvajal-Prieto, M. and García-Avilés, J.A. 2015. "2014 Ranking of journalistic innovation in Spain. Analysis and classification of 25 initiatives." *Profesional de la información, 24*(3), pp. 227–234.

Wilson, S. 2016. "In the living room: Second screens and TV audiences." *Television & New Media, 17*(2), pp.174–191.

Lemon, K.N. and Verhoef, P.C. 2016. "Understanding customer experience throughout the customer journey." *Journal of Marketing, 80*(6), pp. 69–96.

Ansari, S., Garud, R. and Kumaraswamy, A. 2016. "The disruptor's dilemma: TiVo and the US television ecosystem." *Strategic Management Journal, 37*(9), pp. 1829–1853.

Verhoef, P.C., Broekhuizen, T., Bart, Y., Bhattacharya, A., Dong, J.Q., Fabian, N. and Haenlein, M. 2021. "Digital transformation: A multidisciplinary reflection and research agenda." *Journal of Business Research, 122*, pp. 889–901.

Mogyorosi, M. 2021. Sentiment analysis: First steps with Python's NLTK Library.

Loader, B.D., Vromen, A. and Xenos, M.A. 2016. "Performing for the young networked citizen? Celebrity politics, social networking and the political engagement of young people." *Media, Culture & Society, 38*(3), pp. 400–419.

Dudek, D., Woodley, G. and Green, L. 2022. ""Own your narrative": teenagers as producers and consumers of porn in Netflix's Sex Education." *Information, Communication & Society, 25*(4), pp. 502–515.

Loader, B.D. 2007. "Introduction: Young citizens in the digital age: Disaffected or displaced?" In *Young Citizens in the Digital Age* (pp. 15–32). Routledge.

Möller, J., Trilling, D., Helberger, N. and van Es, B. 2018. "Do not blame it on the algorithm: An empirical assessment of multiple recommender systems and their impact on content diversity." *Information, Communication & Society, 21*(7), pp. 959–977.

Helberger, N., Karppinen, K. and D'acunto, L. 2018. "Exposure diversity as a design principle for recommender systems." *Information, Communication & Society, 21*(2), pp. 191–207.

Nagpal, A. and Gabrani, G. 2019, "February. Python for data analytics, scientific and technical applications." In *2019 Amity International Conference on Artificial Intelligence (AICAI)* (pp. 140–145). IEEE.

McKinney, W. 2011. "pandas: A foundational Python library for data analysis and statistics." *Python for High Performance and Scientific Computing*, *14*(9), pp. 1–9.

Bird, S. 2006, July. NLTK: "The natural language toolkit." In *Proceedings of the COLING/ACL 2006 Interactive Presentation Sessions* (pp. 69–72).

Fernández-Morales, M. and Menéndez-Menéndez, M.I. 2016. "When in Rome, Use What You've Got" A Discussion of Female Agency through Orange Is the New Black. *Television & New Media*, *17*(6), pp. 534–546.

Segado-Boj, F., Grandio, M.-d.-M. and Fernandez-Gomez, E. (2015, May/June). Social media and television: A bibliographic review based on the web of science. *El Profesional de la Informacion*, *24*(3), pp.227–234. doi:10.3145/epi.2015.may.02

Chapter 11

- Bag, S., Srivastava, G., Bashir, M. M. A., Kumari, S., Giannakis, M., & Chowdhury, A. H. (2022). "Journey of customers in this digital era: Understanding the role of artificial intelligence technologies in user engagement and conversion." *Benchmarking: An International Journal*, *29*(7), 2074–2098.

- Boddu, R. S. K., Santoki, A. A., Khurana, S., Koli, P. V., Rai, R., & Agrawal, A. (2022). "An analysis to understand the role of machine learning, robotics, and artificial intelligence in digital marketing." *Materials Today: Proceedings*, *56*, 2288–2292.

- Brożek, B., & Janik, B. (2019). "Can artificial intelligence be a moral agent?" *New Ideas in Psychology*, *54*, 101–106.

- Cao, L., Chen, C., Dong, X., Wang, M., & Qin, X. (2023). "The dark side of AI identity: Investigating when and why AI identity entitles unethical behavior." *Computers in Human Behavior*, 107669.

- Cuéllar, M. F. (2019). "A common law for the age of artificial intelligence." *Columbia Law Review*, *119*(7), 1773–1792.

- Gerke, S., Minssen, T., & Cohen, G. (2020). "Ethical and legal challenges of artificial intelligence-driven healthcare." In *Artificial intelligence in healthcare* (pp. 295–336). Academic Press.

- Gonçalves, A. R., Pinto, D. C., Rita, P., & Pires, T. (2023). "Artificial intelligence and its ethical implications for marketing." *Emerging Science Journal, 7*(2), 313–327.

- Haleem, A., Javaid, M., Qadri, M. A., Singh, R. P., & Suman, R. (2022). "Artificial intelligence (AI) applications for marketing: A literature-based study." *International Journal of Intelligent Networks.*

- Hermann, E. (2022). "Leveraging artificial intelligence in marketing for social good – An ethical perspective." *Journal of Business Ethics, 179*(1), 43–61.

- Huang, M. H., & Rust, R. T. (2021). "A strategic framework for artificial intelligence in marketing." *Journal of the Academy of Marketing Science, 49,* 30–50.

- Kertysova, K. (2018). "Artificial intelligence and disinformation: How AI changes the way disinformation is produced, disseminated, and can be countered." *Security and Human Rights, 29*(1–4), 55–81.

- Kumar, V., Rajan, B., Venkatesan, R., & Lecinski, J. (2019). "Understanding the role of artificial intelligence in personalized engagement marketing." *California Management Review, 61*(4), 135–155.

- Legg, S., & Hutter, M. (2007). "A collection of definitions of intelligence." *Frontiers in Artificial Intelligence and Applications, 157,* 17.

- Ljepava, N. (2022). "AI-enabled marketing solutions in marketing decision making: AI application in different stages of marketing process." *TEM Journal, 11*(3), 1308–1315.

- McCollough, C. J., Wallace, A. A., & Luttrell, R. (2022). "Artificial intelligence: The dark side, ethics, and implications." In *The Emerald handbook of computer-mediated communication and social media* (pp. 671–684). Emerald Publishing Limited.

- Perakakis, E., Mastorakis, G., & Kopanakis, I. (2019). "Social media monitoring: An innovative intelligent approach." *Designs, 3*(2), 24.

- Peyravi, B., Nekrošienė, J., & Lobanova, L. (2020). "Revolutionized technologies for marketing: Theoretical review with a focus on artificial intelligence." *Business: Theory and Practice, 21*(2), 827–834.

- Savulescu, J., & Maslen, H. (2015). "Moral enhancement and artificial intelligence: Moral AI?" *Beyond artificial intelligence: The disappearing human-machine divide*, 79–95.

- Theodoridis, P. K., & Gkikas, D. C. (2019). "How artificial intelligence affects digital marketing." In *Strategic innovative marketing and tourism: 7th ICSIMAT, Athenian Riviera, Greece, 2018* (pp. 1319–1327). Springer International Publishing.

- Davenport, T., Guha, A., Grewal, D., & Bressgott, T. (2020). "How artificial intelligence will change the future of marketing." *Journal of the Academy of Marketing Science, 48*, 24–42.

- Fan, A., Lu, Z., & Mao, Z. E. (2022). "To talk or to touch: Unraveling consumer responses to two types of hotel in-room technology." *International Journal of Hospitality Management, 101*, 103112.

- Grewal, D., Guha, A., Satornino, C. B., & Schweiger, E. B. (2021). "Artificial intelligence: The light and the darkness." *Journal of Business Research, 136*, 229–236.

- Ioannou, A., & Tussyadiah, I. (2021). "Privacy and surveillance attitudes during health crises: Acceptance of surveillance and privacy protection behaviors." *Technology in Society, 67*, 101774.

- Hu, Y., & Min, H. K. (2023). "The dark side of artificial intelligence in service: The "watching-eye" effect and privacy concerns." *International Journal of Hospitality Management, 110*, 103437.

- Marr, B. (2021). What are the negative impacts of artificial intelligence (AI)? Bernard Marr & Co. USA. Available at: `https://bernardmarr.com/default.asp?content ID=1827`

- Mikalef, P., & Krogsite, J. (2020). "Examining the interplay between big data analytics and contextual factors in driving process innovation capabilities." *European Journal of Information Systems. 29*(3), 260–287. `https://doi.org/10.1080/0960085X.2020.1740618`

- Conboy, K., Mikalef, P., Dennehy, D., & Krogstie, J. (2020). "Using business analytics to enhance dynamic capabilities in operations research: A case analysis and research agenda." *European Journal of Operational Research, 281*(3), 656–672. https://doi.org/10.1016/j.ejor.2019.06.051

- Davenport, T. H. (2018). "From analytics to artificial intelligence." *Journal of Business Analytics, 1*(2), 73–80. https://doi.org/10.1080/2573234X.2018.1543535

- Huang, M.-H., & Rust R. T. (2018). "Artificial intelligence in service." *Journal of Service Research,* 21(2), 155–172.

- Ioannou, A., Tussyadiah, I., & Miller, G. (2021) "That's private! Understanding travelers' privacy concerns and online data disclosure." *Journal of Travel Research*, 60(7), 1510–1526.

- Mikalef, P., & Gupta, M. (2021). "Artificial intelligence capability: Conceptualization, measurement calibration, and empirical study on its impact on organizational creativity and firm performance." Information Management, 58(3), 103434. https://doi.org/10.1016/j.im.2021.103434

- Vidgen, R., Shaw, S., & Grant, D. B. (2017). "Management challenges in creating value from business analytics." *European Journal of Operational Research*, 261(2), 626–639. https://doi.org/10.1016/j.ejor.2017.02.023

- Davenport, T., & Malone, K. (2021, Winter). "Deployment as a critical business data science discipline." *Harvard Data Science Review* (3.1). https://doi.org/10.1162/99608f92.90814c32

- Sharda, R., Delen, D., & Turban, E. (2016). *Business intelligence, analytics, and data science*: A managerial perspective (4th ed.). Pearson-Prentice Hall.

- Iis P. Tussyadiah, Dan Wang, Timothy H. Jung, M.Claudia tom Dieck. Virtual reality, presence, and attitude change: Empirical evidence from tourism, Tourism Management, Volume 66, 2018, Pages 140–154, ISSN 0261-5177, https://doi.org/10.1016/j.tourman.2017.12.003. (https://www.sciencedirect.com/science/article/pii/S0261517717302662)

Chapter 12

Woodruff, R. B. (1997). "Customer value: The next source for competitive advantage." *Journal of the Academy of Marketing Science*, 25(2), 139–153.

Ulaga, W., & Chacour, S. (2001). "Measuring customer-perceived value in business markets: A prerequisite for marketing strategy development and implementation." *Industrial Marketing Management*, 30(6), 525–540.

Kumar, V., Aksoy, L., Donkers, B., Venkatesan, R., Wiesel, T., & Tillmanns, S. (2010). "Undervalued or overvalued customers: Capturing total customer engagement value." *Journal of Service Research*, 13(3), 297–310.

Nagle, T. T., & Hogan, J. E. (2006). *The strategy and tactics of pricing: A guide to growing more profitably*. Upper Saddle River, NJ: Pearson Education.

Homburg, C., Koschate-Fischer, N., & Hoyer, W. D. (2005). "Do satisfied customers really pay more? A study of the relationship between customer satisfaction and willingness to pay." *Journal of Marketing*, 69(2), 84–96.

Gale, B. T. (1994). *Managing customer value: Creating quality and service that customers can see*. New York, NY: Free Press.

Chapter 13

1) Atenstaedt, R. 2012. "Word cloud analysis of the BJGP." *The British Journal of General Practice: The Journal of the Royal College of General Practitioners* 62 (596), 148.

2) Borges, A. F., F. J. Laurindo, M. M. Spínola, R. F. Gonçalves, and C.A. Mattos. 2020. "The strategic use of artificial intelligence in the digital era: Systematic literature review and future research directions." *International Journal of Information Management* 57: 102225.

3) Cobo, M. J., A. G. López-Herrera, E. Herrera-Viedma, and F. Herrera. 2011. "An approach for detecting, quantifying, and visualizing the evolution of a research field: A practical application to the Fuzzy Sets Theory field." *Journal of Informetrics* 5 (1), 146–166.

4) Dobrescu, E. M., and E. M. Dobrescu. 2018. "Artificial intelligence (Ai)-the technology that shapes the world." *Global Economic Observer* 6 (2): 71–81.

5) Eren, B. A. 2021. "Determinants of customer satisfaction in chatbot use: Evidence from a banking application in Turkey." *International Journal of Bank Marketing* 39 (2): 294–331.

6) Loureiro, S. M. C., J. Guerreiro, and I. Tussyadiah. 2020. "Artificial intelligence in business: State of the art and future research agenda." *Journal of Business Research.* https://doi.org/10.1016/j.jbusres. 2020.11.001.

7) Malali, A. B., and S. Gopalakrishnan. 2020. "Application of artificial intelligence and its powered technologies in the Indian banking and financial industry: An overview." *IOSR Journal of Humanities and Social Science* 25 (4): 55–60. Tarafdar, M., C. M. Beath, and J. W. Ross. 2019. "Using AI to enhance business operations." *MIT Sloan Management Review* 60 (4): 37–44.

8) Rajaobelina, L., and L. Ricard. 2021. "Classifying potential users of live chat services and chatbots." *Journal of Financial Services Marketing* 26 (2): 81–94.

9) Ransbotham, S., D. Kiron, P. Gerbert, and M. Reeves. 2017. "Reshaping business with artificial intelligence closes the gap between ambition and action." *MIT Sloan Management Review* 59(1).

10) Valsamidis, S., L. Tsourgiannis, D. Pappas, and E. Mosxou. 2020. "Digital banking in the New Era: Exploring customers' attitudes." In *European business performance and financial institutions* (pp. 91–104). Springer, Cham.

11) Verma, S., R. Sharma, S. Deb, and D. Maitra. 2021. "Artificial intelligence in marketing: Systematic review and future research direction." *International Journal of Information Management Data Insights* 1: 100002.

Chapter 14

An, M. A., & Han, S. L. (2020). "Effects of experiential motivation and customer engagement on customer value creation: Analysis of psychological process in the experience-based retail environment." *Journal of Business Research, 120,* 389–397. https://doi.org/10.1016/j.jbusres.2020.02.044

Carlson, J., Wyllie, J., Rahman, M. M., & Voola, R. (2019). "Enhancing brand relationship performance through customer participation and value creation in social media brand communities." *Journal of Retailing and Consumer Services, 50,* 333–341. https://doi.org/10.1016/j.jretconser.2018.07.008

Fazidah Elias, N., Mohamed, H., & Arridha, R. R. (2015). "A study on the factors affecting customer satisfaction in online airline services." *International Journal of Business Information Systems, 20*(3).

Grönroos, C., & Gummerus, J. (2014). "The service revolution and its marketing implications: Service logic vs service-dominant logic." *Managing Service Quality,* 24(3), 206–229. https://doi.org/10.1108/MSQ-03-2014-0042

Hollebeek, L. D., & Macky, K. (2019a). "Digital content marketing's role in fostering consumer engagement, trust, and value: Framework, fundamental propositions, and implications." *Journal of Interactive Marketing, 45,* 27–41. https://doi.org/10.1016/j.intmar.2018.07.003

Hollebeek, L. D., & Macky, K. (2019b). "Digital content marketing's role in fostering consumer engagement, trust, and value: Framework, fundamental propositions, and implications." *Journal of Interactive Marketing, 45,* 27–41. https://doi.org/10.1016/j.intmar.2018.07.003

Lee, S. M., & Lee, D. H. (2020). ""Untact": A new customer service strategy in the digital age." *Service Business, 14*(1). Springer. https://doi.org/10.1007/s11628-019-00408-2

Li, F., Larimo, J., & Leonidou, L. C. (2021). "Social media marketing strategy: Definition, conceptualization, taxonomy, validation, and future agenda." *Journal of the Academy of Marketing Science,* 49(1), 51–70. https://doi.org/10.1007/s11747-020-00733-3

Lim, X. J., Mohd Radzol, A. R. bt, Cheah, J.-H. (Jacky), & Wong, M. W. (2017). "The impact of social media influencers on purchase intention and the mediation effect of customer attitude." *Asian Journal of Business Research, 7*(2). https://doi.org/10.14707/ajbr.170035

Matarazzo, M., Penco, L., Profumo, G., & Quaglia, R. (2021a). "Digital transformation and customer value creation in Made in Italy SMEs: A dynamic capabilities perspective." *Journal of Business Research, 123,* 642–656. https://doi.org/10.1016/j.jbusres.2020.10.033

Matarazzo, M., Penco, L., Profumo, G., & Quaglia, R. (2021b). "Digital transformation and customer value creation in Made in Italy SMEs: A dynamic capabilities perspective." *Journal of Business Research, 123,* 642–656. https://doi.org/10.1016/j.jbusres.2020.10.033

North, K., Aramburu, N., & Lorenzo, O. J. (2020). "Promoting digitally enabled growth in SMEs: A framework proposal." *Journal of Enterprise Information Management, 33*(1), 238–262. https://doi.org/10.1108/JEIM-04-2019-0103

Nuseir, M. T., El Refae, G. A., Aljumah, A., Alshurideh, M., Urabi, S., & Kurdi, B. Al. (2023). *Digital Marketing Strategies and the Impact on Customer Experience: A Systematic Review* (pp. 21–44). https://doi.org/10.1007/978-3-031-12382-5_2

Nyagadza, B. (2020). "Responding to change and customer value improvement: Pragmatic advice to banks." *The Marketing Review, 19*(3), 235–252. https://doi.org/10.1362/146934719x15774562877719

Penco, L., Serravalle, F., Profumo, G., & Viassone, M. (2021). "Mobile augmented reality as an internationalization tool in the "Made In Italy" food and beverage industry." *Journal of Management and Governance, 25*(4), 1179–1209. https://doi.org/10.1007/s10997-020-09526-w

Piriyakul, I., & Piriyakul, R. (2022). "The moderating effect of influencer on the causal map of mutual information, coproducer and customer value: A thematic analysis of messages posted by brand communities." *Journal of Marketing Analytics, 10*(2), 131–144. https://doi.org/10.1057/s41270-021-00124-9

Popa, V. (n.d.). *Customer Value Measurement. Proposal for Value Measurement Model Supply Chain Management View project Supply Chain Management View project Customer Value Measurement. Proposal for Value Measurement Model.* www.researchgate.net/publication/361412052

Repoviene, R., & Paz ̌eraite, A. (2018). "Content marketing decisions for the customer value creation in social networks: "Ilzenberg manor" case." *Research for Rural Development, 2,* 271–278. https://doi.org/10.22616/rrd.24.2018.083

Safie, N., Satar, M., Dastane, O., Yusnorizam, M., & Arif, M. (2019). "Customer value proposition for E-commerce: A case study approach school of accounting & business management, FTMS Global Malaysia Block 3420, Persiaran Semarak Api, Cyber 4, 63000 Cyberjaya, Malaysia 2." *IJACSA International Journal of Advanced Computer Science and Applications, 10*(2). www.ijacsa.thesai.org

Sze Wan, W., Dastane, O., Safie, N., Satar, M., & Ma'arif, M. Y. (2019). "What WeChat can learn from WhatsApp? customer value proposition development for Mobile Social Networking (MSN) apps: A case study approach." *Journal of Theoretical and Applied Information Technology, 28*(4). https://ssrn.com/abstract=3345134

Xiao, M., Wang, R., & Chan-Olmsted, S. (2018). "Factors affecting YouTube influencer marketing credibility: A heuristic-systematic model." *Journal of Media Business Studies, 15*(3), 188–213. https://doi.org/10.1080/1652235 4.2018.1501146

Yang, X., Zhao, K., Tao, X., & Shiu, E. (2019). "Developing and validating a theory-based model of crowdfunding investment intention-perspectives from social exchange theory and customer value perspective." *Sustainability (Switzerland), 11*(9). https://doi.org/10.3390/su11092525

Zeithaml, V. A., Verleye, K., Hatak, I., Koller, M., & Zauner, A. (2020). "Three decades of customer value research: paradigmatic roots and future research avenues." *Journal of Service Research, 23*(4), 409–432. https://doi.org/10.1177/1094670520948134

Chapter 15

1. Krittanawong C, Zhang H, Wang Z, Aydar M, Kitai T (2017) "Artificial intelligence in precision cardiovascular medicine." 69(21):2657–2664. `https://doi.org/10.1016/j.jacc.2017.03.571`

2. Hamet P, Tremblay J (2017) "Artificial intelligence in medicine." *Metab Clin Exp* 69:S36–S40. `https://doi.org/10.1016/j.metabol.2017.01.011`

3. Soltani-Fesaghandis G, Pooya A (2018) "Design of an artificial intelligence system for predicting success of new product development and selecting proper market-product strategy in the food industry." *Int Food Agribus Manage Rev* 21(7):847–864

4. Donepudi PK (2014) "Technology growth in shipping industry: an overview." *Am J Trade Policy* 1(3):137–142

5. Vadlamudi S (2018) "Agri-food system and artificial intelligence: reconsidering imperishability." *Asian J Appl Sci Eng* 7(1):33–42. `https://journals.abc.us.org/index.php/ajase/article/view/1192`

6. Kumar I, Rawat J, Mohd N, Husain S (2021) "Opportunities of artificial intelligence and machine learning in the food industry." *J Food Quality* 2021:1–10. `https://doi.org/10.1155/2021/4535567`

7. Mavani NR, Ali JM, Othman S, Hussain MA, Hashim H, Rahman NA (2022) "Application of artificial intelligence in food industry—A guideline." *Food Eng Rev* 14(1):134–175. `https://doi.org/10.1007/s12393-021-09290-z`

8. Borana J, Jodhpur NU (2016) "Applications of artificial intelligence & associated technologies." *Proceeding of International Conference on Emerging Technologies in Engineering, Biomedical, Management and Science [ETEBMS-2016]*, March, 5–6.

9. Narvekar M, Fargose P (2015) "Daily weather forecasting using artificial neural network." *Int J Comput Appl* 121(22):9–13. `https://doi.org/10.5120/21830-5088`

10. Waltham M, Moodley D (2016) "An analysis of artificial intelligence techniques in multiplayer online battle arena game environments." *ACM Int Conf Proceeding Ser* 26–28-Sept. `https://doi.org/10.1145/2987491.2987513`

11. Iqbal J, Khan ZH, Khalid A (2017) "Prospects of robotics in food industry." *Food Sci Technol* 37(2):159–165. https://doi.org/10.1590/1678-457X.14616

12. Ge Z, Song Z, Ding SX, Huang B (2017) "Data mining and analytics in the process industry: the role of machine learning." *IEEE Access* 5:20590–20616. https://doi.org/10.1109/ACCESS.2017.2756872

13. Allawi MF, Jaafar O, Ehteram M, Mohamad Hamzah F, El-Shafe A (2018) "Synchronizing artificial intelligence models for operating the dam and reservoir system." *Water Resour Manage* 32(10):3373–3389. https://doi.org/10.1007/s11269-018-1996-3

14. Kawakami E, Tabata J, Yanaihara N, Ishikawa T, Koseki K, Iida Y, Saito M, Komazaki H, Shapiro JS, Goto C, Akiyama Y, Saito R, Saito M, Takano H, Yamada K, Okamoto A (2019) "Application of artificial intelligence for preoperative diagnostic and prognostic prediction in epithelial ovarian cancer based on blood biomarkers." *Clin Cancer Res* 25(10):3006–3015. https://doi.org/10.1158/1078-0432.CCR-18-3378

15. Nor Muhammad NA, Abdul Jalal AA (2019) "Artificial neural network based ovarian cancer survivability prediction tool." *DSxConference*. https://scholar.google.es/scholar?hl=es&as_sdt=0% 2C5&q=Funcionalidad+Familiar+en+Alumnos+de+1%C2%B0+y+2%C2%B0+grado+de+secundaria+de+la+instituci%C3%B3n+educativa+parroquial+%E2%80%9CPeque%C3%B1a+Bel%C3%A9n%E2%80%9D+en+la+comunidad+de+ Peralvillo%2C+ubicada+en+el+distrito+de+Chancay+-+periodo+2018&btnG=

16. Ramakrishna RR, Hamid ZA, Zaki WMDW, Huddin AB, Mathialagan R (2020) "Stem cell imaging through convolutional neural networks: current issues and future directions in artificial intelligence technology." *PeerJ* 8 https://doi.org/10.7717/peerj.10346

17. Bera S (2021) "An application of operational analytics: for predicting sales revenue of restaurant," in *Machine Learning Algorithms for Industrial Applications*, pp. 209–235, Springer, Cham, Switzerland

18. Tyagi N, Khan R, Chauhan N, Singhal A, Ojha J (2021) "E-Rickshaws management for small scale farmers using big data-Apache spark," in *IOP Conference Series: Materials Science and Engineering*, vol. 1022, no. 1, Article ID 12023, Bandung, Indonesia, April 2021.

19. Kakani V, Nguyen VH, Kumar BP, Kim H, Pasupuleti VR (2020) "A critical review on computer vision and artificial intelligence in food industry." *J Agric Food Res* 2:100033. https://doi.org/10.1016/j.jafr.2020.100033

20. Tiwari S, Zaman H (2010) *The Impact of Economic Shocks on Global Undernourishment*, The World Bank. SSRN: https://ssrn.com/abstract=1559733

21. United nation (2023). www.un.org/development/desa/dpad/publication/un-desa-policy-brief-no-153-india-overtakes-china-as-the-worlds-most-populous-country/

22. Godfray HCJ, Beddington JR, Crute IR, Haddad L, Lawrence D, Muir JF, Pretty J, Robinson S, Thomas SM, Toulmin C (2010) "Food security: the challenge of feeding 9 billion people." *Science* 327:812–818. https://doi.org/10.1126/science.1185383

23. Priest HD, Fox SE, Rowley ER, Murray JR, Michael TP, Mockler TC (2014) "Analysis of global gene expression in Brachypodium distachyon reveals extensive network plasticity in response to abiotic stress." *PLoS One* 9(1):e87499.

24. Reardon T, Taylor JE, Stamoulis K, Lanjouw P, Balisacan A (2000) "Effects of non-farm employment on rural income inequality in developing countries: an investment perspective." *J Agric Econ* 51:266–288

25. Johnston BF, Mellor JW (1961) "The role of agriculture in economic development." *Am Econ Rev* 51:566–593

26. Garver K (2018) 6 examples of artificial intelligence in the food industry. Retrieved from https://foodindustryexecutive.com/6-examples-of-artificial-intelligence-in-the-food-industry/

27. Sharma S (2019) How artificial intelligence is revolutionizing food processing business? Retrieved from: `https://towardsdatascience.com/how-artificial-intelligence-is-revolutionizingfood-processing-business-d2a6440c03`

28. Utermohlen K (2019) 4 Applications of artificial intelligence in the food industry. Retrieved from `https://heartbeat.fritz.ai/4-applications-of-artificial-intelligence-ai-in-the-food-industry e742d7c02948`

29. Funes E, Allouche Y, Beltrán G, Jiménez A (2015) "A review: artificial neural networks as tool for control food industry process." *J Sens Technol* 05(01):28–43. `https://doi.org/10.4236/jst.2015.51004`

30. Correa DA, Montero Castillo PM, Martelo RJ (2018) "Neural networks in food industry." *Contemp Eng Sci* 11(37):1807–1826. `https://doi.org/10.12988/ces.2018.84141`

31. Kondakci T, Zhou W (2017) "Recent applications of advanced control techniques in food industry." *Food Bioprocess Technol* 10(3):522–542. `https://doi.org/10.1007/s11947-016-1831-x`

32. Wang J, Yue H, Zhou Z (2017) "An improved traceability system for food quality assurance and evaluation based on fuzzy classification and neural network." *Food Control* 79:363–370. `https://doi.org/10.1016/j.foodcont.2017.04.013`

33. Alizadeh-Sani M, Mohammadian E, Rhim JW, Jafari SM (2020) "pH-sensitive (halochromic) smart packaging films based on natural food colorants for the monitoring of food quality and safety." *Trends Food Sci Technol* 105(January):93–144. `https://doi.org/10.1016/j.tifs.2020.08.014`

34. Halonen N, Pálvölgyi PS, Bassani A, Fiorentini C, Nair R, Spigno G, Kordas K (2020) "Bio-based smart materials for food packaging and sensors – a review." *Front Mater* 7(April):1–14. `https://doi.org/10.3389/fmats.2020.00082`

35. Sun Q, Zhang M, Mujumdar AS (2019) "Recent developments of artificial intelligence in drying of fresh food: a review." *Crit Rev Food Sci Nutr* 59(14):2258–2275. `https://doi.org/10.1080/10408398.2018.1446900`

36. Bhagya Raj GVS, Dash KK (2020) "Comprehensive study on applications of artificial neural network in food process modeling." *Crit Rev Food Sci Nutr* 1 28 https://doi.org/10.1080/10408398.2020.1858398

37. Poyatos-Racionero E, Ros-Lis JV, Vivancos JL, Martínez-Máñez R (2018) "Recent advances on intelligent packaging as tools to reduce food waste." *J Clean Prod* 172:3398–3409. https://doi.org/ 10.1016/j.jclepro.2017.11.075

38. Mustafa F, Andreescu S (2018) "Chemical and biological sensors for food-quality monitoring and smart packaging." *Foods* 7(10).

39. Chen S, Brahma S, Mackay J, Cao C, Aliakbarian B (2020) "The role of smart packaging system in food supply chain." *J Food Sci* 85(3):517–525. https://doi.org/10.1111/1750-3841.15046

40. Ahmed I, Lin H, Zou L, Li Z, Brody AL, Qazi IM, Lv L, Pavase TR, Khan MU, Khan S, Sun L (2018) "An overview of smart packaging technologies for monitoring safety and quality of meat and meat products." *Packag Technol Sci* 31(7):449–471. https://doi.org/10.1002/pts.2380

41. Ghoshal G (2018) "Recent trends in active, smart, and intelligent packaging for food products." In *Food Packaging and Preservation.* Elsevier Inc. https://doi.org/10.1016/b978-0-12-811516-9.00010-5

42. Alam AU, Rathi P, Beshai H, Sarabha GK, Jamal Deen M (2021) "Fruit quality monitoring with smart packaging." *Sensors* 21(4):1–30. https://doi.org/10.3390/s21041509

43. Rahman MS, Rashid MM, Hussain MA (2012) "Thermal conductivity prediction of foods by Neural Network and Fuzzy (ANFIS) modeling techniques." *Food Bioprod Process* 90(2):333–340. https://doi.org/10.1016/j.fbp.2011.07.001

44. Rahman NA, Hussain MA, Jahim MJ (2012) "Production of fructose using recycle fixed-bed reactor and batch bioreactor." *J Food Agric Environ* 10(2):268–273 33. Mozafari MR, Khosravi-Darani K, Borazan GG, Cui J, Pardakhty A, Yurdugul S (2008) "Encapsulation of food ingredients using nanoliposome technology." *Int J Food Prop* 11(4):833–844. https://doi.org/10.1080/10942910701648115

45. Jayasooriya SD, Bhandari BR, Torley P, D'Arcy BR (2004) "Effect of high power ultrasound waves on properties of meat: a review." *Int J Food Prop* 7(2):301–319. https://doi.org/10.1081/JFP-120030039

46. Saha D, Bhattacharya S (2010) "Hydrocolloids as thickening and gelling agents in food: a critical review." *J Food Sci Technol* 47(6):587–597. https://doi.org/10.1007/s13197-010-0162-6

47. Belluco S, Losasso C, Maggioletti M, Alonzi CC, Paoletti MG, Ricci A (2013) "Edible insects in a food safety and nutritional perspective: a critical review." *Compr Rev Food Sci Food Saf* 12(3):296–313. https://doi.org/10.1111/1541-4337.12014

48. Corney D (2002) "Food bytes: intelligent systems in the food industry." *Br Food J* 104(10):787–805. https://doi.org/10.1108/00070700210448890

49. Perrot N, Ioannou I, Allais I, Curt C, Hossenlopp J, Trystram G (2006) "Fuzzy concepts applied to food product quality control: a review." *Fuzzy Sets Syst* 157(9):1145–1154. https://doi.org/10.1016/j.fss.2005.12.013

50. Doganis P, Alexandridis A, Patrinos P, Sarimveis H (2006) "Time series sales forecasting for short shelf-life food products based on artificial neural networks and evolutionary computing." *J Food Eng* 75(2):196–204. https://doi.org/10.1016/j.jfoodeng.2005.03.056

51. Szturo K, Szczypinski PM (2017) Ontology based expert system for barley grain classification. *Signal Processing – Algorithms, Architectures, Arrangements, and Applications Conference Proceedings, SPA,* 2017-Septe:360–364. https://doi.org/10.23919/ SPA.2017.8166893

52. Leo Kumar SP (2019) "Knowledge-based expert system in manufacturing planning: state-of-the-art review." *Int J Prod Res* 57(15– 16):4766–4790. https://doi.org/10.1080/00207543.2018.1424372

53. Sipos A (2020) "A knowledge-based system as a sustainable software application for the supervision and intelligent control of an alcoholic fermentation process." *Sustainability* 12(23):10205. https://doi.org/10.3390/su122310205

54. Ardiansah I, Efatmi F, Mardawati E, Putri SH, Padjadjaran U, Info A, Testing F, Product F, Chaining F, Industries M (2020) "Feasibility testing of a household industry food production certificate using an expert system with forward chaining method." *J Inform Frequency* 5(2):137–144. https://doi.org/10.15575/join. v5i2.579

55. Filter M, Appel B, Buschulte A (2015) "Expert systems for food safety." *Curr Opin Food Sci* 6:61–65. https://doi.org/10.1016/j. cofs.2016.01.004

56. Skjerdal T, Tessema GT, Fagereng T, Moen LH, Lyshaug L, Gefferth A, Spajic M, Estanga EG, De Cesare A, Vitali S, Pasquali F, Bovo F, Manfreda G, Mancusi R, Trevisiani M, Koidis A, Delgado-Pando G, Stratakos AC, Boeri M, Halbert C (2018) "The STARTEC decision support tool for better tradeoffs between food safety, quality, nutrition, and costs in production of advanced ready-to-eat foods." *Biomed Res Int* 2018:1–13

57. Mahdi MS, Ibrahim MF, Mahdi SM, Singam P, Huddin AB (2019) "Fuzzy logic system for diagnosing coronary heart disease." *Int J Eng Technol* 8(1.7):119–125.

58. Zadeh LA (2015) "Fuzzy logic – a personal perspective." *Fuzzy Sets Syst* 281:4–20. https://doi.org/10.1016/j. fss.2015.05.009

59. Hannan MA, Ghani ZA, Hoque MM, Ker PJ, Hussain A, Mohamed A (2019) "Fuzzy logic inverter controller in photovoltaic applications: issues and recommendations." *IEEE Access* 7:24934–24955. https://doi.org/10.1109/ACCESS. 2019.2899610

60. Mutlag AH, Mohamed A, Shareef H (2016) "A nature-inspired optimization-based optimum fuzzy logic photovoltaic inverter controller utilizing an eZdsp F28335 board." *Energies* 9(3). https://doi.org/10.3390/en9030120

61. Rajesh N, Yuh LC, Hashim H, Abd Rahman N, Mohd Ali J (2021) "Food and bioproducts processing fuzzy Mamdani based user-friendly interface for." *Food Bioprod Pro*

62. Isaqour R, Abdelhaq M, Saeed R, Uddin M, Alsukour O, Al-Hubaishi M, Alahdal T (2015) "Dynamic packet beaconing for GPSR mobile ad hoc position-based routing protocol using fuzzy logic." *J Netw Comput Appl* 47:32–46. https://doi.org/10. 1016/j.jnca.2014.08.008

63. Naf'an E, Universiti KM, Mohamad Ali N, Universiti PIP (2018) "Modelling of robot bunker based on fuzzy logic." *Digital Transformation Landscape in the Fourth Industrial Revolution (4IR) Era* 177–190.

64. Ali JA, Hannan MA, Mohamed A, Abdolrasol MGM (2016) "Fuzzy logic speed controller optimization approach for induction motor drive using backtracking search algorithm." *Meas.: J Int Meas Confed* 78, 49–62. https://doi.org/10.1016/j. measurement.2015.09.038

65. Zareiforoush H, Minaei S, Alizadeh MR, Banakar A, Samani BH (2016) "Design, development and performance evaluation of an automatic control system for rice whitening machine based on computer vision and fuzzy logic." *Comput Electron Agric* 124:14–22. https://doi.org/10.1016/j.compag.2016.01.024

66. Al-Mahasneh M, Aljarrah M, Rababah T, Alu'datt, M. (2016) "Application of Hybrid Neural Fuzzy System (ANFIS) in food processing and technology." *Food Eng Rev* 8(3):351–366.https://doi.org/10.1007/s12393-016-9141-7

67. Baliuta S, Kopylova L, Kuievda I, Kuevda V, Kovalchuk O (2020) "Fuzzy logic energy management system of food manufacturing processes." *Process Equipment* 9(1):221–239.https://doi.org/10.24263/2304-974X-2020-9-1-19

68. Cebi N, Sagdic O, Basahel AM, Balubaid MA, Taylan O, Yaman M, Yilmaz MT (2019) "Modeling and optimization of ultrasound-assisted cinnamon extraction process using fuzzy and response surface models." *J Food Process Eng* 42(2):1–15. https://doi.org/10.1111/jfpe.12978

69. Butler KT, Davies DW, Cartwright H, Isayev O, Walsh A (2018) "Machine learning for molecular and materials science." *Nature* 559(7715):547–555. https://doi.org/10.1038/s41586-018-0337-2

70. Sharp M, Ak R, Hedberg T (2018) "A survey of the advancing use and development of machine learning in smart manufacturing." *J Manuf Syst* 48:170–179. https://doi.org/10.1016/j.jmsy.2018.02.004

71. Erickson BJ, Korfatis P, Akkus Z, Kline TL (2017) "Machine learning for medical imaging." *Radiographics* 37(2):505–515. https://doi.org/10.1148/rg.2017160130

72. Mullainathan S, Spiess J (2017) "Machine learning: an applied econometric approach." *J Econ Perspect* 31(2): 87–106. https://doi.org/10.1257/jep.31.2.87

73. Deo RC (2015) "Machine learning in medicine." *Circulation* 132(20):1920–1930.   https://doi.org/10.1161/CIRCULATIONAHA.115.001593

74. Carleo G, Cirac I, Cranmer K, Daudet L, Schuld M, Tishby N, Vogt-Maranto L, Zdeborová L (2019) "Machine learning and the physical sciences." *Rev Mod Phys* 91(4):45002. https://doi.org/10.1103/RevModPhys.91.045002

75. Rajkomar A, Dean J, Kohane I (2019) "Machine learning in medicine." *N Engl J Med* 380(14):1347–1358. https://doi.org/10.1056/NEJMra1814259

76. Estelles-Lopez L, Ropodi A, Pavlidis D, Fotopoulou J, Gkousari C, Peyrodie A, Panagou E, Nychas GJ, Mohareb F (2017) "An automated ranking platform for machine learning regression models for meat spoilage prediction using multi-spectral imaging and metabolic profiling." *Food Res Int* 99:206–215. https://doi.org/10.1016/j.foodres.2017.05.013

77. Lu NV, Vuong TN, Dinh DT (2020) "Combining correlation based feature and machine learning for sensory evaluation of Saigon beer." *Int J Knowl Syst Sci* 11(2):71–85. https://doi.org/10.4018/IJKSS.2020040104

78. Li B, Lin Y, Yu W, Wilson DI, Young BR (2020) "Application of mechanistic modelling and machine learning for cream cheese fermentation pH prediction." *J Chem Technol Biotechnol.* https://doi.org/10.1002/jctb.6517

79. Kim DH, Zohdi TI, Singh RP (2020) "Modeling, simulation and machine learning for rapid process control of multiphase flowing foods." *Comput Methods Appl Mech Eng* 371:113286. https://doi.org/10.1016/j.cma.2020.113286

80. Alaiz-Rodriguez R, Parnell AC (2020) "A machine learning approach for lamb meat quality assessment using FTIR spectra." *IEEE Access* 8:52385–52394. https://doi.org/10.1109/ACCESS.2020.2974623

81. Tsoumakas G (2019) "A survey of machine learning techniques for food sales prediction." *Artif Intell Rev* 52(1):441–447.https://doi.org/10.1007/s10462-018-9637-z

82. Garre A, Ruiz MC, Hontoria E (2020) "Application of machine learning to support production planning of a food industry in the context of waste generation under uncertainty." Oper Res Perspect 7(January):100147. https://doi.org/10.1016/j.orp.2020.100147

83. Kumar K (2016) "Intrusion detection using soft computing techniques." *Int J Comput Commun* 6(3):153–169. www.ijcscn.com

84. Al-Waeli AHA, Sopian K, Yousif JH, Kazem HA, Boland J, Chaichan MT (2019) "Artificial neural network modeling and analysis of photovoltaic/thermal system based on the experimental study." *Energy Convers Manag* 186(November 2018), 368–379. https://doi.org/10.1016/j.enconman.2019.02.066

85. Gandhi N, Petkar O, Armstrong LJ (2016) "Rice crop yield prediction using artificial neural networks." *Proceedings – 2016 IEEE International Conference on Technological Innovations in ICT for Agriculture and Rural Development, TIAR 2016,* 105–110. https://doi.org/10.1109/TIAR.2016.7801222

86. Gonzalez-Fernandez I, Iglesias-Otero MA, Esteki M, Moldes OA, Mejuto JC, Simal-Gandara J (2019) "A critical review on the use of artificial neural networks in olive oil production, characterization and authentication." *Crit Rev Food Sci Nutr* 59(12):1913–1926. https://doi.org/10.1080/10408398.2018.1433628

87. Maladkar K (2018) 6 types of artificial neural networks currently being used in machine learning. Retrieved from: https://analyticsindiamag.com/6-types-of-artificial-neural-networkscurrently-being-used-in-todays-technologies/

88. Abdul Aziz FAB, Rahman N, Mohd Ali J (2019) "Tropospheric ozone formation estimation in Urban City, Bangi, Using Artificial Neural Network (ANN)." *Comput Intell Neurosci* 2019:1–10. https://doi.org/10.1155/2019/6252983

89. Khamis N, Mat Yazid MR, Hamim A, Rosyidi SAP, Nur NI, Borhan MN (2018) "Predicting the rheological properties of bitumen-filler mastic using artificial neural network methods." *J Teknol* 80(1):71–78. https://doi.org/10.11113/jt.v80.11097

90. Funes E, Allouche Y, Beltrán G, Jiménez A (2015) "A review: artificial neural networks as tool for control food industry process." *J Sens Technol* 05(01):28–43. https://doi.org/10.4236/jst.2015.51004

91. Ismail M, Jubley NZ, Ali ZM (2018) "Forecasting Malaysian foreign exchange rate using artificial neural network and ARIMA time series." *Proceeding of the International Conference on Mathematics, Engineering and Industrial Applications 2018.* https://doi.org/10.1063/1.5054221

92. Rashmi W, Osama M, Khalid M, Rasheed A, Bhaumik S, Wong WY, Datta S, Tcsm G (2019) "Tribological performance of nanographite-based metalworking fluid and parametric investigation using artificial neural network." *Int J Adv Manuf Technol* 104(1–4):359–374. https://doi.org/10.1007/s00170-019-03701-6

93. Said M, Ba-Abbad M, Rozaimah Sheik Abdullah S, Wahab Mohammad A (2018) "Artificial neural network (ANN) for optimization of palm oil mill effluent (POME) treatment using reverse osmosis membrane." *J Phys Conf Ser* 1095(1). https://doi.org/10.1088/1742-6596/1095/1/012021

94. Correa DA, Montero Castillo PM, Martelo RJ (2018) "Neural networks in food industry." *Contemp Eng Sci* 11(37):1807–1826. https://doi.org/10.12988/ces.2018.84141

95. da Silva CET, Filardi VL, Pepe IM, Chaves MA, Santos CMS (2015) "Classification of food vegetable oils by fluorimetry and artificial neural networks." *Food Control* 47:86–91. https://doi.org/10.1016/j.foodcont.2014.06.030

96. Silva SF, Anjos CAR, Cavalcanti RN, Celeghini RMDS (2015) "Evaluation of extra virgin olive oil stability by artificial neural network." *Food Chem* 179:35–43. https://doi.org/10.1016/j.foodchem.2015.01.100

97. Stăncioiu A (2017) "The fourth industrial revolution "industry 4.0."" *Fiabilitate Şi Durabilitate* 1:74–78. www.utgjiu.ro/rev_mec/mecanica/pdf/2017-01/11_Alin STĂNCIOIU-THE FOURTH INDUSTRIAL REVOLUTION INDUSTRY 4.0".pdf

98. Morrar R, Arman H, Mousa S (2017) "The fourth industrial revolution (Industry 4.0): a social innovation perspective." *Innov Manag Rev* 7(11):12–20. https://doi.org/10.22215/timreview/1323

99. Bai C, Dallasega P, Orzes G, & Sarkis J (2020) "Industry 4.0 technologies assessment: a sustainability perspective." *Int J Prod Econ* 229:107776. https://doi.org/10.1016/j.ijpe.2020.107776

100. Pan Y (2016) "Heading toward artificial intelligence 2.0." *Engineering* 2(4):409–413. https://doi.org/10.1016/J.ENG.2016.04.018

101. Tao D, Yang P, Feng H (2020) "Utilization of text mining as a big data analysis tool for food science and nutrition." *Compr Rev Food Sci Food Saf* 19(2):875–894. https://doi.org/10.1111/1541-4337.12540

102. Wang X, Puri VM, Demirci A (2020) "Equipment cleaning, sanitation, and maintenance." *Food Saf Eng* 333–353. https://doi.org/10.1007/978-3-030-42660-6_13

Chapter 16

Alvarez, C., & Fournier, S. (2016). "Consumers' Relationships with Brands." *Current Opinion in Psychology*, *10*, 129–135. https://doi.org/10.1016/j.copsyc.2015.12.017

Aniskova, A. (2020). *Stakeholders' Perceptions of Purpose-Driven Brands: The Case of Nike's "Dream Crazy" Advertising Campaign*. Lund University.

Banerjee, S., & Shaikh, A. (2022). "Impact of Brand Nostalgia on Intention to Purchase Brand Extensions: Moderating Role of Brand Attachment." *Journal of Product & Brand Management*, *31*(7), 1005–1017. https://doi.org/10.1108/JPBM-10-2020-3149

Chen, H. (2022). "Coca-Cola's Gains from Digital Marketing." *Highlights in Business, Economics and Management*, *1*, 31–35. https://doi.org/10.54097/hbem.v1i.2314

Eyada, B. (2020). "Brand Activism, the Relation and Impact on Consumer Perception: A Case Study on Nike Advertising." *International Journal of Marketing Studies*, *12*(4), 30. https://doi.org/10.5539/ijms.v12n4p30

Feldman, R. (2013). "Techniques and Applications for Sentiment Analysis." *Communications of the ACM*, *56*(4), 82–89. https://doi.org/10.1145/2436256.2436274

Feng, Y., & Chen, H. (2022). "Leveraging Artificial Intelligence to Analyze Consumer Sentiments Within Their Context: A Case Study of Always #LikeAGirl Campaign." *Journal of Interactive Advertising, 22*(3), 336–348. https://doi.org/10.1080/15252019.2022.2126337

Gladson Nwokah, N., & Ahiauzu, A. I. (2009). "Emotional Intelligence and Marketing Effectiveness." *Marketing Intelligence & Planning, 27*(7), 864–881. https://doi.org/10.1108/02634500911000199

Goik, R., & Tanazefti, A. (2016). *Recycling Your iPhone Can You Fix Your iPhone and if You Can't Fix It, Do You Really Own It? Capturing the Moment The Ever-Evolving, World's Most Popular Camera.* www.

Heffernan, T., O'Neill, G., Travaglione, T., & Droulers, M. (2008). "Relationship Marketing: The Impact of Emotional Intelligence and Trust on Bank Performance." *International Journal of Bank Marketing, 26*(3), 183–199. https://doi.org/10.1108/02652320810864652

Hwang, J., & Kandampully, J. (2012). "The Role of Emotional Aspects in Younger Consumer-Brand Relationships." *Journal of Product & Brand Management, 21*(2), 98–108. https://doi.org/10.1108/10610421211215517

Jorfi, H., Fauzy Bin Yacco, H., & Md Shah, I. (2012). "Role of Gender in Emotional Intelligence: Relationship Among Emotional Intelligence, Communication Effectiveness and Job Satisfaction." *International Journal of Management, 29*(4).

Kidwell, B., Hardesty, D. M., Murtha, B. R., & Sheng, S. (2011). "Emotional Intelligence in Marketing Exchanges." *Journal of Marketing, 75*(1), 78–95. https://doi.org/10.1509/jm.75.1.78

Lin, H.-C. K., Wang, T.-H., Lin, G.-C., Cheng, S.-C., Chen, H.-R., & Huang, Y.-M. (2020). "Applying Sentiment Analysis to Automatically Classify Consumer Comments Concerning Marketing 4Cs Aspects." *Applied Soft Computing, 97*, 106755. https://doi.org/10.1016/j.asoc.2020.106755

Liu, X., Shin, H., & Burns, A. C. (2021). "Examining the Impact of Luxury Brand's Social Media Marketing on Customer Engagement: Using Big Data Analytics and Natural Language Processing." *Journal of Business Research, 125*, 815–826. https://doi.org/10.1016/j.jbusres.2019.04.042

Medvedeva, N. (2021). "Belong Anywhere? Airbnb's Corporate Narratives as Emotional Governance." *Feminist Studies, 47*(3), 700–728. https://doi.org/10.1353/fem.2021.0036

Menapace, D. C. (2019). "Airbnb: Powerful Global Branding in Action." *Management, IT, Finance and Marketing, 11*(2).

Millard, J. (2009). "Performing Beauty: Dove's "Real Beauty" Campaign." *Symbolic Interaction*, *32*(2), 146–168. `https://doi.org/10.1525/si.2009.32.2.146`

Mowen, J. C. (1988). "Beyond Consumer Decision Making." *Journal of Consumer Marketing*, *5*(1), 15–25. `https://doi.org/10.1108/eb008214`

Munoko, I., Brown-Liburd, H. L., & Vasarhelyi, M. (2020). "The Ethical Implications of Using Artificial Intelligence in Auditing." *Journal of Business Ethics*, *167*(2), 209–234. `https://doi.org/10.1007/s10551-019-04407-1`

Murray, D. P. (2013). "Branding "Real" Social Change in Dove's Campaign for Real Beauty." *Feminist Media Studies*, *13*(1), 83–101. `https://doi.org/10.1080/14680777.2011.647963`

Niessen, N. (2021). "Shot on iPhone: Apple's World Picture." *Advertising & Society Quarterly*, *22*(2). `https://doi.org/10.1353/asr.2021.0023`

Patterson, M., & O'malley, L. (2006). *Brands, Consumers and Relationships: A Review*.

Peter, P. C. (2010). "Emotional intelligence." In *Wiley International Encyclopedia of Marketing*. John Wiley & Sons, Ltd. `https://doi.org/10.1002/9781444316568.wiem04017`

Shankar, V., & Parsana, S. (2022). "An Overview and Empirical Comparison of Natural Language Processing (NLP) Models and an Introduction to and Empirical Application of Autoencoder Models in Marketing." *Journal of the Academy of Marketing Science*, *50*(6), 1324–1350. `https://doi.org/10.1007/s11747-022-00840-3`

Thomson, M., MacInnis, D. J., & Whan Park, C. (2005). "The Ties That Bind: Measuring the Strength of Consumers' Emotional Attachments to Brands." *Journal of Consumer Psychology*, *15*(1), 77–91. `https://doi.org/10.1207/s15327663jcp1501_10`

Tien, Dr. N. H., Vu, Dr. N. T., & Tien, Dr. N. Van. (2019). "The Role of Brand and Brand Management in Creating Business Value Case of Coca-Cola Vietnam." *International Journal of Research in Marketing Management and Sales*, *1*(2), 57–62. `https://doi.org/10.33545/26633329.2019.v1.i2a.18`

Turner, J. (2020, June 2). *How Emotional Intelligence Can Impact Your Marketing Strategy*. `www.forbes.com/sites/theyec/2020/06/02/how-emotional-intelligence-can-impact-your-marketing-strategy/?sh=32be10c0267d`

Vredeveld, A. J. (2018). "Emotional Intelligence, External Emotional Connections and Brand Attachment." *Journal of Product & Brand Management*, *27*(5), 545–556. `https://doi.org/10.1108/JPBM-10-2017-1613`

Willman-Iivarinen, H. (2017). "The Future of Consumer Decision Making." *European Journal of Futures Research*, 5(1), 14. https://doi.org/10.1007/s40309-017-0125-5

Yoga, I. M. S., Sistadyani, N. P. I., Sharah Fatricia, R., Rani Yulianti, D., & Basmantra, I. N. (2022). "Indonesian Consumers' Emotional and Psychological Factors in the Nexus of Fear of Missing Out (FOMO)." *BISMA (Bisnis Dan Manajemen)*, 14(2), 144–159. https://doi.org/10.26740/bisma.v14n2.p144-159

Zhang, L., Wang, S., & Liu, B. (2018). "Deep Learning for Sentiment Analysis: A Survey." *WIREs Data Mining and Knowledge Discovery*, 8(4). https://doi.org/10.1002/widm.1253

I

Index

Printed in the United States
by Baker & Taylor Publisher Services